John Matthews has spent thirty years studying the Western Mystery traditions and is an internationally acknowledged authority on the Arthurian and Grail legends. This, combined with his personal involvement in the poet's craft, has led him to research the deepest levels of the native Shamanic tradition which lies at the heart of the Bardic works of Taliesin. He has contributed widely to literary journals such as *Literary Review, New Celtic Review, From Avalon to Camelot* and his many books include *At the Table of the Grail* (Arkana, 1987), *The Grail, Quest for Eternal Life* (Thames and Hudson, 1981), *Gawain, Knight of the Goddess* (Aquarian, 1990). Forthcoming titles include *Choirs of the God* and *The Song of Taliesin*, both to be published in 1991.

The Celtic Shaman from the Gundestrup Cauldron

TALIESIN

Shamanism and the Bardic Mysteries
in
Britain and Ireland

JOHN MATTHEWS

with additional material
by Caitlín Matthews

The Aquarian Press
An Imprint of HarperCollins*Publishers*

The Aquarian Press
An imprint of Grafton Books
A Division of HarperCollins*Publishers*
77–85 Fulham Palace Road,
Hammersmith, London W6 8JB

Published by The Aquarian Press 1991

10 9 8 7 6 5 4 3 2 1

A CIP catalogue record for this book
is available from the British Library

ISBN 1–85538–109–5

Printed in Great Britain by
Collins Manufacturing, Glasgow

His voice was exceptionally beautiful, and his song had a strange and wondrous stamp. It dealt with the origin of the earth and stars, the rise of plants, animals, and man; with the all-powerful sympathy of nature; with the primeval golden age and its sovereigns – love and poetry; with the emergence of hate and barbarism and their battles with those benevolent goddesses; and finally with the coming triumph of those divinities, the end of calamities, the rejuvenation of nature, and the return of an everlasting golden age.

Novalis, Heinrich von Ofterdingen

There will be again a certain . . . wise man, a bard,
whom all call the wisest among men,
by whose noble mind the whole world will be educated,
For he will write the chief points with power and
    intelligence
and at various times he will write clearly, very wondrous
    things,
having mastered my words and metres and phrases.

The Sibylline Oracles, translated by J. J. Collins

I can frame what no tongue utters.

Cad Goddeu

ACKNOWLEDGEMENTS

My greatest debt is expressed in the dedication of this book, but I wish to express my thanks to the following people who have helped in one way or another to bring this volume to completion:

To my wife, Caitlín Matthews, as always thanks and love for her tireless support, and especially for allowing me to pillage her notes. Without her work on the poems alone this would have been in every way a poorer book.

To the late Robert Graves, with whom I first discussed the mysteries of Taliesin in 1968. I hope he likes what I have done with the matter in hand.

To Philip le Galoise, for reading and commentating on the manuscript and for his many helpful suggestions regarding material in Welsh.

To R. J. Stewart, Kaledon Naddair, Gareth Knight, Philip Carr-Gomm, and the legendary Company of Hawkwood (class of '88) for their encouragement.

To Alan Haymes, for drawing my attention to various articles and for providing copies of them.

To Nigel Suckling for sharing his vision of **Gwyddbwyll**.

To Stuart Littlejohn for his inspiring work on the cover and internal designs.

To the legion of scholars who have contributed to the understanding of Celtic and specifically matters relating to Taliesin. The present book would have been infinitely poorer without them. None, of course, are responsible for my own failures or mistakes in the present book.

CONTENTS

To Master Taliesin himself, for all that he has taught me, and in the hope that this study may help to re-establish his once great fame.

Ceridwen's Boast

Nine are my natures
through many spheres.
Who dares meet the sow and her nine?
Lleu Llaw Gyffes was a tasty feast
at the foot of the pine.

It was the son of the Hazel
who brought me to shore.
Then was sown wheat and barley –
bread and beer for women and men.
Amathaon's store.

But best is the ferment of bees:
only their honey shall sweeten
the mead in the high cup.
Best for the honey-isle
a dragon who drinks deep of the draught.

And my fine eagle,
fosterling of the Wood-Seer:
he shall himself endure,
baiting on a high tree
'til a ladder of words shall lure.

My bright one, my dark one,
contentious to the end,
brothers of one womb,
I am your beginning
and your sure doom.

In the northern court of Don,
my lawful chair is set:
giver of wisdom's gift,
keeper of the caers,
weaver of the weft.

My shifting fingers
reckoning all rents,
counting each herb and flower
to their own potency,
shall stew to the hour.

And ninefold the waves
shall batter the land.
The cauldron overset
shall poison the honey isle,
its swift horses fret.

In every turning of the caer,
in every shaping's shift –
I am the Mistress of the Brew,
Ceridwen of the Chair,
in acorns, milk and dew.

                    Caitlín Matthews

FOREWORD

Mircea Eliade, in his classical study of shamanism (1951) points out that the use of the word 'shaman' to describe all magicians, sorcerers and prophets is misleading, and can confuse or blur any true definition we might wish to propose. The same may be said to apply to the central subject of this book. It is a simple task to extract material from works relating to Taliesin and relate it to the world of shamanic activity. Thus, it may be thought that even to attempt to bridge the gap between such a widely recognised and much explored realm and its less frequently explored Celtic aspect is a dangerous one, which may only be undertaken in the full realisation that much of the material is speculative. Nevertheless, I am satisfied that a close scrutiny of extant Celtic records, together with the texts and later commentaries, shows beyond reasonable doubt that Celtic shamanism did exist, and that elements of it are still to be found in more recent folk-culture.

Shamanism is, anyway, notoriously difficult to define. The best we can expect to do, since the existence of such basic beliefs is beyond question, is to point to certain common shamanic practices which are found within the Celtic world. Shamanism is therefore used very much as a blanket term throughout this book. More specific aspects must await further study. Once we have established some common basis from which to work, we can then proceed to investigate the elements of shamanism which lie embedded in Celtic literature and folk-lore. Doubtless, much more can, and will, be said about each of the aspects dealt with herein. It is hoped that the present work will serve as a springboard for future investigation, which is greatly needed.

Few people would claim to have read everything in the extensive literature of shamanism. I certainly have not. My findings are based on more than twenty years of research into the Celtic and Arthurian traditions, and rather less than that in shamanic practice, both ancient and modern. I have read, as far as I am aware, every text or commentary relating to the subject from this point of view, and have drawn my own conclusions. This book is aimed at all who wish to

1

explore further, and I hope I have supplied bibliographical apparatus for them to do so.

Time, and the limitations of space, have necessitated that this book deals largely with Welsh and Irish material. The vast, and still largely uncharted, area of Scots Gaelic lore and literature remains to be investigated on another occasion.

Taliesin has long been a personal obsession of mine, and I hope to extend the materials presented here in a number of ways. Among the books planned to appear in the next few years are a collection of magical narratives (*The Song of Taliesin*, Unwin Hyman, 1991), an epic of the Arthurian world (*Broceliande*), a practical workbook (*The Celtic Shaman*, Element Books, 1991), and an account of a modern quest for the 'Hallows' of the Grail. These will collectively form *The Books of Broceliande*, and will hopefully provide a steadily deepening appreciation and awareness of the figure of Taliesin. The present book is offered in a spirit of scholarly detective work. I am aware of my shortcomings in many areas and have relied on the help and support of others, especially my life partner and frequent collaborator Caitlín Matthews. I am, however, ultimately responsible for the direction and faults in the book. My hope is that it will persuade others, many of them better able than I, to pursue the Quest for Celtic Shamanism and the Bardic Mysteries even further.

John Matthews
London, 1990

INTRODUCTION

Symbols, whether they be myths or ceremonies or objects,
reveal their full significance only within a particular tradition;
one must be part and parcel of that tradition to experience
fully the power and illumination of the myth.

Celtic Heritage, Alwyn and Brynley Rees

Taliesin **Pen Beirdd**, the 'Primary Chief Bard of the Island of
Britain', is a real figure who lived in Wales during the latter
half of the 6th Century and composed songs and poems which
have survived to the present time – though in a fragmentary
and sometimes confused form. Lost and forgotten for many
years in private libraries and collections, they were rediscovered in the 18th Century, and efforts were made to translate
them from medieval Welsh into English. Unfortunately, the
antiquarians and scholars who worked on them possessed
insufficient knowledge of the language or, more importantly,
the background from which the writings sprang. This resulted
in uneven and sometimes extremely unreliable material which
has remained, until now, largely unexplored and generally
unexplained.

The reasons for this are several. A great deal of the material
attributed to Taliesin is, in fact, not by him at all, but is part of
a much later cycle of medieval stories, poems and lore which
came to be attributed to him, due to the fact that he was a
representative figure who spoke for the ancient mystery religion of the native British people. As Professor Simms-Williams
noted in a recent article, the poems probably formed part of

> . . . a cycle of poems put into the mouth of the arch-bard
> Taliesin which relate to his legendary omniscience and his
> legendary reincarnations at various periods in history. The
> main aim of the poet, or school of poets . . . [being] to enhance
> the prestige of the traditional bardic order, represented by
> Taliesin, and to do so by being deliberately esoteric in style
> and content. (280)

Thus, many of the statements contained within the material
were taken quite literally, while in fact they were references to
ancient practices and beliefs. An added difficulty was brought

3

about by the fact that the medieval writers and collectors of the 'Taliesin' material often did not understand what they were writing down, as much of their material came from oral traditions which stretched back in unbroken lines for many generations.

As Dr Rachel Bromwich stated in her 1968 J. G. Williams Memorial Lecture (35), while referring to the Welsh Triads in words which apply very well to the works of Taliesin and the Bardic Traditions:

> As the centuries progress, new influences become embodied in the successive versions of the text, and these reflect the political, ecclesiastical, or literary interests, either of the individual scribe, or the source from which he copied. But all such variants and additions are subsidiary, and they do not alter the fact that [. . . they] refer to a body of tradition which has remained fixed and constant in its main outlines and in its essential character.

The writings of Taliesin thus fall into two groups. Group one consists of actual poems composed by the 6th Century bard, and group two contains a vast body of mythical allusion, story and song *attributed* to Taliesin but actually *pre-dating* him by several hundred years.

Within this second group of material can be found nothing less than the foundation stones of the ancient shamanic mystery teachings of Britain and Ireland. There are references to methods of divination, to the Secret Language of Poets which kept the ancient mysteries in a coded form, and to the rites and rituals which formed an essential part of the worship of the Celtic deities.

The question of authenticity is one which necessarily accompanies any body of ancient textual matter. As long ago as the era of Classical Greece, when the two greatest libraries in the Western world, at Alexandria and Pergamun, vied with each other for the possession of original works by the early philosophers and orators, there was much forgery and scholarly dispute. Two distinct methods, identified by Luciano Canfora in his book *The Vanished Library* (44), make clear the widely differing approaches to the material.

> The Alexandrians toiled long and hard to reach what they regarded as incontrovertible conclusions, making careful

4

lexical studies and accurate collations ... Such subtleties
held no attraction for the men of Pergamun ... What interested
them was the 'hidden' meaning, the meaning that lay 'behind'
the classical ... texts – the 'allegory' as they called it ...
The Alexandrians, by contrast, patiently found line-by-line
and word-by-word explanations, halting whenever sense was
not plain to them.

In the present book much is taken for granted, and the
hidden meanings have indeed been sought out. At the same
time, scrupulous attention has been given to the sense of
words and lines within the writings attributed to Taliesin. It
cannot always be said that we have 'halted whenever sense
was not plain' – indeed we have often had to take a leap
in the dark, finding, on many occasions, that the necessary
illumination was given to make the sense clear. So we may be
seen as taking a course somewhere between the two extremes
of Alexandria and Pergamun, finding truth where it exists, and
hopefully adding nothing to the already considerable volume
of invented matter.

Nonetheless, it must also be remembered that what, for want
of a better phrase, we may call the 'Taliesin Tradition' is a still
living one, in which the creation (or re-creation) of the past
is a viable method for arriving at a better understanding of the
ancient mystery teachings of this land. From this remarkable,
and still virtually unknown, body of authentic material, it has
been possible to reconstruct what may be seen as the bones of
the original shamanic and Bardic mystery teachings of Britain
and Ireland, lost for thousands of years amid the dust of history
and the intractable thicket of pied language.

The use of the words 'shaman' and 'shamanism' requires
some explanation in the context of this book, and it is
important to establish at this point exactly what is meant
by it. The word is such a fashionable one, and used so
easily by so many different groups, that it has become open
to misuse and misinterpretation. On the one hand, there are
those who believe that shamanism (which is a word of eastern
origin) is a foreign system 'imported' into this country in the
last few years to describe something which never happened
here. This is manifestly nonsense. Shamanism is simply a word
for something which took place all over the ancient world.
Shamans were the interpreters of the gods, the doctors and

5

inner guides of their people; they kept the records (orally) of every family in their tribe – important when intermarriage could so easily occur in small communities – and they were the recorders of the life of the tribe itself, both inner and outer. They were, in fact, performing much the same function as the Bards, Druids and Ovates of Britain and Ireland.

On the other hand, there are many people currently practising a kind of neo-shamanism which, though firmly based on the old ways, has been intermingled with modern psychological teachings and 'New Age' therapy. A third kind of shamanism is that written about by the anthropological community who (rightly, in a certain sense) regard it as a kind of window on the past, but for whom the realities of shamanism are still very far from confirmed.

The word 'shaman' actually derives from Siberia and Central Asia, from the Tungusc **saman**. It has been applied widely, however, and there seems no reason to be pedantic in using alternative words belonging to individual cultures.

Shamans are more usually male (though by no means exclusively so), perhaps because they originated in typical hunter and herder societies. There are records of female shamans in certain cultures, but these are few compared with those of the male shamans. This does not, of course, mean that shamanism is an exclusively male preserve. It can be practised by either sex with the same degree of success or failure. Within this book I have adopted the word to mean either male or female practitioners, rather than opting for the female word for shaman 'shamanka'. In the same way, 'he', 'his', etc should be seen as applying equally to 'her', 'hers', etc – once again this has been adopted to avoid the unnecessary 'he or she', 'him or her self', throughout the book.

The shaman is not exactly a magician, not exactly a visionary, healer, or a poet but he often performs all of these functions, along with those of inner guide and remembrancer. It is the *intensity* of his experience that makes him unique. His ability to extend his consciousness beyond that of the ordinary human being, and to control his movement through inner, as well as outer, space is without parallel. That he is able, also, to exercise some degree of control over his physical state is important. He can, so to speak, choose the moment of his own death, alter the circumstances of his day-to-day existence, and cross barriers that are normally insurmountable. In each

6

of these respects we will see that Taliesin – who may here be said to represent *all* similar Celtic figures – possesses the same ability in one form or another.

Finally, a word must be said about the versions of the poems found within these pages. Whilst many are translated word for word, we have not hesitated, where it seemed appropriate, to manifest the meaning through the metaphors of the poems. Much of the material attributed to Taliesin was written in a verse form called **awdl**, which is more or less untranslatable in modern English. We have, therefore, opted for a more literal and flexible form, rather than attempt a word order which would appear, in English, strained. One of the reasons why the Taliesin material has never been fully appreciated is because of the way earlier writers have sought to provide versions which are as exact as possible, without ever taking into account the meaning *behind* the words, which are indeed often obscure and difficult. The approach we have taken is that of a painstaking study both of the words *and* their meaning, often with astonishing results. Our translations should, therefore, be looked upon as 'versions', rather than perfect translations (though we have taken care to be as exact as possible), which help to illuminate this frequently dark corner of Celtic lore and learning. In certain cases we have included other versions already extant, where we felt unable to improve on them. These are clearly indicated in the text. For a more strictly scholarly version of the Taliesin corpus (though limited to the so-called 'historical' poems), readers are referred to the works of Sir Ivor Williams listed in the Bibliography. Patrick K. Ford's eagerly awaited work on Taliesin has yet to appear, though this will doubtless add significantly to the interpretation of the material, as has his recently published translation of the *Mabinogion* (2).

PART ONE

Chapter One

THE STORY OF TALIESIN: GWION'S TRANSFORMATIONS

> The Emergence of the child from the sea is [important] . . .
> because it is this moment which is every moment, changing,
> powerfully potential, elusive but precise. The child found in
> the fisherman's net is given a name, a new name, for the new
> shape is the new thing and therefore a new word, which stands
> for the thing itself. He is called Taliesin.
>
> *Cordelia and the Button*, Idris Parry

The Bright Singer

Most of what we know about Taliesin the Bard comes from
two sources: a 16th Century text called the *Hanes*, or story,
of Taliesin; and the seventy-seven poems contained in a 14th
Century volume known as *The Book of Taliesin*, one of the
Four Ancient Books of Wales (10). Apart from these there are
some references in the Mabinogion story, 'Branwen Daughter
of Llyr', in the *Welsh Triads* (334), and in the following passage
from the *Historia Brittonum* (225), attributed to the 9th Century
monk Nennius.

> Tunc Outigirn in illo tempore foriter dimicabat contra gentem
> Anglorum. Tunc Talhaern Tataguen in poemate claruit; et
> Neirin, et Taliessin, et Bluchbard, et Cian, qui vocatur Gueinth
> Guaut, simul uno tempore in poemate Brittanico claruerunt.
> (At that time Outigern then fought bravely against the English
> nation. Then Talhaearn Tad Awen was famed in poetry;
> and Aneirin and Taliesin and Bluchbard and Cian, known
> as Gueinth Guaut, were all simultaneously famed in Bri-
> tish verse.)

Several details are notable here. The dating of the *Historia*
(actually compiled in the 9th Century AD) seems to indicate
a period within the 6th Century as Taliesin's *floreat*, yet the

11

Figure 1 The World of the Shaman *Four inner plates from the
Gundestrup cauldron depicting a) the Goddess surrounded by
animals, b) the Shaman with his attendant creatures, c) the
God of the Year with fantastic (zodiacal?) animals and
d) dead warriors inserted into the cauldron of rebirth and
emerging alive.*

actual wording of the text is ambiguous. Does it mean that
Taliesin, along with the other bards mentioned, was famous
for his poetry at that time, or that he was a famous character *in*
the poetry of the time? The former would seem, on the strength
of internal evidence, to be the case. Yet the secondary meaning
is very much in line with the belief that Taliesin actually dated
from a much earlier period – or even that there was already,
at this comparatively early date, some confusion between
the historical figure and a more primitive, semi-mythical
personality, to whose name had become attached a vast body
of floating lore, much of which was transmitted orally and thus
had no specific author.

These memories were still locked in the unconscious minds
of the people who lived in these lands during the 6th Century,
and who were still half-conscious of a more primitive self as
late as the 16th Century, when a Welsh writer named Llewellyn
Sion transcribed the text known as *Hanes Taliesin*. We are,
indeed, very firmly in the magical world of the *Mabinogion*
which, as one of its translators put it, 'probably dates back
to the dawn of the Celtic world.' (2)

Not only the Celtic world however. The foundations on
which these stories, especially that of Taliesin, rest, are built
of both older and wider materials than any single culture,

part of the world-wide practice of shamanism which we shall discuss in the next chapter. There are certainly references enough within both the *Hanes Taliesin* and the poems to prove that Taliesin, whether or not he was their author, was the inheritor of a British shamanic tradition which was possibly still flourishing in the 6th Century and was at least partly known about in the 16th.

So let us begin by looking in detail at the *Hanes* and seeing exactly where it will lead us. Its textual history is complex, there being no less than four distinct versions, found in numerous manuscript editions, each with their own variants. The following summary is based on all the extant versions. Unlike Lady Charlotte Guest's early version of the *Mabinogion* in 1849 (5), more recent editions have tended to omit 'The Story of Taliesin', on the grounds of its lateness, while the most recent translation, by Professor Ford (2), deals with a fragmentary text by Elis Gruffydd, which will be discussed below. The poems which form an integral part of this text have been translated separately and will be found at the pages indicated.

In the time of Arthur there lived in the region of Llyn Tegid [Bala Lake] a nobleman named Tegid Foel [the Bald]. And he had a wife who was named Ceridwen, who was skilled in the magical arts. Tegid and Ceridwen had two children: one who was so ugly that they called him Morfran (Great Crow), but who came to be known as Afagddu (Utter Darkness), because of his extreme ugliness. The other child was a daughter, whose name was Creirwy (Dear One), and she was as fair as Morfran was dark. Ceridwen thought that her son would never be accepted in the world because of his hideous looks, so she cast about for a way to empower him with wisdom, so that none would care about his appearance. And so she resolved to boil a Cauldron of Inspiration and Wisdom according to the Books of the Fferyllt, and the method of it was this: she must first gather certain herbs on certain days and hours, and put them in the Cauldron, which must then be kept boiling for a year and a day, until three drops of Inspiration were obtained. For the task of maintaining the fire beneath the Cauldron, Ceridwen chose an old blind man named Morda, who was lead by a youth named Gwion Bach (Little), the son of Gwreang of Llanfair Caereinion in Powys.

At the end of the year Ceridwen stationed herself, with her son, close by the Cauldron, and there she fell asleep [alternatively she is still out gathering more herbs and making incantations]. And while she slept [or was away], it happened that three drops flew out of the Cauldron and landed on the thumb of Gwion Bach, and so great was the pain therefrom that he put his thumb into his mouth and sucked it. And at once he knew all that there was to know, and foremost of that knowledge was that Ceridwen would destroy him as soon as she learned what had happened. And thus he fled. But the Cauldron gave a great cry and cracked in two, and the waters flowed from it into a nearby stream and poisoned the horses of Gwyddno Garanhir. And Ceridwen awoke [returned] and when she saw what had occurred her anger knew no bounds. She struck the blind Morda so hard that one of his eyes fell out on his cheek, but he said that she had injured him wrongly. Then Ceridwen knew all that had occurred and went in pursuit of Gwion, running. And he was aware of her and changed himself into the semblance of a hare; and she, perceiving that, turned herself into the semblance of a black greyhound. He ran to a river and became a fish; and she pursued him as an otter-bitch, until he turned himself into a bird of the air and she into a hawk. Then, in fear for his life, he saw where a heap of winnowed wheat lay on the floor of a barn, and dropping amongst them, turned himself into one of the grains. Then Ceridwen turned herself into a black, red-crested hen and swallowed the grain of wheat, which went into her womb, so that she became quickened and bore Gwion in her womb for nine months. And when she gave birth to him he was so fair and beautiful that she could not bear to kill him, or to have another kill him for her. And so she placed him in a leather bag [or in a bag within a coracle] and set him adrift on the sea [in a river or on a lake] on the 29th day of April [or on **Calen Gaef**, the 31st Oct].

Now there lived at that time, in the lordship of Maelgwn Gwynedd, a nobleman named Gwyddno Garanhir. He had a weir on the shore of the river Conwy [between Dyfi and Aberystwyth] close to the sea. And on every May Eve [All Hallows] he was accustomed to take from it salmon to the value of a hundred pounds. And Gwyddno had one son who was named Elffin, a hapless youth who had nothing but evil luck. Therefore his father told him that on this particular year he should have all that he could find in the weir. So Elffin went to the weir on May Eve and when he and his servants arrived they could see that there was not so much as a single salmon in the nets. Then Elffin began to lament, until one of the men with him pointed out where a leather bag hung upon a pole of the weir [or where a coracle lay in the arms of the weir]. Then

15

Elffin took the bag from the water and cut a slit in it with his knife. And within he saw a bright forehead and cried aloud, 'Behold, a radiant brow (**tal iesin**). And the child within the bag replied, 'Tal-iesin it is!' [And it is said that he had been floating in the bag for nearly 40 years.] Thereupon Elffin took the child up and placed it before him on the crupper of his saddle and rode for home. And as he rode the child made a poem for him, which was **The Consolation of Elffin** (pages 280–1), and it is told that this was the first poem that Taliesin made. And Elffin was filled with wonder, and asked the child how he came to compose poetry, as he so young; and Taliesin replied with another poem, which is called **Taliesin's Song of his Origins** (pages 281–2), and by the time he had sung it they were back at Gwyddno's court.

Now when Gwyddno heard how Elffin had failed to find any salmon in the weir he bemoaned the ill-luck of his son, but Elffin replied that he had from the weir something of far greater value. 'And what is that?' demanded Gwyddno. 'A bard' replied his son. And when Gwyddno asked how that would profit him, Taliesin himself replied, 'He will get more profit from me than the weir ever gave to you.' 'Are you able to speak, and you so little?' demanded Gwyddno, and Taliesin replied, 'I am better able to speak than you to question me.' Whereupon Gwyddno asked him what more he had to say, and Taliesin replied with another song, which began, 'Water possesses the power to bless . . .' And so Elffin gave the child to his own wife to raise, which she did most lovingly. And from that day forth Elffin's luck turned, and he grew prosperous and was much favoured by his uncle Maelgwn Gwynedd.

Time passed until Taliesin was a child no longer and, in the year that he became thirteen, Elffin journeyed to the Christmas court at Deganwy, where he heard many things said in praise of Maelgwn, that he was the most powerful and handsome and generous Prince, and that his wife was more fair than any other, and that his bards were the wisest in all the land. And Elffin happened to remark that though this was true, he believed his own wife was fairer and more chaste than Maelgwn's, and that his Bard was far more skilful than those of his uncle. When Maelgwn heard of this he at once ordered that Elffin be thrown into prison, until such time as his words were proved true or false, and he sent his own son, Rhun, who had a reputation as a womaniser, to test the faithfulness of Elffin's wife. And Elffin himself was shut up in a tower with a chain about his feet, which some said was a silver chain because he was, after all, Maelgwn's nephew.

Now Taliesin knew all that had occurred, and he told Elffin's wife that Rhun was coming to bring disgrace upon her. And he caused his mistress to put on the dress of her own maidservant, and to give to the girl her own things, and her ring, which had been given to her by Elffin. And so Rhun was made welcome and shown to the lady's chamber, where she was taking supper, but it was the maidservant that he saw, while Elffin's wife pretended to be her own maid. Thus over supper, while Rhun engaged the girl in seductive talk, and saw to it that she drank heavily, the girl fell soundly asleep, and Rhun cut off her little finger, with the ring still upon it, and left quietly to return to Maelgwn.

Then Maelgwn had Elffin brought before him and presented him with the ring, still upon the finger, and challenged him with the disgrace of his wife's infidelity. But Elffin merely looked at the ring and said that while he did not deny it was his ring, he did deny that the finger belonged to his wife. For it was, he said, a fact that the ring would scarcely fit his wife's thumb, whereas the ring had been forced upon this little finger. Also, his wife had been wont to pare her nails at least once a week, while this nail had not been cut for a month. What was more it had bread-dough under it and his wife had not kneaded any dough since she became his wife.

Even more outraged, Maelgwn ordered Elffin thrown back into prison, determined that he must prove the wisdom of his bard before he would be let out. Knowing this, Taliesin told all that had occurred to Elffin's wife and then set out to Maelgwn's court. Before he departed he sang the song called **Journey to Deganwy** (pages 282–3). He arrived just before the feast was about to begin and seated himself in a dark corner. And, as the Bards of the Court filed in, he pouted his lips at them and played **blerwm, blerwm** on them with his fingers, so that when they stood at last before Maelgwn, instead of uttering praises to him, all they could do was pout their lips and say, **blerwm, blerwm**. This made Maelgwn furious, and he ordered one of his squires to strike the chief bard, who was called Heinin Fardd. This broke his trance, and then he was able to tell his lord that the cause of their speechlessness was the spirit in the form of a child who sat in the corner.

Then Maelgwn ordered Taliesin brought before him, and questioned him as to his origin and what he was. And Taliesin replied with his great song which begins, Primary Chief Bard am I (pages 283–6). In this he claimed to have been present at certain key events in the history of the world; the building of the Tower of Babel; the Crucifixion, and the Conquests of Alexander, etc. All were amazed at his eloquence and wisdom, and Maelgwn called forth his own bards to contend with the youth, but they were unable to do more than mouth noises as before. Then Maelgwn asked the boy his errand and Taliesin replied that he had come for Elffin. Then he sang the song called **The Contention of the Bards** (pages 289–90), in which he mocked all who knew less than he. And while he sang, a great wind arose, which shook the castle to its foundations, so that Maelgwn called hastily for Elffin to be brought before them. And at once Taliesin sang a verse which caused the chains to fall off him. Then he turned once more to Maelgwn and his bards and sang first **The Interrogation of the Bards** and then **The Rebuke of the Bards** (pages 290–1), and then a third song called **The Satire of the Bards**. And all were so amazed at the power of his words that they were silenced.

Then Taliesin called for Elffin's wife to enter the hall, and she showed all that she had ten fingers, at which Rhun and his father were most discomfited. Then Taliesin asked Elffin to wager that his horse was swifter than all Maelgwn's steeds, and to wager against him. And this Elffin did, and on a day appointed there was a race held at a site that had been agreed. Taliesin came, and gave to the lad who was to ride Elffin's horse twenty-four sticks of holly which he had burned black. And he said to the youth to let all of Maelgwn's horses pass him at first, and then, as he overtook each one, to strike it across the rump with one of the twigs, letting the twig fall to the earth afterwards. And he further said that when the race was won, to be sure and notice where the horses stopped and to throw down his cap to mark the spot. And all this was done as he had requested, and Elffin's horse won. And at the spot where the horse came to a halt, a hole was dug, and there was found a cauldron filled with gold. Then Taliesin gave the gold to Elffin and thanked him for bringing him from the water and for caring for him since that day.

Thus was Maelgwn discomfited utterly, and in humility he called for Taliesin to sing of the order of the world, of its creation and its end. And Taliesin sang the song which has ever since been called one of **The Four Pillars of Song**. And after that he told many other things that would come to pass, including Maelgwn's own death.

Thus ends this extraordinary text – part folk-tale, part romance, part myth. Before we look at its meaning we need to examine in more detail the complex history of the work itself. The reason for this will become obvious when we come to deal with the question of authenticity within the Taliesin tradition, which is far from straightforward.

A Tangle of Traditions

To begin with, Lady Guest did not translate the work unaided. She had the help of the Rev. John Jones, who also wrote under the Bardic name 'Tegid'. When it came to the text of the *Hanes*, Lady Guest wrote, 'No perfect copy of the *Mabinogi* of Taliesin being accessible, it has been necessary to print it in the present series from two fragments. The former of the two is contained in a manuscript in the Library of the Welsh School, in London ... The second fragment is from a manuscript in the library of the late Iolo Morgannwg, and was kindly communicated by his son, the late Mr Taliesin Williams (Ab Iolo).' She then went on to point out that the text had already appeared in a translation by Dr Owen Pughe, to which she had made certain amendments, particularly within the texts of the poems.

The version published in Lady Guest's *Mabinogion*, which is familiar to thousands of readers, should therefore be seen as deriving, by a number of stages, from that generally supposed to have been composed, from still earlier fragments, by Llewelyn Sion (1540–*c*. 1615), worked upon further by Iolo Morgannwg (1747–1826), Dr Owen Pughe (1759–1835), and finally Lady Guest (1812–1895) and her silent collaborator John Jones (1792–1852). We may see that all of the last named were roughly contemporary, and that only a little over 150 years separated Llewelyn Sion from Iolo Morgannwg. The vitality of the oral tradition in Wales over this period meant that in all probability the material changed little in form, which may possibly indicate that the manuscripts to which Iolo claimed to have access were in all likelihood authentic. That he also executed forgeries is beyond doubt, as we shall see in Chapter Five. Professor Ford is also of the belief that 'the manuscript tradition of the *Hanes* was paralleled by the oral tradition' (84), an idea which is further strengthened by Juliette Wood in a recent article (332).

Independent of the version attributed to Llewelyn Sion, though in all probability recorded at roughly the same time, there exists a fragmentary re-telling of the story set down by Elis Gruffydd (*c*. 1490–*c*. 1552). This forms part of his *Chronicle of the World* (National Library of Wales, MS.5276D) in which he recorded a considerable amount of oral tradition – although, since he was in fact 'compiling' his Chronicle, and clearly had access to more ancient materials, he may well have copied the Taliesin story from one of these. If he did so, he felt no compunction about making changes, omitting the full transformation sequence and including various asides whenever he saw fit to disagree with the story. That he also inserts the tale into the part of his Chronicle dealing with the 6th Century, may or may not be seen as further evidence for Taliesin having lived at this time.

In summary, the various manuscripts fall into four groups:

1 Ellis Gruffydd's text   (NLW 5276)
2 A copy by John Jones   (Peniarth 111)
3 Llewellyn Sion's version   (NLW 13075)
4 Variant copy by Owen Jones   (NLW 13081, 1–4v.)
5 Variant version by Lewis Morris (Cwrt mawr 14)

Owen Jones used an archaic script for *Hanes Taliesin*, at variance with his usual hand, suggesting that he regarded the material as appreciably archaic (332).

The many variations in the spellings of personal names in the various manuscripts indicate local versions and demonstrate that the work was widely diversified. A comparison of the various texts indicates that this is a tale of largely oral and folk-loric tradition which has not undergone 'literalization' (332), as is the case with the other texts included in the *Mabinogion*. This makes it likely to have been more primitive than the rest and to have preserved more ancient material.

We have already noticed that in certain of the texts of *Hanes Taliesin* there is a distinct break, suggesting that there were once two separate stories. The division appears at the point where Gwion is re-born from Ceridwen's womb and cast adrift in the sea. The second part of the story, which is sometimes printed separately, concerns the early adventures of Taliesin from his appearance in the weir to his triumph over Maelgwn. Apart from this, it has been recognised (330) that the Gwion story was influenced by two recognisable international folk-tale themes called 'The Magician and His Pupil' and 'The White Snake'. When one pauses to consider this, several important facts make themselves known.

Firstly, we have no evidence to suppose that Gwion and Taliesin were originally connected at all. This would explain the (otherwise puzzling) tradition of Taliesin being the son of St. Hennwg, of whom virtually nothing is known (336).

It also presupposes certain facts about Gwion himself. Who, exactly, was this child who, by seeming chance, imbibed the three drops of wisdom from the Cauldron? On one level, he is an initiate shaman who, by submitting to the tests of the Cauldron, is made a fully-fledged practitioner of the shamanic arts. On another level he is, perhaps, not human at all, but an Otherworld child whose first adventures take place *in* the Otherworld but who, once he has undergone a human birth, must go out into the world of men and become human. There, he takes upon himself the persona of the arch-poet Taliesin. If this is more or less what occurred, then we have a better understanding of the whole Taliesin tradition. The poet, we may assume, was indeed a real man, who lived towards the end of the 6th Century, was unusually learned, and practised a form of shamanism whilst paying lip-service to Christianity. At some point, probably not long after his death, a body of floating lore began to be attached to him. We may imagine a story-teller who knew the story of Gwion Bach and felt that it needed to be extended, wondering what occurred to his hero after he had been reborn. Hearing, perhaps, other stories then circulating, about Gwyddno Garanhir and his son Elffin, one of whom may indeed have been Taliesin's patron, he put the two stories together and thus provided the vehicle for an even greater collection of tales and lore, which gradually transformed the figure of the old Bard into that of the god-like poet and shaman of the *Hanes Taliesin* and *The Book of Taliesin*.

The Wondrous Child

But what does all this tell us about Taliesin himself, as we meet him in the account of his early life? It says, quite clearly, that he was one of several Wondrous Children who appear regularly in Celtic myth, and who include Fionn Mac Cumhail, Pwyll, Pryderi, Gwair, Goreu, and Mabon son of Modron (183). Each of these was either born with or obtained magical powers as children. All were either imprisoned or, as with Taliesin, helped set free a prisoner. In more than one instance, as in the **Preiddeu Annwn**, quoted later, a cauldron is involved.

We have already discussed these themes elsewhere at length, and so will not repeat them here (183). The important fact is that Taliesin demonstrates not only his ability to perform magical acts – the releasing of the chains which bound Elffin, the 'blerwm, blerwm' episode with Maelgwn's bards, and the discovery of treasure after the race make this clear – he also demonstrates his powers as a prophet and makes some extraordinary claims to having been in many places and times throughout history.

These boasts, the 'I have beens' as they are known, are echoed throughout much of the poetry, as we shall see. We may view these statements as elliptical references to a certain kind of inner knowledge, which was a product of Bardic/shamanic initiation and training. It is this which is most clearly indicated by the *Hanes* account of Taliesin's re-birth from Gwion Bach. This whole episode is, as we have seen, almost certainly a product of two stories, one at least of which (The Tale of Gwion Bach) dates from very ancient Celtic belief-systems, and offers a clear description of a shamanic initiation. There are parallel references in several of the poems attributed to Taliesin. In the **Cad Goddeu**, 'Battle of the Trees', translated in full on pages 296–301, the poet says:

> I have been in many shapes
> Before I assumed a constant form.

Later in the same work (which is really a miscellany of poems) we find:

> Not of mother, nor of father was my creation.
> I was made from the ninefold elements:
> From fruit-trees, from paradisal fruit;
> From primroses and hillflowers,
> From blossom of the trees and bushes;
> From the roots of the earth I was made;
> From the bloom of the nettle,
> From water of the ninth wave.
> Math enchanted me before I was made immortal;
> Gwydion created me by his magic wand;
> From Emrys and Euryon, from Mabon and Modron,
> From five fifties of magicians and masters like Math
>   was I made.
> I was made by the master in his highest ecstasy;
> By the wisest of druids I was made before the world
>   began.

This has for a long time been taken as a description of the making of the Flower-Woman Blodeuwedd by the magicians Math and Gwydion, but there is a sense in which it could apply to Taliesin also. He partook of many elements indeed, and was not, in a real sense, born 'of father or mother'. The elements referred to are all of a poetic or magical nature, with the speaker claiming to be of the substance of 250 magicians – surely a more appropriate reference to the Bard than to Blodeuwedd. However, this remains a matter for speculation until further evidence comes to light.

Elsewhere, in one of his many riddling songs the poet says:

> I am old, I am young, I am Gwion,
> I am universal . . . I am a bard.

And in still another poem (No. vi in Skene's translation of the *Black Book of Carmarthen*):

> With seven created beings I was placed for purification;
> I was gleaming fire when I was caused to exist.

While in a memorable passage from the important **Hostile Confederacy** (translated on pages 312–19) he relates:

> A second time I was formed
> I have been a blue salmon.
> I have been a dog;
> I have been a stag;
> I have been a roebuck on the mountain . . .
> I have been a grain discovered . . .
> A hen received me . . .
> I rested nine nights
> In her womb a child . . .
> I have been dead, I have been alive . . .
> I am Taliesin.

The references are numerous, and we shall see their like many times throughout the course of this book.

In another poem, **The Chair of Taliesin** (translated on pages 319–21) he gives some, if not all, of the ingredients of a sacred drink (akin to that of Eleusis) which was imbibed by all who underwent the rigorous ceremony resulting in

23

a series of visions. In Taliesin's case, this took the form of transformation into bird, beast and fish. Later, we may suppose, further self-induced trances gave him access to the pattern of history – hence his ability to be 'present' at many events which took place long before his time.

This is all in line with our premise that Taliesin is the repository of an age-old common tradition, shared in part by all initiates. We can learn more of his particular role from two sources: the Branwen story already mentioned, and another poem from *The Book of Taliesin*, which has become perhaps the best known of the works attributed to him. This is the **Preiddeu Annwn**, or 'Spoils of Annwn', which describes a raid on the Otherworld, led by Arthur. In both texts the objective of the search is a cauldron with special properties which relate it to the Cauldron of Ceridwen, as well as to other cauldrons which will be examined in more detail in Chapter Three.

The poem (translated in full on pages 251–2) is important for a number of reasons. It links Taliesin with Arthur and with the raid on Annwn to steal the magical Cauldron of Rebirth – which is perhaps a way of saying that Taliesin the Shaman led his Chieftain and his Chieftain's warriors on an interior journey to seek the Wisdom of the Cauldron. It claims a breadth of wisdom unequalled by the 'weak-willed clerics' or 'bards of the cowardly circuit' (a reference to the travelling singers whom Taliesin so roundly attacks in many of his poems such as **The Rebuke of the Bards**).

The repeated refrain is interesting. It is echoed by two other such lists: that which relates to the seven men (amongst them Taliesin) who returned from Bran's voyage to Ireland in search of the magical Cauldron which restored life (and which is closely related to Ceridwen's cauldron); and to the list of seven men who survived Camlan – one of whom was Ceridwen's offspring Morfran (334). The references to the imprisoned youth, Gwair, to the Cauldron warmed by the breath of nine maidens or muses, and to the visits to the seven mysterious Caers, are all part of an intricate cosmology and will be dealt with fully in Chapter Nine.

The Family of the Black Crow

When we come to look at the family of Ceridwen, we begin to glimpse something like a native British pantheon. Although

24

Tegid Foel is, in some senses, reduced to the figure of an ordinary man, we may be able to find a larger figure behind him. As for Morda, Gwion, Creirwy, and Morfran/Afaggdu, here we have all the possible signs of a 'family' of Gods and Goddesses.

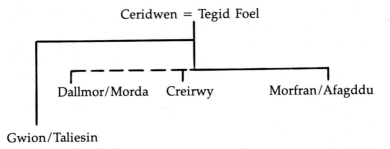

Ceridwen = Tegid Foel

Dallmor/Morda   Creirwy   Morfran/Afagddu

Gwion/Taliesin

Figure 2   The Family Tree of Taliesin.

Little is known of Tegid Foel 'The Bald'. It is possible that he is to be equated with the gigantic possessor of the Cauldron mentioned in **Branwen** and discussed in Chapter Three. Llyn Tegid, where he was stated to have dwelled with Ceridwen, is now associated with Bala Lake in modern-day Wales. It is said to have been formed by the overflowing of a well which was left uncovered so that the waters escaped. It flooded the original town of Bala, now supposedly under the waters of the lake. This is a typical folklore theme, but here the wellspring may refer to the Cauldron itself which, as we know, when left untended, burst. It may be that we have a distant memory of such a magical inundation in this story; the fact that the lake is named after Tegid, rather than Ceridwen, suggests that he was once of greater importance than in the *Hanes Taliesin*, where he is simply a name.

In the figure of Morda (or Dallmor Dallme as he is sometimes called), the mysterious blind man mentioned in some of the versions of *Hanes Taliesin*, there may well be, as noted by Professors Bloomfield and Dunn (29), the last vestige of 'the mysterious blind person who, in an earlier understanding of the myth, may well have symbolised an otherworld divine counterpart of the human poets who, like Homer, are blind.' Where Afagddu is concerned there may be something more than a hint of a 'hideous youth' character who parallels the

25

'hideous hag' of Celtic myth. The name Afagddu means literally 'utter darkness' (**Y Fagddu**), possibly derived from **Afanc Ddu** (Black Beaver), and seems to have been a title rather than an actual name. His real name seems to have been Morfran, which means 'Black Crow' (or possibly 'Sea Raven'), suggesting part of the tradition referring to the crow as a totem of war Goddesses like the Irish Morrigan and Badb. In the version of *Hanes Taliesin* copied by John Jones (Penniard 111) he is described as follows:

> There was a well-born man in Penllyn in former times who was named Tegid the Bald . . . and his wife was called Ceridwen; and from that wife there was born a son who was called Morfran vab Tagid, and a daughter who was called Creirwy, and she was the fairest maiden in the world; and they had a brother who was the ugliest man in the world, who was called **Y Vagddu** . . .
>
> (Trans. Bromwich, 334)

From this we can see that in all probability the original name of Ceridwen's son was Morfran and that, subsequently, the epithet **Afagddu** was attached to him, before the two names became separated again, giving Ceridwen two sons rather than one. A further reference in the *Mabinogion* story of 'Culhwch ac Olwen' (144), seems to confirm this, as well as adding other valuable details. The passage, which is part of a kind of pseudo-triad, reads as follows.

> Morfran son of Tegid (no man placed his weapon in him at Camlan, so exceedingly ugly was he; all thought he was a devil helping. He had hair on him like the hair of a stag) and Sandde Angel-Face (no one placed his spear in him at Camlan, so exceeding fair was he; all thought he was an angel helping) . . . (144)

We notice that here the figure of Morfran is set against that of Sandde or Sendaf 'Angel-Face', and this may well offer a clue to a deeper level of the myth, as we shall see.

In a late, and not necessarily reliable, source, *Cambrian Popular Antiquities* by the Rev. Peter Roberts (266), we find the following story, the source of which, according to the author, was a manuscript in the collection of Mr Jones of

Gelly Lyfdy. In this the hero, Arthur, loses his way in the mountains around Eryri (Snowdon) and finds his way to a cave in which are three gigantic beings: an old woman, her son and her daughter. The old woman and the son want to kill Arthur in case they are discovered, but the daughter pleads for him and he is offered freedom on one condition – that he remain there that night and deliver a triad of truths next day. The son places a heavy ox-hide over the hero and in the morning Arthur says to him, 'You are the best harper I ever heard.' To the old woman he says, 'You are the ugliest hag I ever saw.' And to the daughter he says, 'If I were once from hence I would never come hither again.' These things are all allowed to be irrefutable truths and Arthur is set free.

Roberts identifies the three giants as Ceridwen, Avagddu and Creirwy, which does not seem unlikely. If this is a genuine folkloric episode – and there seems no reason to doubt that it is – then we have a most interesting memory which reinforces our earlier contention as to the nature of Ceridwen and her family. This will be discussed further in Chapter Three. For the moment we should note that the gigantic stature of the threesome indicates otherworldly origin, while the fact that Afagddu is described as a brilliant harper suggests that, as in Taliesin's poem **The Chair of Ceridwen** (pages 304–8), the Goddess' dark son achieved some status in the world!

In another story, from Irish tradition, we hear of Amairgen, the father of Conall Cernach. His story is told in the *Book of Leinster* (260).

There was in Ulster a famous smith called Eccet or Eccen, surnamed **Salach** the 'Sooty'. He had a beautiful daughter and a hideously ugly son called Amairgen, who had reached the fourteenth year of his age without uttering a word. It happened that one day, when Eccet was away, Aitherne the master poet sent his man Greth on an errand. Greth saw the daughter with the hideous child near by. Looking at him grimly the child suddenly asked him if he liked eating curds and scraps. The child spoke in such allusive language that Greth fled and told his master what had occurred. Meanwhile, the smith came home and was told of the events of the day. He at once guessed that the ingenious wording of the boy's question betokened coming poetic greatness, and that Aitherne would make the same assumption and come to kill a possible rival. Eccet therefore told his daughter to take the child away to the sea near Slieve Mis in the South, while his father made an image of earth which so looked like the boy that when Aitherne came, ostensibly to ask for an axe to be mended, he was fooled and struck the boy suddenly so that he appeared dead. Pretence was made of pursuing him and demanding an **eric** (honour price), which was finally set that Aitherne must educate a child of Eccet until he should be equal in poetic craft to himself. When this was agreed, Amairgen was brought back. Afterwards he lost his hideous looks and became one of the foremost poets of Ulster.

Finally, in the story of the master-poet Senchan, contained in *Cormac's Glossary* (233), we learn how Senchan journeys to the Isle of Man in search of a famous lost poetess. He is accompanied by a hideous youth and on arrival is met by an old woman on the shore. Hearing that the leader of the party is Senchan she offers to help them if he can answer a poetic riddle. She then speaks one half of a poem and invites Senchan to complete it. While he hesitates, the ugly youth supplies the missing words, and in due course the old woman is recognised as the missing poetess. Senchan clothes her in fine raiment and returns with her to Ireland. There they meet again with the ugly youth, who had vanished after the contest. Now he is 'a young hero, kingly, radiant ... fairer than the men of the world was he, both in form and dress' (233). He is later identified as the Spirit of Poetry itself but, as we have suggested elsewhere (187), it is easy to see that the roles have been exchanged and that at one time the old woman (the Hag) was the Spirit of Poetry, or the initiatrix, and that in all probability the ugly youth who transforms into a beautiful, fair and radiant man, is a younger version of Senchan, who was transformed after winning a poetic contest.

This underlying theme of the ugly youth who is transformed as an outward form of his inner, poetic transformation, runs through each of these stories. It may well be a lost strand in the history of Taliesin, where Gwion begins life as a hideous youth rather than Afagddu, and that the whole matter of the transformation and chase by Ceridwen is a description of his growth into poetic manhood. In which case it is even possible that Gwion was, at one point in the development of the myth, the actual **son** of Ceridwen, rather than her reborn offspring by the method of swallowing the grain of wheat. Elsewhere we have stated that:

The pursuit of the youthful god by the hag is a perennial theme in Celtic tradition. The interaction of their roles and the subtle polarities which affect them have often been wilfully misunderstood ... It is plain ... that the Hag or Cailleach, typified by Ceridwen, is the Mother of Creation whose role is that of opposer and initiator of the candidate. The Son of Wisdom, typified by Gwion, is pursued throughout all his transformations, just as a tutor pushes a student through harder and more varied forms of learning until a synthesis of knowledge is acquired. Only then does the Hag rest and send the newly-born seer-poet out into the world. (183)

Afagddu, Amairgen, and the youth who advises Senchan, all possess an earlier, hideous self who, in each case, undergoes a change from ugly to beautiful, which was maybe Taliesin's original change. Amairgen's name seems to mean 'wonder child' (260), and Gwion/Taliesin is certainly this. The suggestion is that Afagddu-Gwion-Taliesin, the ugly youth who represents all the darkness in the individual, sought wholeness through the initiation of the Cauldron, and was reborn afterwards with the bright brow of fairness and the understanding of poetry.

Rhys remarks (260) that Goddesses of the Ceridwen type usually give birth to dark and light twins, who represent the darkness and light of the world. In 'Culhwch and Olwen' we saw Morfran linked with Sendaf Bright Angel. Were these, at one time, the children of Ceridwen? And what of the description of Morfran as being 'covered in hair like a stag'? Does this literally mean that, like Merlin, he was born with a thick pelt of hair, or could it possibly be a reference to a shaman's dress of deerskin cloak and horned head-dress? We will see, in Chapter Four, how this possibly equates the learning of the Bright Knowledge of the poets with its other, darker side, reflected in the kind of *un*wisdom of Maelgwn's bards. This is further confirmed by the date and manner of Taliesin being set adrift. These vary from script to script: in Llewelyn Sion's version it is 20th April; in Owen John's version it is 29th April; in Gruyffydd's version it is 31st October (Calan Gaeaf). **Calan Gaeaf** means, literally, 'the first day of winter', and Gwion/Taliesin's crossing over from one world to the other at this time is significant. This is because Samhain was traditionally the time when the people of the Otherworld were known to make such crossings, and it was said that upon this night the doors between the worlds were open. The other dates, 20th or 29th April, relate to the other great festival of the Celtic year, Beltain, at which time new beginnings were celebrated. Thus, the moment of Taliesin's nascence takes place at one or other of the most important festivals, when life itself changed pace and meaning and when the dwellers in the Otherworld were closest at hand. These two festivals are associated with Dark and Light, with the Beginning and the End of the Celtic year, and seem wholly appropriate to one who is so closely related to the theme of the Dark and Light twins.

The Birth of the Poet

The central theme of *Hanes Taliesin* is rebirth, however one decides, ultimately, to view this. Our thesis is simply that the information contained in this reputedly late work, together with that provided by the poems attributed to Taliesin, shows evidence of a continuing shamanic tradition in Britain during the Heroic Age and earlier, and that this tradition, together with parallel beliefs in Ireland, lies at the heart of Celtic myth and religion. That it includes the various beliefs and practices of the Druids is probable, and enables us to view their existence with new eyes.

The doctrine of metempsychosis, or transmigration of souls, has been attributed to the Celts ever since the classical writers discovered them. In the *De Situ Orbis* of Pomponius Mela (Book III, pages 2, 18, and 19) and in the writings of Ammianus Marcellinus (Book XV, pages 9 and 8), we find references to this. Caesar himself discussed it in his account of the Gaulish Druids. Traces are also to be found in actual Celtic texts. In **The Festivities of the House of Conan** (Trans. of Ossianic Society vol 2, 1854), for example, we find the following dialogue:

'Tell me,' says Conan to Fionn, 'who among the Fenian heroes is he who leaps over his own gravestone every day, whose own daughter is his mother, and who is demanding **eric** and reparation from the man who killed him, though he is himself alive?'

'I will tell you about that,' says Fionn. 'Two Fenian chiefs of my people, namely Oscur the son of Criomthann, and

Daoglas son of Cairrill Cas, one day quarrelled about a fight that occurred between two dogs, and Daoglas was slain on that occasion. The beautiful marriageable daughter of Daoglas came over to him, and having stooped down to kiss him, a red spark of fire flew from his mouth into hers, and she became pregnant in consequence, and brought forth a broad-crowned son in due time; and, since no other name was found for him, he was called by the name of his father. He was nurtured in fitting manner until his seventh year; and the first feat of youthful folly that he performed was to leap over his own gravestone; and he is now demanding **eric** from Oscur, son of Criomthann.

The Thumb of Wisdom

Taliesin imbibes the wisdom of the Cauldron when he places his burned thumb into his mouth. This simple fact hides a maze of references which will be more fully explored in Chapter Seven, which deals with prophetic inspiration. Taliesin is not alone in receiving power or insight by this method (we may call it a method in the light of evidence relating to the mysterious skills known as **Teinm Laida, Dichetel do Chenaib** and **Imbas Forosnai** to be discussed later). The principal character who shares this unusual mode of magical transmission is the Irish hero Fionn Mac Cumhail, who is sometimes called a poet, but who certainly possesses wisdom at least in some ways equal to that of Taliesin – though never so totally expressed as in the *Hanes Taliesin* or the *Book of Taliesin*.

The story of Fionn's childhood, and his acquiring of wisdom, is told in an Irish text *The Boyhood Exploits of Fionn* (202), which has been dated to at least the 10th Century, although, as with the Taliesin material, the story it tells dates from a much earlier period.

Fionn's father, Cumaill, was the leader of the Fianna, a picked band of warriors who served the High Kings of Ireland. His place was much sought after by one Aed, son of Morna (later called Goll, One Eye). In a battle fought at Cnucha (now Castleknock, Co. Dublin) he slew Cumaill and took his place. Cumaill's wife, Muirne, was pregnant, and in due time brought forth a son who was named Demne. Because of the threat to him from Goll and the other sons of Morna, the infant was given into the keeping of two ancient women-warriors, Bodbmall the Druidess, and the Grey One of Luachaire. They took him to the forest of Sleive Bloom and reared him in secret. Then, when he was grown to young manhood, he went with a group of friends to a place called Crotta, where he caught scurvy *and therefrom became a scald* and was known as Demne the Bald.

Later he was at a place called Moy Liffey, in Kildare, when he spied some youths playing hurly and, joining in, defeated them all. When they complained to their lord, he told them to kill the stranger, but they declared that they would be unable to do so because of his strength. Asked to describe the youth, they said that he was 'a shapely fair youth'. The lord said he should henceforth be called Fionn (**finn** 'the fair') and the name stuck to him. He had many more adventures, including one where he slew a great sow which had been devastating the midlands of Munster. After this he left his female fosterers, because the sons of Morna were coming close. Soon after, he encountered a woman mourning the death of her son who had been slain by Liath Luachra, the very man who had struck the first blow at Fionn's father. Fionn ambushed Liath and slew him, at the same time recovering from him the crane-bag which Liath had stolen from Cumaill. Because of this act, 'he durst not remain in Ireland else he took to poetry, for fear of the son of Uirghriu and the sons of Morna.' (202)

Fionn thus went to learn poetry from Finneces (White Wisdom), who lived on the shores of the magical river Boyne, and who had been, for seven years, seeking the Salmon of Wisdom which swam in Fec's Pool, since it had been prophesied that he would find it, eat it and know everything. However, when it was found, Finneces entrusted its cooking to Fionn who, though cautioned to eat nothing of the fish, nevertheless thrust his burnt thumb into his mouth when it was splashed by some of the liquor in which the salmon was cooked. So it was the boy, not Finneces, who received the wisdom of the salmon. The old poet immediately recognised the boy as Fionn (The Fair One), naming him as the prophesied receiver of wisdom. In aftertimes, Fionn had only to put his thumb into his mouth to have prophetic knowledge.

It is that which gave the knowledge to Finn, to whit, whenever he put his thumb into his mouth, and sang through **teinm laida**, then whatever he had been ignorant of would be revealed to him. (202)

Other versions of the story say that Fionn's thumb was trapped in the door of a **sidhe** mound (faery mound) when he chased a woman of the Otherworld there, and that it was thus that he acquired his wisdom. Both accounts go to show how Fionn, ostensibly a warrior, became known for his great wisdom and poetry.

The way in which both men exercise their abilities varies, since Fionn's knowledge is dependent upon his putting his thumb into his mouth. Taliesin is shown to be universally omniscient. However, it seems clear that both Fionn and Taliesin correspond to the archetype of Oengus or Mabon, the Young God, whose youth and wisdom totally overset the ingrained cunning or venerable knowledge of either ancestral gods or sage Druids. They are both capable in the combat of knowledge since they have imbibed from its very source. This youthful ability to confound wise men was later celebrated in the Celtic Church in the episode where Christ disputes with the elders of the Temple.

It is interesting to notice that as well as receiving the wisdom of the salmon, Fionn is already a poet (scald), which occurs through his falling ill with scurvy. It is well known that in many instances shamanic abilities manifest themselves after illness, so that Fionn may be seen as both a poet *and* a shaman, just as is Taliesin. He also becomes bald as a result of this, which makes one think at once of Tegid the Bald and of the ugly youth who becomes fair. The fact that Fionn seeks to become a poet in order to escape the vengeance of Goll and his brothers refers to the indemnity enjoyed by poets whose honour-price was so high that few men would injure or kill a poet knowingly.

There is a very good case for the etymological derivation of both Fionn and Gwion from the same source (109). Apart from the obvious similarity of the names – and the analogous adventures of the two characters – the Welsh root **Gwi** and the Irish **Fi** seem to be compatible. This lends support to the belief that at one time the story of the shaman-poet who acquired wisdom through drops that fell on his thumb was widespread, and that it later became attached to the stories of the Irish Fionn and the Welsh Gwion (or Gwynn). We have asserted that Taliesin's life is a reflection of the role of the shaman-poet and we shall hope to show how this is so in the next chapter. To summarise the evidence so far collected, we have shown that Gwion/Taliesin derives from extremely primitive sources, that he may well be the offspring of Ceridwen in her guise as Goddess of Poetry, and that he is the possessor of a unique store of wisdom derived from shamanic and bardic sources which he shares with figures such as Fionn. We may also list Taliesin's major roles within the tradition:

1) He is a mediator who describes numerous visits to various parts of the Otherworld.
2) He is a guardian of poetic and shamanic lore, including the natural sciences.
3) He is also a seer and prophet – fulfilling the role of ovate (**vatus**), a master of the shamanic mysteries of foretelling the future and remembering the past.

We shall now examine the evidence for the existence of such a shamanic tradition in the Celtic world, before proceeding to show how the material relating to Taliesin conforms to this.

Chapter Two

SHAMANISM AND THE CELTS: THE FELLOWSHIP OF THE WISE

Frenzy, trance, and shape shifting, all point to some generic connection between the Celtic magician, of whatever name, and the shaman of the Northern Eurasiatic zone. It is not at all unlikely that this remounts to the early period of contacts over the Pontiac steppes.

The Celts, T. E. G. Powell

The Lord of the Beasts

The image of the Celtic shaman stares back at us from one of the most familiar icons of the Celtic world – a relief from one of the inner panels of the Gundestrup Cauldron (see frontispiece). It shows him in a pose traditionally assumed by shamans the world over: cross-legged; upright; staring forth at a world only he can see. On his head are antlers, which may be seen either as a head-dress, or as actually growing from his head. He is surrounded by beasts of all kinds, the spirit helpers which enable him to enter and travel unharmed through the realm of the Otherworld, and in his left hand he grasps the head of a serpent, a creature long associated with wisdom and magic. The name of this figure, long-accepted by historians, archaeologists and mythographers alike, is 'The Lord of the Beasts'. He appears dramatically in several texts, nowhere perhaps as vividly as the following account from 'The Lady of the Fountain', one of the stories contained in the medieval collection of Welsh myths and legends known as *The Mabinogion* (144). In this the hero, Cynon, relates the story of his adventures, in which, having entered an obvious Otherworldly place and met with one of its denizens, he is instructed to go into a wood and there follow a path to a large sheltered glade with a mound in the centre.

And thou wilt see a black man of great stature on top of the mound. He is not smaller in size than two men of this world. He has but one foot; and one eye in the middle of his forehead. And he has a club of iron, and it is certain that there are no two men in the world who would not find their burden in that club. And he is not a comely man, but on the contrary he is exceedingly ill-favoured; and he is the woodward of that wood. And thou wilt see a thousand wild animals grazing around him . . .

Cynon follows these instructions and there, as foretold, is the strange figure of the woodward.

Huge of stature as the man had told me that he was, I found him to exceed by far the description he had given me . . . And he only spoke to me in answer to my questions. Then I asked him what power he held over those animals. 'I will show thee, little man' said he. And he took his club in his hand and with it struck a stag a great blow so that it brayed vehemently, and at his braying the animals came together, as numerous as the stars in the sky, so that it was difficult for me to find room in the glade to stand among them. There were serpents, and dragons, and divers sorts of animals. And he looked at them, and bade them go and feed; and they bowed their heads and did him homage as vassals to their lord.

This whole passage is rife with shamanic overtones. It is clearly a very primitive story, despite the fact that it was not recorded until the Middle Ages. The depiction of the figure with one eye and one foot derives from a manner of casting a spell, in which the shaman or magician would stand upon one leg, with one hand behind his back and one eye tightly closed, before uttering his incantation. Interestingly, also, there are references in Siberian tradition to the birth of the shaman, where the Mother of Animals, who is responsible for all shamans, gives them, new-born – that is, into their shamanic abilities – into the keeping of a spirit named Burgestez-Udagan, who has one eye, one hand and one leg. This clearly relates to an ancient idea of the shamanic initiator being hideous which, as we shall see in the next chapter, is very much a part of the emerging picture. The fact that the figure is also black denotes his connection with the earth and with the underworld. Like all shamans he only answers when questioned directly. He is a master of beasts, including serpents and dragons – both of which are depicted on the Gundestrup Cauldron. His method of summoning the animals, by striking the stag so that it in turn calls the rest, seems to relate to an earlier scenario in which the shaman probably adopted the skin and antlers of the stag and summoned them by calling in the language of the beasts.

In a passage immediately following the one quoted above, the woodward instructs Cynon that if he would seek adventure he should go to a certain very tall tree in the midst of an open space 'whose branches are greener than the greenest pine tree'.

> Under this tree is a fountain, and by the side of the fountain is a marble slab, and on the marble slab a silver bowl, attached by a chain of silver, so that it may not be carried away. Take the bowl and throw a bowlful of water upon the slab, and thou wilt hear a mighty peal of thunder, so that thou wilt think that heaven and earth are trembling with its fury. With the thunder will come a shower so severe that it will be scarce possible for thee to endure it and live. And the shower will be of hailstones; and after the shower the weather will become fair, but every leaf that was on the tree will have been carried away by the shower. Then a flight of birds will come and alight upon the tree; and in thine own country thou didst never hear a strain so sweet as that which they will sing . . .

This whole passage reads like an account of a shamanic initiation. First Cynon must go to a great tree in the midst of a glade. This equates very closely to the idea of the World-Tree common to all shamanic beliefs (see below). There he finds a silver vessel which may well have been a cauldron of the kind from which inspiration and knowledge were derived. Then he is instructed in the uses of weather magic which invokes a storm of hail so fierce that it will almost destroy him. Finally there is the wonderful image of the tree, stripped of its leaves, suddenly clothed again in the living bodies of birds, whose song is the sweetest he will ever have heard. Accounts of shamanic visions abound with such descriptions, and the birds themselves are found throughout Celtic myth as the bringers of inspiration, or as conductors of the seekers into the Otherworld. Coming so close upon the description of the Lord of the Beasts, it can hardly be coincidental, and we can only believe that we are reading a very ancient description, preserved in folk-memory, of real shamanic activity.

Figure 3 Horned figure with hands in attitude of receiving inspiration. He is apparently tattooed with serpentine decorations.

The figure depicted on the Gundestrup Cauldron is usually accepted as being that of a god, referred to – on the most slender of evidence – as 'Cernunnos'. However, he would have been more generally recognised, among the Celts of Britain, Ireland and Gaul, as a shaman, a walker between the worlds, who in varying degrees became the tribe's remembrancer, their physician, and their poet. It is this figure, in all his many guises, which we shall be tracing throughout this book. And because, within the writings attributed to Taliesin and within the legends which grew up about his character, we find the last vestiges of shamanic practice among the Celts, our investigation will concentrate on the figure of the great Bard as a manifestation of that tradition.

As to the identification of the horned figure who appears, not only on the Gundestrup Cauldron, but on carved stones throughout the Celtic world, it is perhaps worth noting at this point that the usual ascription of the name Cernunnos to this character has little real foundation. It is based primarily on a single inscription, found on an altar-stone in Gaul, to: '[C]ERNUNNOS', the 'horned', or 'peaked', one. From this the assumption has been made that *all* the depictions of horned, squatting figures, like that found on the Gundestrup Cauldron, represent this same figure. Cernunnos is, however, equally likely to have been the name of a local tribal deity, whilst the collection of antlered figures may just as easily be seen as representations of the shaman figure among the Celts.

We might wish, here, to consider some actual definitions of shamanism. These are taken from *Dreamtime and Inner Space* (152), a remarkable book by Holger Kalweit, who, though he is a trained anthropologist, keeps an open mind about the deeper aspects of the subject. Put alongside descriptions from Celtic records, we will at once see just how closely they resemble each other.

> The shaman is part of the age-old tradition of the Perennial Philosophy – the mystical teaching of unity of all things and all being. In the realm of magic everything is interrelated; nothing exists in isolation. Here rules the principle of pars pro toto. This level of consciousness, like a gigantic telephone exchange, affords access to all other realms of awareness. All mystical paths are agreed that such a way of experiencing requires a suspension of normal awareness and of rational thought by means of special techniques of mind training. An empty mind allows an alternative level of transpersonal experience.

This is the key to understanding the mysteries referred to again and again in the works attributed to Taliesin. They are by no means unique in the Celtic world, and it will be said that an examination of the traditions of other figures like Taliesin would provoke a similar conclusion. However, this is to strengthen rather than weaken our case. This significantly shamanic tradition, of which Taliesin is a prime representative, is at the heart of the Celtic world. To quote Holger Kalweit again:

> Those that have returned from this world [the inner place of the Shaman] say that present, past, and future exist simultaneously, and that to enter this world is tantamount to enlightenment. Many people felt that in some inexplicable way they had gained *total knowledge* ... One person who returned said: 'It seemed that all of a sudden, all knowledge – of all that had started from the very beginning, that would go on without end – that for a second I knew all the secrets of the ages, all the meaning of the universe, the stars, the moon – of everything. (My italics)

How better can we explain – if an explanation is required at all – Taliesin's extravagant claims to have been present at the great events in the life of the cosmos, to know, literally, everything, to be familiar at once with the course of the heavens, the lives of stone and river and plant, to have penetrated so deeply into the essence of creation that he is able to state that he has been an endless number of things: a spade; a spear; a tree; a flower; a bird; a beast; a fish; a drop of water . . . the catalogue goes on for ever.

And all of these things are part of the shaman's world. He, too, sees through everything, dies and is reborn, suffers the pangs of the world and sees into its darkest corners. As the Augustine monk Abraham of Santa Clara puts it, 'Someone who dies before he dies does not die when he dies' (152). The almost-death of initiation, the moment when Gwion becomes Taliesin, is the common experience of shamans the world over. Afterwards, they are never the same; everything has changed. They have known total knowledge and, to a degree according to their skills and strengths, have permanent access to it from that moment on. Some, like Fionn Mac Cumhail, have to reactivate their wisdom through a ritual act – Fionn chews his thumb. Others, like Taliesin, seem able to command their store of knowledge at any time. It makes them unique, and it is not surprising that we find them awe-inspiring today. They must have seemed so in their own time, when the understanding and appreciation of the inner realms was more generally recognised than it is now. But what is so astounding is that, in most cases, their words, where these have been recorded, still elicit a response from us today. We may not understand the poems of Taliesin at a first reading, but they speak to us at a level of which we are scarcely aware. We can still, if we wish, recover something of that original response, and of the miraculous knowledge that was part of the shamanic tradition. As we begin our journey through the labyrinth of words which make up the Taliesin tradition, we cannot help but be aware that we are walking in a world of crystalline wonder, a world where all things are possible and only the unexpected is to be expected.

The Shamanic Experience

Mircea Eliade, the greatest contemporary writer on the subject of shamanism, defines the shamanic experience as follows:

In the sphere of shamanism in the strict sense, the mystical experience is expressed in a ... trance ... The shaman is preeminently an ecstatic. Now on the plane of primitive religions ecstasy signifies the soul's flight to heaven, or its wanderings about the earth, or, finally, its descent to the subterranean world ... (74)

Shamanic abilities are generally brought on by personal crisis. However, where this was not naturally forthcoming, initiations designed to produce the effects of such a state were used to bring about this rebirth as a shaman. In the story of Taliesin, of course, this is clearly instanced by the episode of the Cauldron. Though elaborated into the form of a story, there can be little doubt that it hides a description of a shamanic initiation, in which the candidate was given a drink which caused him to undergo the kind of experience alluded to in the poems. The characteristic experience of the shaman may be tabulated as follows:

1   He falls ill/becomes unconscious/ecstatic;
2   He encounters Otherworld personages;
3   He enters the Otherworld itself;
4   He journeys there for some time;
5   He receives teachings;
6   He faces dangers/initiations;
7   He returns 'to life' at the moment he left.

Each and every one of these points are encountered in the Taliesin tradition, which represents a kind of shamanic practice which seems to have been still in vogue during the 6th Century, and which became associated gradually with the figure of the (by then) semi-mythical Bard. That is to say, it was not 'made up' by the clerics who copied the poems, but simply recorded by them, often without understanding, and with some disapproval. Quite simply, Taliesin's original experiences and teachings, contained in his inspired utterances, became overlaid by layers of complex manuscript transference. However, traces of their original shape and substance can still be observed when one looks at the poems line by line and verse by verse. For the moment let us look at a sample of quotations from various of the poems.

I have become a predicting Bard ...
I have been with skilful men,

With Math and Govannon,
With Eunydd and Elestron . . .

I have been a sow, I have been a buck,
I have been a sage, I have been a snout,
I have been a horn, I have been a wild sow,
I have been a shout in battle . . .

I have been a cat with a speckled head on three trees
I have been a well-filled crane-bag, a sight to behold.
I am a harmonious one; I am a clear singer;
I am steel, I am a Druid.
I am an artificer, a scientist;
I am a serpent [of wisdom]; I am love . . .
I am the depository of song . . .
I am a bard in the hall, a chick of the Chair [i.e. a fledgeling of
   Ceridwen, the Great Hen].

Three times I have been born, I know by meditation;
Anyone would be foolish not to come and obtain
All the sciences of the world from my breast.
For I know what has been, what in future will occur.
I know all the names of the stars from North to South;
I have been in the galaxy at the throne of the Distributor
I have been three periods in the Prison of Arianrhod . . .

I am a wonder whose origin is not known.
I have obtained the muse from the Cauldron of
   Ceridwen . . .

I have been an instructor to all intelligences,
I am able to instruct the whole universe.
I shall be until the day of doom on the face of the earth;
Nor is it known if my body is flesh or fish.

Firstly I was formed in the shape of a handsome man,
In the hall of Ceridwen where I was refined.
Though small and modest in my behaviour,
I became great in her lofty sanctuary.

While I was held prisoner, sweet inspiration educated me
And laws were imparted to me in speech without words;
But I had to flee from the angry, terrible hag
Whose outcry was terrifying.

42

Conspicuous when came from the cauldron
The three inspirations of Ceridwen . . .

My tongue is not free in the place of the Goddess . . .
For her glory is the offering
Of milk, of dew, of acorns . . .

I praise the one
who, to keep guard over me,
did bestow my seven senses,
from fire and earth, water and air: . . .
one is for instinct,
two is for feeling,
three is for speaking,
four is for tasting
five is for seeing
six is for hearing,
seven is for smelling . . .

Figure 4   Prehistoric Shaman wearing horns and a skin robe,
accompanied by an ithiphallic spirit-helper.

43

And so on. All totally in line with the role of the shaman, who must know the heavens, the gods and the secrets of the elements, who must use all of his senses, including instinct and feeling, to act as a bridge between this world and the other. Three times, Taliesin tells us, he has been a prisoner in the court of Arianrhod, which is also known as the Northern Crown, the Corona Borealis – and now he is able to instruct all creatures, indeed the whole of the universe. He has learned the secrets of transformation, he has dwelled in the Court of Ceridwen and drunk from her Cauldron – in other words he has received initiation and is able to prophesy all the things that will be as well as knowing all the things that were. We shall be returning to these statements again throughout this book, as we examine the evidence for predictive skills, shapeshifting, and the magic of song itself.

Battle of the Shamans

If wisdom and cunning are seen as weapons wielded by a shaman-poet of skill and power, other aspects of his redoubtable abilities are not hard to find. A poem known as **The Siege of Drom Damhgaire** provides us with a unique description of a magical battle, fought between two shamans: Ciothruadh, in the service of the great king Cormac Mac Airt, and Mogh Ruith (Servant of the Wheel) on the side of Fiacha Muilleathan, the King of Munster. (Although the term used throughout is 'druid', to all intents we may substitute 'shaman'.)

Cormac was king of Tara. His hospitality was so prodigious that his royal revenue was soon exhausted. He sought to get a double tribute out of the kingdom of Munster; since Munster had two provinces, he believed it should give him double measure. King Fiacha disputed the justice of this claim and offered what he considered ample tribute to Cormac.

Cormac then called together his druids to give him an augury concerning the outcome of a foray against Munster and, though the druids could give only unfavourable replies, set off to Damhghaire. Cormac's druids caused springs and streams to dry up in Munster. But Mogh Ruith, Fiacha's druid, came against the army of Cormac. He had been trained in the East, in the school of Simon Magus himself – for Simon was of the race of the Gaels.

Mogh Ruith relieved the drought on Munster. Then, Cioth-ruadh said that their last resort was to use the Druidic Fire against the enemy. He ordered Cormac's men to go and each cut down a quickbeam (mountain ash or rowan) and make a great fire from the resulting wood. If the smoke drifted south, then Cormac would be victorious, but if it came northwards, then Munster would overcome him.

Mogh Ruith perceived their purpose and ordered the men of Munster to bring out of the forest a faggot of rowan wood. Then he ordered that the king should himself bring out a special bundle of wood that had grown in the shelter of three things; sheltered from the north-east wind of March, sheltered from the sea-winds, and sheltered from the winds of conflagration which were being lit against them. Mogh Ruith's apprentice, Ceannmhair, built up this wood in the shape of a triangle, with seven vents into it. (Ciothruadh's fire was only heaped up roughly with three vents.) Then Mogh Ruith asked each of the Munster troop to give him a shaving from the handle of his spear which he then mixed with butter, and rolled into a great ball saying all the while:

'I mix a roaring powerful fire;
It will clear the woods; it will blight the grass;
An angry flame of powerful speed;
It will rush up to the skies above;
It will subdue the wrath of all burning wood;
It will break a battle on the clans of Conn'.

Then he threw the ball into the fire whence it exploded with great force. Saying that he was about to bring a rout upon the enemy, Mogh Ruith told all to stand ready and watch if the fires blew northwards against their foe. Then 'he blew his druidical breath up into the sky, and it immediately became a threatening black cloud, which came down in a shower of blood upon the plain before him, and moved onwards from that to Tara, the Druid all the time pronouncing his rhythmical incantations.'

Mogh Ruith asked what effect the flames were having, because he was blind. They reported that the fires were chasing over each other West and North, and that not a tree in mid Munster was left standing. When he asked again, the fires had risen up into the sky like angry warriors. 'Then Mogh

Ruith called for his dark-grey hornless bull's hide and his white speckled bird head-piece and he flew up into the air to the verge of the fires, and commenced to turn them northwards. When Cormac's druid, Ciothruadh, saw this, he also ascended to oppose Mogh Ruith.' But Mogh Ruith knocked Ciothruadh to the ground, and turned the fires north.

Cormac's army retreated, hotly pursued by Mogh Ruith in his chariot drawn by wild oxen. He asked who were the men at the rear of the enemy's army.

'They are three tall grey-headed men,' said they. 'They are Cormac's three Druids, Cecht, Ciotha and Ciothruadh,' said he, 'and my gods have promised me to transform them into stones, when I should overtake them, if I could but blow my breath upon them.' And then he blew a druidic breath upon them, so that they were turned into stones; and these are the stones that are called the Flags of Raighne at this day. (232)

This extraordinary text gives a vivid portrait of the power wielded by the shaman. He is, like many of the great poets or seers of the Celts, blind. Yet despite the fact that he has to ask about the direction of the fires he is apparently able to see the three grey headed men at the rear of the opposing army. (Were the druids disguised in the form of cranes?) This leads one almost to suppose that perhaps he was only *temporarily* blind – while he was actually performing his incantations. (See also Chapter Six, on the darkness sought by poets.)

But it is the description of Mogh Ruith's 'dark grey hornless bull's hide and his white speckled bird head-piece' which really gives one pause. If this is not a shaman's dress what is? The power of flight, and the power over the flames, as well as the choice of wood, are all a part of the shaman's control of the elements discussed below. Such magical battles as this are described in almost every tradition that possesses a shamanistic element.

The Inner Sight

The most important single aspect of shamanism is atunement with the Otherworld. All shamans are in touch with the inner self who is wiser, stronger, more balanced than they may appear in their normal selves. Trance states are used a great deal to keep in touch with the spirit world, including chant, drumming, and various hallucinatory substances. (The use of the last is not recommended except under the most rigorously controlled circumstances and under the guidance of a trained shaman.) Drumming, the most commonly practised way of entering trance, does not seem to have been part of Celtic practice, despite the use of the **bodhran** by contemporary folk musicians, which seems to have no ancient tradition attached to it.

The shaman possessed unique abilities to enter and leave the spirit world. Celtic literature abounds with descriptions of this place – descriptions which possess so many common elements that they could only derive from the very deepest levels of consciousness. We shall have occasion to look in more detail at what we may call 'The Shamanic Universe' throughout this book (see especially Chapters Six, Seven and Nine). For the moment we shall confine ourselves to noticing a single theme, and the way in which it is reflected in the material with which we are engaged.

Amongst the various attributes of the shaman discussed by Eliade (76) is the pole (originally from a tent) used by most Siberian shamans to represent the Centre of the Universe or the Cosmic Tree. (We have already caught a glimpse of this in the passage concerning the Lord of the Beasts quoted above.) Whilst climbing this the shaman would pause at various points to describe what he saw, each level representing a further stage in a voyage to an Otherworldly state of being. Similarly, the many stories of **Immrama** 'voyages', from island to island across uncharted seas, represented a kind of map of the soul's voyage through life (191). In Ancient Egypt the same idea was current in the journey of the soul *after* death, in the Boat of Millions of Years.

The Celtic view of the Otherworld is extraordinarily detailed. Perhaps in no other part of the world do so many full and varied descriptions exist that we can actually tabulate them and relate them to different states of being (165). David Spaan, in his study of the Otherworld in early Irish literature (285), lists over a hundred different *names* for the Otherworld. The three central divisions were into the Otherworldly Paradise, which is usually situated on an island; the Land-Beneath-the-Wave, and the Underworld, which centred mainly on the lands beneath the various **sidhe** mounds. All three are at once very distinctive and yet so mutable in outline that they often overlap or blur into each other in a bewildering way. A single example of each must suffice to illustrate this point – though there will be many other references to these realms throughout the book.

1 The Celtic Paradise

There was a large fortress in the midst of the plain with a wall of bronze around it. In the fortress was a house of white silver, and it was half-thatched with the wings of white birds. A fairy host of horsemen were at the house, with lapfuls of the wings of white birds in their bosoms to thatch the house ... Cormac saw a man kindling a fire, and the thick-boled oak was cast upon it, top and butt. When the man came again with another oak, the burning of the first oak had ended. Then he saw another royal stronghold, and another wall of bronze around it. There were four palaces therein. He entered the fortress and saw the vast palace with its beams of bronze, its wattling of silver, and its thatch of the wings of white birds. Then he saw in the enclosure a shining fountain, with five streams flowing out of it, and the hosts in turn drinking its water ... He entered the palace. There was one couple inside awaiting him. The warrior's figure was distinguished owing to the beauty of his shape, the comeliness of his form, and the wonder of his countenance. The girl along with him, mature, yellow-haired, with a golden head-dress, was the loveliest of the world's women. Cormac's feet were washed by invisible hands. There was bathing in a pool without the need of attendance. The heated stones themselves went into and came out of the water.

Cormac's Adventures in the Land of Promise, (59)

2 The Land-Beneath-the-Wave

That which is a clear sea
For the prowed skiff in which Bran is,
That is a happy plain with profusion of flowers
To me from the chariot of two wheels.

Bran sees
The number of waves beating across the clear sea:

I myself see in Mag Mon
Rosy coloured flowers without fault.

Sea-horses glisten in summer
As far as Bran has stretched his glance:
Rivers pour forth a stream of honey
In the land of Manannan son of Lir.

The sheen of the main, on which thou art,
The white hue of the sea, on which thou rowest,
Yellow and azure are spread out,
It is land, it is not rough.

Speckled salmon leap from the womb
Of the white sea, on which thou lookest:
They are calves, they are coloured lambs
With friendliness, without mutual slaughter.

Though but one chariot-rider is seen
In Mag Mell of many flowers,
There are many steeds on its surface,
Though them thou seest not.

The Voyage of Bran mac Ferbal, (209)

3 The Underworld

My chair is in Caer Siddi,
Where no-one is afflicted with age or illness.
Manawydden and Pryderi have known it well.
It is surrounded by three circles of fire.
To the borders of the city come the ocean's flood,
A fruitful fountain flows before it,
Whose liquor is sweeter than the finest wine.

The Defence of the Chair

This last example is by Taliesin himself, and is translated in full
on pages 294–6. It is a simple but telling statement, in keeping
with the poet's laconic style, which tells of his own sojourn
in the Otherworld, from where his poetic spirit (his Chair)
comes. It shares some details with the previous examples,
both of which are from Irish tradition. It is not difficult to

imagine the shaman-poet conducting his listeners through the stages of the Otherworld whilst climbing the World-Tree, leaving them with a series of magical images upon which to draw.

A shaman recorded by the anthropologist M. A. Castren, and reported by F. M. Cornford (58) stated:

> God has appointed that I must wander both beneath and upon the earth, and has bestowed on me such power that ... I can [know] the future, the past and everything which is taking place in the present, both above and below the earth.

The journey to the Underworld has been described and explored comparatively rarely (291), yet its obvious importance to the Celts is clear enough. In numerous instances the hero who visits the Otherworld does so by entering a faery mound or **sidhe**, beyond which he finds another world *within* or *beneath* the earth. In other stories the way is again downward, by way of wells or lakes which offer admittance to an Otherworldly realm. Such approaches are so commonly observed among shamans that they scarcely require comment. The evidence of Celtic folklore and myth is unified in its presentation of the ancient gods (for example the Irish Tuatha de Danaan) as retiring beneath the 'hollow hills' after their conquest or expulsion by succeeding tribes who possessed their own families of gods. The shaman went into the earth to visit the ancestors, and so, in a sense, did the Celtic shaman-hero. Again and again we find evidence of this. The ancient dead are recalled to tell of some past great event (cf. the example of Caolte on page 112), or to advise the visitor on the direction of his own life. The Roman author Tertullian (*De Anima*, 57), recording the words of Nicander, reports that the Celts spent nights at the tombs of their heroes in order to obtain special oracles. Archaeological evidence abounds for the existence of ancestor 'cults' or 'worship' among the Celts, who made offerings to their great dead in much the same way as to the gods themselves. Indeed, it is even possible that they saw the famous ancestors as, in some senses, attaining the status of gods themselves – or at least as holding a place of honour among the denizens of the Otherworld. The suggestion by R. J. Stewart, in his illuminating book *The Underworld Initiation* (291) which places the whole concept on a realistic basis, is

that the ancient grave sites contained guardian spirits attached to them, partly for the purpose of consultation. This seems wholly in keeping with the evidence of folk-lore and myth.

Swearing by the Elements

'I have been a torrent on the slope . . . a wave on the long shore . . . rain in a great deluge . . .' sings Taliesin, in the poem called **Horses**, indicating at once the degree of intimacy with the living elements of Creation. In the *Hanes Taliesin* we saw how his command of the wind contributed to the freeing of Elffin; even his patron's chains obeyed his voice and fell from Elffin's wrists and ankles. It could be said, without exaggeration, that **all** of the Celtic mysteries, and especially those of the poet-shamans, are concerned, in one way or another, with the elemental world. It is recorded that the most powerful and binding oath a man or woman could swear was:

> May the earth open and swallow me,
> May the sky fall upon me,
> May the sea rise and cover me,
> May fires consume me,
> If I am forsworn.

It is told of Leaghire, King of Ireland in the time of Patrick, that he swore 'by the sun and moon, water and air, day and night, sea and land', not to invade the neighbouring kingdom of Leinster, and that when, two years later, he broke this oath, 'the elements passed a doom of death upon him – to wit, the earth to swallow him up, the sun to burn him, and the wind to depart from him', and that 'the sun and wind killed him because he had violated them' (**Book of the Four Masters**, quoted Joyce, 149).

Another example is found in the **Dindsenchas**. Dub, the wife of Enna, discovered that her husband had another wife, Aide, the daughter of Ochenn. In jealousy, then, Dub chanted a sea-spell before Ochenn's house, so that Aide was drowned with all her family (267).

The shaman poet possesses four unique abilities:
1   Mastery of Fire;
2   Mastery over the Winds;
3   Divination Through Entering the Earth;
4   Inspiration by Water.

He is thus a master of all the elements, and derives much of his power from them. We have already seen how the Druid Mogh Ruith commanded the powers of air and fire in his battle against Ciothruadh. His ability to take to the air with his bull's cloak and feathered head-dress is but another aspect of this. In later chapters we shall see how the shaman, by entering the body of the earth, finds the secrets of the past and future; and how he discovers inspiration through the interaction of water and light. For the moment let us look at some of the ways in which mastery over the elements plays a part in the shaman's world and his work in it.

Taliesin's mastery over the elements is well-attested through the poems, especially water, of which there are more references than any other. In a poem from *Black Book of Carmarthen* (10) (No. vi in Skene's ordering), he declares:

> Along with seven created beings
> I was placed
> In a fire of purification.
> I was myself gleaming fire,
> When I was first given life.
> I was dust on the earth,
> And grief could not reach me;
> I was a great wind –
> Less evil than good;
> I was mist on a mountain
> A shelter for game;
> I was blossom on every tree
> On the face of the earth.

Fire, earth, wind and water (mist) again. Here the poet seems to be speaking – the lines are unusually hard – of a primal time, perhaps seeing himself as present at the very birth of the world. Elsewhere, in the great *Cad Goddeu*, he says:

> I have been a tear-drop in the air . . .
> I have been a drop in a shower of rain . . .
> I have been a sponge in the fire . . .

> I travelled in the earth
> Before I was learned ...
>
> (Trans. Skene)

This theme of weather is continued even in the medieval poem by Geoffrey of Monmouth, **The Vita Merlini** (54), which is full of elemental and cosmological lore (the latter is discussed more fully in Chapter Nine). Indeed, we first meet Taliesin in this source coming to visit Merlin in his observatory, having lately come from Brittany, where he had been studying with 'Gildas the Wise'. The Prophet, we are told, 'sent for him to find out what wind or rainstorm was coming up, for both together were drawing near and the clouds were thickening.' Taliesin gives voice to a long and complicated dissertation on the creation of the Universe, mostly drawn by Geoffrey from the writings of the 6th Century encyclopedist, Isadore of Seville. The most important point is that, even at his late date (the **Vita** was composed *c.* 1220), Taliesin is firmly associated with the weather lore and the elements.

The Song of Amairgen

The Irish *Book of the Invasions* (170) contains the epic story of successive waves of conquerors: the Children of Nemed, the Fir Bolg, the Tuatha de Danaan, and finally the Milesians or Children of Mil. These last-named were probably a tribe of Iberian Celts, who found their way to the rich lands of *Eriu* (the earliest name for Ireland) sometime in the 3rd Century BC, and settled there after overcoming the native population. But their coming was certainly not unopposed, and had it not been for the presence of the great poet Amairgen, who in many ways parallels Taliesin, and who showed himself the master of the elements of wind and water and earth, their conquest would have been much harder.

On their arrival in the land the Milesians were met by the Tuatha de Danaan, and first Amairgen had to encounter and placate the triple-aspected Goddess of the land: Banba, Fodla, and Eriu. This he did by promising each of them that the land would be named after them – the secret names of the land and its Goddesses being all important. Then, according to the complex laws of the time, the Milesians demanded either submission, or battle, or a judgement from their foes. The Danaans replied that they could remain for nine days, and that at the end of that time they should either depart, or give battle, or give themselves up. Then, when the Milesians sought to reject this, they offered them 'the judgement of your own poets . . . for if they give false judgement against us they will die on the spot.' Here we see the power and sanctity of the shaman-poet, who was held in such respect that even his enemies considered themselves bound by his word. In this instance Amairgen gave the judgement, which was that the land should be left to the Danaans 'till we come again to take it by force.' When his fellows asked where they should go then, Amairgen replied 'over nine waves', and then sang a song:

> The men you have found are in possession:
> Over the nine green-necked waves
> Of the sea advance ye:
> Unless by you power then be planted,
> Quickly let the battle be prepared.
> I assign the possession
> Of the land you have found:
> If you love concede this award,
> If you love not concede it not –
> It is I that say this to you.
>
> trans. Cross and Slover, 59

The Milesians therefore departed and sailed away from the land a short distance. There they were plagued by powerful winds raised against them by the Danaan Druids. When he understood this, Amairgen rose and sang:

> I invoke the land of Ireland.
> Much coursed be the fertile sea,
> Fertile be the fruit-strewn mountain,
> Fruit-strewn be the showery wood,
> Showery be the river of water-falls,
> Of water-falls be the lake of deep pools,
> Deep-pooled be the hill-top well,
> A well of tribes be the assembly,
> An assembly of the kings of Tara,
> Tara be the hill of the tribes,
> The tribes of the sons of Mil,
> Of Mil of the ships, the barks,
> Let the lofty bark be Ireland,

> Lofty Ireland, darkly sung,
> An incantation of great cunning . . .
> I invoke the land of Ireland (ibid.)

At once, the wind dropped and the sea became flat calm. The Milesians sailed on and, despite some losses, landed finally at Inber Colptha. There Amairgen spoke this rhapsody:

> I am the wind upon the sea,
> I am a wave upon the ocean,
> I am the sound of the sea,
> I am a stag of seven points,
> I am a bull of seven fights,
> I am a hawk upon a cliff,
> I am a teardrop of the sun,
> I am the fairest of blossoms,
> I am a boar of boldness,
> I am a salmon in a pool,
> I am a lake on a plain,
> I am the mound of poetry,
> I am a word of skill,
> I am a battle-waging spear of spoil,
> I am a God who fashions fire in the mind.
> Who but I knows the secrets of the stone door?
> Who has seven times sought the Places of Peace?
> Who, save I, knows the ages of the moon,
> The place and time the sun sets?
> Who calls the kine from Tethra's house,
> And sees them dance in the bright heavens?
> Who shapes weapons in a fort of glass,
> In a fort that harbours satirists?
> Who but the poet, the singer of praises,
> Who but I divides the Ogam letters,
> Separates combatants, approaches the Faery mound?
> I, who am a wind upon the sea.

> Based on the original Irish, and on the translations of
> R. A. S. Macalister, Eleanor Hull, T. P. Cross and
> C. H. Slover, 170, 130, 59

This remarkable poem, which puts us at once in mind of Taliesin, is filled with a sense of elemental power. Amairgen is master of the weather, of winds and waves; he has the strength of the bull, the keenness of sight that belongs to the hawk, the wisdom of the salmon who has swum in the Pool of Knowledge; and he knows the way to and from the Places of Peace – that is the Faery Mounds – where he has learned to wield the fire of inspiration that burns in the head. He is wise also, in the lore of the heavens, knowing the ages of the moon (its quarters), the rising and setting of the sun, and the dancing of the stars (Tethra's kine) in the heavens. It is his power which subdues the Druid winds, which calms the angry sea, and which placates the Triple Goddess by knowing her names and her desire to keep her place in the land. Thus he wields air, water, and earth, and binds all to him through the elemental fire of his inspiration.

There are many other instances of poets or shamans who have power over the elements – particularly the weather. In the *Mabinogion* (144) Caswallawn summons up a magical mist – a common form of weather witching – while the great wizard Gwydion ap Don, is able to exert extraordinary power over the earth and the heavens (182). We shall look further at the subject of the elements and of the shaman's power over them in Chapter Nine.

The Healing Dream

A primary function of the shaman was that of healing, often carried out through the medium of a trance or dream state in which the shaman encountered the spirit causing the sickness, and either did battle with it, or returned with information which could aid the sufferer. Evidence of similar practice among the Celts is to be found in two very different sources. Firstly, the Romano-British temple to the god Nodens at Lydney in Gloucestershire, and secondly, the presence within certain ancient sites in Ireland, of the implements necessary to create 'sweat lodge' conditions.

Lydney's dedication is to Nodens. Little is known about this god, who has been alternatively described as a solar deity and a god of sea or river. Sir John Rhys first pointed out (259) the links between Nodens and the Irish Nuada Argetlam (Nuada of the Silver Hand) and the Welsh Llud Llaw Ereint through the earlier Brythonic version, *Ludons Lamargentios*. Llud in turn can be plausibly identified as Llyr Lledyeith (Llyr Half-Speech). All this is interesting since it implies connections both with physical defects and water. Nuada receives an artificial hand after losing the original at the first battle of Mag Turid; Llyr, we may presume, had a stammer (though his name could also mean 'Foreign Accent') and is also a god of the sea.

Figure 5   Reconstruction of the Temple of Nodens at Lydney.

At Lydney an object believed to have been a priestly diadem was found, bearing a picture of the god, mounted on a chariot drawn by horses and surrounded by neriads and spirits of the winds. From this, some commentators have been led to assume Nodens (assuming this is a depiction of him) to be a sun god of the same type as Phoebus Apollo, who also rides about in a four-horse chariot (321). However, the presence of the water beings suggests a sea god more like Neptune – or like Llyr. The temple itself bears a remarkable resemblance to the Asklepion at Epidaurus in Greece, where a kind of healing ritual known as 'incubation' was practised. In this the sufferers, having first sacrificed to the god of the place, then entered a special bath house and, after purifying themselves, were taken to a building which contained a number of small cubicles. There the subject slept and, if the god willed it, received a dream which conveyed to them the means by which they were to be healed.

The temple at Lydney is laid out along almost identical lines, including bath house and incubation cells. In the excavation of the site a cast of a human hand showing signs of disfigurement, and a statue of a heavily pregnant woman were found, along with several images of dogs. At the Asklepion, casts of the afflicted parts of sufferers were often hung up in the temple, while dogs were allowed to roam free – another method of healing being to have a dog lick the affected area. The possible totemic significance of this is not to be ignored.

Certainly, the importance of dreams among the Celts may be judged by the following episodes, one from an Irish source, the other from the *Mabinogion*. In the first, from the **First Battle of Moytura** (88), Eochaid, the High King of Ireland, dreams that he sees 'A great flock of black birds . . . coming from the depths of the Ocean. They settled over all of us, and fought with the people of Ireland. They brought confusion on us, and destroyed us . . .' Cesard, the king's shamanic advisor, when questioned as to the meaning of this dream, replies: 'I have tidings for you: warriors are coming across the sea, a thousand heroes covering the Ocean; speckled ships will press in upon us; all kinds of death will they announce, a people skilled in every art . . . They will be victorious in every stress.' (88)

The second example is found in **The Dream of Macsen Wledig** (144), in which the Emperor Macsen (founded on the real figure of Magnus Maximus, the Roman general who became ruler of the Empire) has a dream in which he crosses the Alps and, reaching the shore of Britain, sees a beautiful woman seated on a throne. He at once falls in love with her and, on waking, sets out to find and marry her.

In both these stories there is implicit belief in the truth of the dream, which is shown to have been accurate in every detail. The raven-warriors of the first story are the Tuatha de Danaan, who conquer Ireland soon after; Macsen's dream also proves true, and the girl in his dream becomes his Empress.

The Lydney temple itself dates from the period between the departure of the Romans and the influx of Saxon mercenaries (c. AD 400–600); however, evidence of ritual activity there dates back much earlier, and almost certainly involved the worship of Nodens or an earlier but similar archetype. Thus, although there is no precise evidence for the practice of incubation before the date of the temple, it would not be too unreasonable to suppose that it did take place there at a much earlier time. Certainly, we should note that at certain ancient sites in Ireland, boat shaped bath-stones have been found, together with collections of smaller, circular stones. These smaller stones, it has been suggested, were intended to be heated over a fire and, when they had attained a sufficient temperature, were placed in the baths and cold water poured over them to create steam. This would have produced an effect identical to that of the shamanic sweat lodges used by both American Indian and Siberian shamans to assist them in reaching a trance state (32).

It does not seem to be stretching the evidence too far to believe that this could have formed part of a healing ritual equivalent to that of ritual incubation. Given the similar methods of Celtic shaman-poets to attain inspiration (see Chapter Four) we can assume that at a much earlier time – possibly as early as the Megalithic period – the subject, either sick patient or aspiring poet, was brought to the outer chamber of the old site, from which all air and light had been excluded by plugging the gaps with mud and turf, and that there, having made an offering to the numen or tutelary spirit of the place, the subject underwent a ritual cleansing in the steam-filled atmosphere. Then, as the steam slowly dispersed, he or she was taken into an inner chamber and allowed to sleep on a sacred bull's hide (see Chapter Six) and in a dream state received either healing or inspiration (188).

Much of this is speculation, but seems to fit the facts available. It is certainly in keeping with the shamanic practices of the Celts, and is borne out by the accumulation of evidence presented here.

A further aspect of the shaman's healing activity – a task for which he will often undertake unusual, even outrageous, actions to bring about a cure – may be illustrated by the following example from Celtic literature, specifically Irish. Here the 'shaman' may be seen to follow closely on the heels of another universal figure, the Trickster or Guiser (112).

In *The Vision of Mac Conglinne* (208) we learn of an affliction suffered by the King of Ireland, Cathal Mac Finguine (an historical King of Munster in the 8th Century), who was possessed by a demon of gluttony which lived in his belly and which caused him to make excessive demands on the hospitality of his neighbours. We then hear of Mac Conglinne himself, a 'scholar' from Armagh, who travels by magic from the North to the South in a single day and arrives at the monastery of Cork expecting hospitality. When this is refused he satirises the monks who, in reply, bind and throw him into a dark cell. There he experiences a vision of the landscape of Ireland made entirely from food! When he repeats this to the monks, the abbot hits on the idea of having Mac Conglinne repeat the poem he has composed to King Cathal. Mac Conglinne dresses in an extravagant costume and dances before the King whilst recounting his poem. The result of this is that as it hears the mouth-watering descriptions of food the demon emerges and is trapped by Mac Conglinne.

Apart from the fact that Mac Conglinne's vision happened while he was in a darkened cell (see Chapter Seven), this is precisely the kind of remedy we should expect from a shaman, who often performs magical songs before an audience – and whose repertoire includes outrageous acts or strange costumes – before exacting a cure. In many cases demons or spirits believed to be the cause of the sickness are drawn forth as a result of the shaman's caperings. We may also recognise the archetype of the fool in this character, whose task it was to entertain and distract the monarch in whose service he belonged. Alan Harrison, in his study of *The Irish Trickster* (112), gives several valuable instances of this figure who, in the light of the evidence collected here, will be seen as performing part of the shaman's function (significantly, perhaps, the Irish word for fool is *druth*, and that for druid *drui*).

The Shaman Saints

Professor Daniel Melia has argued, persuasively it seems to me, that the practice of shamanism lingered on in Irish culture long after the advent of Christianity. He cites the case of the Irish Saint Adamnan, an abbot of Iona, of whom the following story is told (196).

Adamnan and his mother, Ronnat, were travelling near the site of modern day Drogheda (North-Eastern Ireland) when they arrived at the site of a battle. Many dead women were amongst the dead, including a decapitated nursing mother. At his own mother's request Adamnan rejoined the head to the body and brought her back to life. The resuscitated woman was none other than the King of Tara's wife, and she laid on Adamnan a **gaesa** (injunction) that he should neither eat nor drink until he had 'freed all the women of the Western world.' Ronnat gave Adamnan a chain to put round his neck and a piece of flint to put in his mouth. The saint then stood in Loch Swilly for eight months until he was almost dead from cold, exhaustion and lack of food. The object of this was presumably to coerce God into improving the state of women. When it failed to have any effect Adamnan's mother upbraided him for his lack of success. He requested that she should change the method of his torture to something worse, and this she did, having him buried alive in a stone chest, 'so that worms devoured the root of his tongue, so that the slime of his head broke forth through his ears . . .' (quoted Melia). After eight months the chest was reburied, and after a further period of four years an angel appeared to Adamnan (apparently still alive!) and removed him from the chest. He was told that his efforts had been rewarded, but was promptly attacked by a coalition of Kings, whom he defeated solely with the power of his Saint's bell. The remainder of the text is taken up primarily with a list of women's rights, attributed to the angel.

As Professor Melia has indicated, the obvious shamanic elements in this story are 1) the initiatory character of Adamnan's ordeal, 2) the fact that it is instigated by a woman, 3) the fact that 'Adamnan is able to revive the decapitated woman . . . but is unable to converse with, tap or otherwise manipulate the **source** of this power until after his shamanic initiation', and 4) that he is afterwards endowed with greater power, including the magical bell, which is itself recognisable as part of a shaman's equipment. Adamnan's enforced starvation, his standing in cold water, and finally, his burial, are all part of a genuine shamanic inheritance, presumably remembered and attributed to the Saint along with all his other Christian trappings.

To this story may be added another, also associated with Iona, which was, long before its Christian foundation, recognised as an Otherworldly island of the type discussed above. In this story, a monk named Oran was buried alive and after three days dug up and found to be still alive. He at once began to mediate what he had seen of the Otherworld, including:

> Nor is Heaven as it is alleged,
> Nor is Hell as it is asserted,
> Nor is the good eternally happy
> Nor is the bad eternally unhappy

To which Columba replied:

> Earth! earth on the eye of Oran,
> Before he wakes more controversy . . .

This is a clear enough indication of the way shamanic beliefs (i.e. paganism) were treated at this time, yet there is little doubt that a study of the lives and deeds of the Celtic Saints reveals a considerable degree of shamanic activity.

Finally, we would mention a story concerning St Aengus, to whom a child made plaint that he could not learn the Psalms as he had been told to do. The Saint requested him to 'put thy head on my knee, and go to sleep.' The boy did so and when he awoke he not only knew the Psalms by heart, but also much more.

This kind of mantic sleep is very much part of the shaman's ability (see above); that it should be ascribed to a Christian Saint is doubly interesting, and suggests that the practice continued for much longer than is generally believed.

To summarise the foregoing material, we have seen that, in many instances, shamanic techniques are described in some detail by the compilers of Celtic mythology; that the figure of the shaman, as possibly depicted on the Gundestrup Cauldron, and of the shaman-poet, as instructed by such figures as Taliesin himself, Amairgen, and the wizard Mogh Ruith, date back ultimately to a very distant period of time; and that there exists substantial evidence to support the continuance of shamanic activity well into Christian times. In the chapters which follow we shall examine in depth various techniques and abilities common to both the ancient shamans and to the figures of Celtic myth, as represented particularly in the figure of Taliesin.

Chapter Three

THE CAULDRON-BORN: CERIDWEN AND THE GODDESSES OF INSPIRATION

What is the ever-full cauldron? Answer. A Cauldron which should be always kept on the fire for every party that should arrive ... which returns in a perfect state whatever is put into it, while every other cauldron would dissolve it ...

Senchus Mor

Keepers of the Cauldron

The figure of the Goddess, in her many guises, dominates Celtic culture and mythology at every level. Though there are many important Gods, these are almost always seen as secondary to the female deities who represent the land itself, and who are to be found personified in its rivers and hills. The Goddess gave life with one hand and took it away again with the other. She alternatively counselled, cajoled and cursed every hero who came to her notice. She was the inspirer of poets, and sometimes she loved them to death and beyond. She had as many forms as the land itself, appearing as lovely maiden, glorious mother and hideous hag. She is the powerful initiator of Taliesin and her name is seldom far from his lips in his finest poems. One of these, **The Chair of Ceridwen** (translated in full on pages 304–6) is put into her own mouth.

We may dismiss lines 1–9 and 39–44 as clerkly interpolations. This leaves us with two possible poems, of which lines 10–28 constitute one and 29–38 the other. The first refers clearly to the Taliesin/Gwion episodes, though interestingly, here Avagddu is praised as though he had indeed revived the gifts of the Cauldron. Lines 14–22 refer to Gwydion ap Don,

63

the wizard-God who features largely in the *Four Branches of the Mabinogion*, who made the woman Blodeuwedd (Flower or Owl Face) from flowers, cheated Pryderi of the sacred pigs from the underworld kingdom of Annwn, and who created the illusion of horses and saddles from leaves (as opposed to earth in the poem).

Ceridwen then states that:

> When all the Chairs are compared
> Mine is pre-eminent.
> My Chair, my Cauldron, my Laws.
> My searching speech gives them constancy.

And adds that she is 'an initiate of the Court of Don', referring to the great Chair of Llys Don, the constellation of Cassiopeia.

Ceridwen thus refers to a series of wise initiates, of which she herself is paramount. She includes Avagddu among them defiantly, as though he, rather than Taliesin, had imbibed the fruits of her wisdom. (If the poet really composed this song we must smile at his audacity!)

Lines 29–38 may or may not be part of the same poem. Certainly they stand up as a separate work. However, it is possible, by looking beneath the surface, to perceive a deeper pattern which links the two. In the Fourth Branch of the *Mabinogion* (144), Arianrhod refuses to give her son either a name, a wife, or weapons, without which he cannot pursue his life. Gwydion, nominally his uncle, but almost certainly his father also (183), undertakes to get all three for him, making him a wife from flowers (see above) and tricking Arianrhod into giving him both arms and a name, Llew Llaw Gyffes. We seem to be hearing of the two assaults made upon Arianrhod by Gwydion and Llew together for this purpose. Certainly she was for a time out of favour with her uncle, Math, which presumably explains the reference to her in the poem as 'a great disgrace to the land of Britain' (line 35).

But another, older stratum of story seems to lie beneath the surface here. Arianrhod herself is a Goddess of the Moon (her name means 'Silver Wheel') and she is also associated with the Corona Borealis. Gwydion himself is sometimes said to rule over the Milky Way. So that what we seem to have here is a reference to an ancient star myth, perhaps embodying the story of Arianrhod and Gwydion, which was once current in

Celtic mythology, but is now lost except in the version we find in the *Mabinogion*. In the poem, Arianrhod defends herself with the rainbow of the Corona Borealis, which is seen as encircling the world and giving forth poison – a reference, perhaps, to the poison which leaked from Ceridwen's Cauldron after Gwion had imbibed the three drops. The Cauldron itself can be seen as a metaphor for the heavens, as in numerous other mythologies, where a cup or bowl is used by the Gods to mix the stuff of Creation.

The word **Gwythaint** (line 31), which translates as 'the Angry One', may be a reference to Arianrhod, or to Ceridwen herself, who might well have been referred to thus in the same manner as Demeter **Erinnys**, 'the Fury' in Classical myth. The references to Arianrhod are important also because of Taliesin's boast that he was 'Three times in the prison of Caer Arianrhod'. This almost certainly refers to his initiation, which was a triple one, perhaps because of the three drops of inspiration.

Gwydion was in Caer Arianrhod three times:

1   When he fathered Llew;
2   When he became a shoemaker to get Llew a name;
3   When he became a poet to get arms for Llew.

So that when Taliesin says in 'Primary Chief Bard', 'I was in Llys Don *before* the birth of Gwydion' (my italics), he is claiming a superior revelation. Ceridwen herself (and, through her, Taliesin) may intend the whole poem to be seen as a metaphor of her own overcoming by Taliesin, who frequently likens himself to Gwydion. Like Arianrhod, Ceridwen is tricked into giving up what she would rather keep. If we are correct in believing this, then Ceridwen's own comment that she was an initiate of the Court of Don backs up both her own, and Taliesin's, claims even further.

We can see from the analysis of this single poem how deeply embedded the myth of Ceridwen is in the story of Taliesin. That myth itself is not easily traced, and we have to look at a number of widely scattered references before we can begin to see its outline.

The Myth of Ceridwen

In another poem, curiously entitled **The Hostile Confederacy** (translated in full on pages 312–19), Taliesin refers directly to his 'rebirth' from the womb of Ceridwen:

I have been a grain discovered,
   growing on a hill.
The Harvester took me,
To free my essence
In a place full of smoke.

I have known great suffering.
A red hen took me.
She had red wings and a
   double comb.
I rested nine months
As a child in her belly . . .

While in **Taliesin's Song of his Origins** (translated in full pages 281–2) we read:

First I was formed as a handsome man,
Refined in Ceridwen's Hall;
Though seeming small and modest
I grew great in her lofty sanctuary.

While thus imprisoned,
Sweet inspiration taught me,
Laws were imparted
In a speech without words.
But I had to flee from the angry hag
Whose cries were terrible.

★ ★ ★

Floating like a boat on water,
I was thrown into a dark bag,
And on an endless sea, set adrift.

Here we have all the metaphors for the birth of the child-poet from the womb of the Goddess, where he has learned inspiration (see Chapter One). Ceridwen is referred to as an 'angry hag', and as the 'Harvester', and as 'a hen with red wings and a double comb'. All of these are appropriate to a Goddess who is elsewhere referred to as the patroness of Harvests. But Ceridwen is far more than this, as we shall see.

The latest recorded version of Taliesin's story is that by Lewis Morris dated 1726. (This appears in Manuscript Cwrtmawr 14, folio 10, and has been recently edited by Dr. Juliette Wood (332).) It is, unusually, written in English, and is given here in a modernised version, slightly abridged.

Y Man Gofion
(The Little Remembrancer)

The best account of this Taliesin is as follows. This is he whom the Latin writers call Telesinus. He was born about the year 510, and was poet laureate to Maelgwn Gwynedd, the

British prince who lived at Conway. This Maelgwyn was the son of Caswallon Lawhir, ap Einion Yrth ap Cynedda Wledig etc. Aneurin Wawdrydd otherwise called Anairf Wawdydd: i.e. Aneurin the Satyr, was contemporary with this Taliesin . . .

There are strange stories related of this Taliesin, but scarce credible, for the superstitious monks have so mixed them with lies that they are not worth relating. But that there is some truth in them it cannot be doubted, and the common tradition amongst the British nation through all Wales [is] that Taliesin was found by Elffin (Maelgwyn's brother as some say) on the sea side in a place called Cored Wyddno, in the Comot of Creuddun in Carnarvonshire. He was wrapt up in a leather bag (or rather, a leather boat such as our Cwrwgl's) which made the man who found him think at first that it was some rich treasure that he had found, but having torn the leather, it was a pretty boy. The man being amazed asked him some questions: to which he replied [with the words of **The Consolation of Elffin**] . . .

So the man brought him home with him and instructed him with his own children; and being of a notable genius to poetry and inspired with the spirit of prophecy, he attained to the greatest perfection of that age. The cause of casting him into the sea was this: he being a poor boy begging his bread, came by chance to Creigiau'r Eryri where there were two **Gwiddans** [enchantresses], boiling a panful of enchanted liquor which they could not bring to perfection for want of fuel. Taliesin asked them if he should boil the liquor, and told them that he had a particular way to make much water boil with little fuel, which they easily granted. Taliesin gathered the fuel together and bound it in little faggots, and so in a little time (and before they were aware of him) he boiled the liquor to perfection, and took the first three drops to himself. The virtue of the water was such that he that had the first three drops of it when boiled should properly be inspired with the spirit of divining. And this water the Gwiddans intended to give to their own sons (and Taliesin having heard of it) he endeavoured to make his escape but was caught by them and cast into the sea in a leather bag.

This is a substantially different account of Taliesin's apotheosis from that found in the *Hanes*. To begin with Taliesin (who is not referred to as Little Gwion) seems to know about the enchanted brew of the two 'Gwiddans', and consciously sets out to obtain it for himself. Pretending to beg for bread he offers himself as someone in possession of a unique ability to heat the water with little fuel. Just how he does so is not precisely explained, but he manages to obtain the three drops of wisdom unnoticed, and to make his escape. There is none of the chase and transformation sequence, nor is he said to be reborn from the Gwiddans; he is simply cast into the sea in a leather bag and discovered by Elffin as in most of the other versions.

The other aspect of particular interest for us here is the fact that instead of Ceridwen, we have the two Gwiddans. The word is most often used as a colloquial term for hag, witch or giant. Thus in the **Aberdar I** manuscript, which contains a number of Taliesin poems, the name Ceridwen is glossed as 'a she giant that lived in North Wales'. While in another poem the name Gwydion (the premier enchanter of Welsh myth) is glossed as a 'giant' also (332).

This suggests a memory of a prehistoric race of giants, traces of whose existence are to be found scattered throughout the Celtic tradition. Almost certainly there must have been at one time three Gwiddans, rather than two, and it is fascinating to speculate whether this does not in fact contain the germ of an even older level of Taliesin material (paradoxically emerging in this late MS) in which the bard was initiated not by one Goddess, but by three (or at least one of triple aspect), who were possibly remembered as giantesses as well!

Also of note is the term **man gofion**, applied to Taliesin in the title of the piece. As a shaman-poet, one of the most important functions he would have performed would have been as remembrancer of the history, genealogy and myths of the tribe. That he is still referred to by this title as late as the 17th Century, indicates even more clearly the way in which primitive material can be caught up in much later manuscripts.

Another gigantic figure, the God Bran, possessed a wondrous vessel which had the property of bringing the dead to life when they were placed within it – though they came forth dumb and unable to speak of what they have seen. When one of Bran's brothers, Efnissien, caused insult to the King of Ireland, Bran gave him, by way of recompense, this same cauldron which had, in fact, come originally from Ireland. The story of its discovery is especially interesting.

One day when Matholwch, the King of Ireland, was hunting near the Lake of the Cauldron, he saw a huge yellow-haired man coming from the Lake with a cauldron on his back. A woman followed him, who was also of great size. And because she was with child and the couple had nowhere to live, Matholwch invited them to return with him to his court. He soon regretted this, because the woman gave birth not to one child but to hundreds – one every month, in fact, and every one a fully armed warrior. Needless to say this made them very unpopular, especially as their general behaviour was also terrible. Matholwch soon tried to get rid of them, having a specially built house prepared, made of iron, which was sealed as soon as the couple entered and its walls heated until they glowed white, but the terrible couple broke out and fled, taking the Cauldron with them. When they arrived in Britain, Bran received them using the woman's seemingly endless reproductive ability to garrison fortresses all over the land. Later on in the same story, when Bran and Matholwch were in conflict, the Irish used the Cauldron to restore their dead warriors, and it was only finally broken when Efnissien, who had caused all the trouble to begin with, crawled inside and stretched himself out, killing himself in the process. Of that fateful war only seven men escaped, including Taliesin.

Now if we look beneath the surface of this story it can be used to explain a number of things from both the **Preiddeu Annwn** and the *Hanes Taliesin*. Although the giant couple are called by other names in the Branwen text, they are clearly a reflection of Tegid Voel and his wife Ceridwen. She herself was originally a Goddess of gestation and birth, a Mountain Mother who, in some stories, is seen as letting fall from her skirt great stones which become mountains and hills.

The endless stream of warriors born by her confirm this identification, and it is perhaps possible to see the Cauldron itself as a symbolic womb – from which not only is life given, but also knowledge, wisdom, and the **awen** or inspiration of the Poet. When the Cauldron is in the hands of other men, they are unable to *create* life, only restore those who were dead.

Comparison with the following description, from **The Destruction of Da Derga's Hostel** (59), adds to this:

As Conaire was going to Da Derga's hostel, a man with black cropped hair, with one hand and one eye and one foot overtook them ... A pig, black-bristled, singed, was on his back, squealing continually, and a woman, big mouthed, huge, dark, ugly, hideous, was behind him. Though her snout was flung on a branch, the branch would support it. Her pudenda reached to her knees. (59)

Their names are Fer Caille and Cichuill and they are clearly related to Llassar Llaes Gyfnewidd and Cymeidei Cymeinfoll (whose name suggests that she shares at least one of the characteristics of Cichuill!), though here they possess no cauldron. The description of the man as having one foot, one eye and one hand recalls the method of cursing or casting spells, which involved standing on one foot, closing one eye and putting one hand behind the back (cf. Chapter Two). The description of the woman, with her enlarged sexual organs, leaves us in no doubt as to her purpose – like Cymeidei Cymeinfoll she is made to bear an endless stream of children (or warriors), just as in the Welsh story.

It is clear that at some stage in the transmission of the various tales which went into the making of **Branwen**, the original story concerned a voyage to capture the fabled Cauldron of Rebirth and Inspiration, and that Taliesin, as an initiate of its secrets (The Cauldron-Born), of course went along, and was, naturally enough, one of the seven (mystic number) who returned from the Otherworld to tell the tale.

Taliesin is, then, someone who has access to the kind of knowledge which enables him to travel and return from the Otherworld. He experiences self-induced trances which give him insight into events both past and future. He is closely connected with a probable cult of initiates who traced their source of inspiration to the Goddess Ceridwen, the same who was the possessor of a cauldron from which Taliesin was said to have been reborn. He thus resembles in several points the shamans we considered in Chapter Two, who had the ability to visit the Otherworld, who had visions of past and future, and who underwent various forms of initiation in which they were 'reborn' with extended powers and deepened knowledge.

Ordeals by Fire and Water

Of all the descriptions of initiations involving both a Cauldron and a hag, that pertaining to the greatest Irish hero,

Cuchulainn, is the most dramatic. It occurred while he was still a child, happening to overhear the Druid Cathbad saying that, 'The little boy that takes up arms this day shall be splendid and renowned for deeds of arms . . . but he shall be short-lived and fleeting.' (72) Cuchulainn at once demanded arms and a chariot from his uncle and set off for the castle of the three sons of Necht, who were the worst enemies of Ulster. Though they were said to be invincible the boy killed them all and took their heads. But the famous battle madness had come upon Cuchulainn during the struggle, and he had become so overheated because of this that one of his uncle's female druids warned him that unless something were done, he might accidentally kill all the warriors of Ulster. So the King decided to send a troop of naked women to meet the child, and the text says:

> Thereupon the young women all arose and marched out . . . and they discovered their nakedness . . . to him. The lad hid his face from them and turned his gaze on the chariot, that he might not see the nakedness . . . of the women. Then the lad was lifted out of his chariot. He was placed in three vats of cold water to extinguish his wrath; and the first vat into which he was put burst its staves and its hoops like the cracking of nuts around him. The next vat into which he went boiled with bubbles as big as fists therein. The third vat into which he went, some men might endure it and others might not. Then the boy's wrath went down . . . and his festive garments were put upon him.
>
> (quoted Eliade, 74)

Both Dumézil and Eliade have noted (72, 74) that this represents an initiation ceremony. Examples of mystical heat or light in this connection are widely attested by shamans in many parts of the world, including India, Africa and North America. Indeed, the very root of the word, 'sham', carries with it the idea of heat or burning. We may note the reference to the first vat (for which we may read Cauldron) bursting 'like the cracking of nuts', which may or may not be a distant echo of the consuming of the hazels of Wisdom (see Chapter Seven et al.) to bring on just such a fit as Cuchulainn suffers. And at the end he had his 'festive garments' put upon him in the manner of an initiate who has survived the ordeal.

The whole subject of ordeals is an interesting one. There are, of course, a number of such rites which we may detect among the Celtic myths. We might instance the passage of Pwyll into the Otherworldly kingdom of Annwn (First Branch of the *Mabinogion*), or the visionary period spent by the seven heroes in the house of Bran the Blessed (in 'Branwen ferch Llyr') as well as, of course, the adventures of Taliesin and Fionn. Another text, *The Irish Ordeals* (299), lists a number of further tests. Among the objects listed in connection with this are the following:

The Collars of Morann Mac Main   The first of these was the caul with which Morann was born (see Chapter One) which became a collar after it was removed from his head. If anyone spoke falsehood whilst it was upon him it shrank and strangled him. The second was a fairy collar, brought out of the **Sidhe** by Morann's fool. This had the same property as the first collar but was placed around wrist or ankle, shrinking until it cut off the limb in question if truth were untold.

Mochta's Adze   It was put over a fire of blackthorn until red hot then passed over the tongue of the person suspect of falsehood. If it burned the person was guilty, if not, the suspect would be freed.

Sencha's Lot-Casting   Lots were cast out of a fire. If the accused were guilty they cleft to his palm. If not they would fall to the earth. Sencha used to make a poet's incantation over them.

The Vessel of Badurn   Badurn was a king, whose wife had entered a faery mound and obtained a magical crystal cauldron which, if three untruths were uttered in its presence, would burst asunder. Then, if three truths were uttered it would reassemble itself.

The Three Dark Stones   Three stones, one white, one black and one speckled were put into a bucket filled with black stuff from a bog. If the accused were guilty he would bring out the black stone; if innocent the white; if only partially guilty, the speckled.

The Cauldron of Truth   This was a vessel of silver in which water was heated to boiling point. The accused then put in his or her hand and if scalded was deemed guilty, if not, innocent.

Luchta's Iron   This was a sacred iron which Luchta the Wizard brought back from Brittany. It was heated and put into the hands of the accused. As in later medieval tests, if the iron burned them the accused was deemed guilty, if not, innocent.

Waiting at an Altar In this ordeal the accused had to go nine times around the altar before drinking a cup of water over which an incantation had been chanted. If he or she were guilty their guilt became manifest upon them. We are not told how this happened, but presumably either the guilty one fell dead or was forced to speak the truth.

Cormac's Cup of Truth (see Chapter One) This more or less repeats the idea of 'The Vessel of Badurn'.

It will be seen that in five of these examples a vessel of some kind is involved, and that the ordeal consisted of either burning the hand or tongue or of drinking water which had been heated in such a vessel. All of this points very directly to the idea of the Cauldron as an initiatory vessel concerned with knowledge and truth. There is an aura of poetic and shamanistic activity in all of these cases, and in at least one of them the vessel in question was brought out of the Otherworld.

In the **Coir Anmann** (Fitness of Names) (299), the following story is told of the way in which the hero Conall Corc received his name. On the night he was born a number of hags (witches?), who were in the habit of killing children, came to the house. Feidlim, a wise Druidess in the service of the house, saw them and though she had an argument with the visitors not to offer resistance to them, nonetheless hid the baby under a cauldron. One of the hags became aware of him and darted 'a flame of fire on the little boy, and burnt his ear, and reddened it.' Hence he was called Conall **corc**, 'The Red'. On the face of it this is a simple story made to explain a physical trait – important because Conall would have been a king, and only unblemished men might rule. Yet beneath this we catch a glimpse of another cauldron myth, involving a number of hags, a cauldron and an initiation of sorts. Perhaps at one point the initiate's ear was painted red as a sign that he had emerged from the ordeal unscathed?

Suibhne and the Hag

Another story which offers parallels to that of Taliesin and Ceridwen concerns the mad shaman-poet Suibhne Geilt who,

73

during his madness, was shut up with 'The Hag of the Mill'. She, for no clear reason, taunted him with his recent wandering experiences. Suibhne replied:

> 'O hag', said he, 'great are the hardships I have encountered if you but knew; many a dreadful leap have I leaped from hill to hill, from fortress to fortress, from valley to valley.' 'For God's sake,' said the Hag, 'leap for us now one of the leaps you used to leap . . .' Thereupon he bounded over the bedrail so that he reached the end of the bench. 'My conscience' said the hag, 'I could leap that myself', and in the same manner she did so. He took another leap out through the skylight of the hostel. 'I could leap that, too' said the hag, and straightway she leaped. This however, is the summary of it: Suibhne travelled through five cantreds [regions] of Dal Araidhe that day until he arrived at Glen na nEachtach in Fiodh Gaibhle, and she followed him all that time. When Suibhne rested there on the summit of a tall ivy-branch, the hag rested on another tree beside him. (239)

The hag continued to pursue Suibhne until they reached Dun Sobairce in Ulster.

> Suibhne leaped from the summit of the fort sheer down in front of the hag. She leaped quickly after him, but dropped on the cliff of Dun Sobairce, where she was broken to pieces, and fell into the sea. In that manner she found death in the wake of Suibhne. (ibid.)

The story is not exactly the same, but there are certainly enough parallels to give one pause. Here we have Suibhne, the mad, inspired poet, driven to his madness, like Merlin, by the sight of the carnage during a battle. In this episode he is pursued by a hag, and part of the sequence of the text (omitted here) includes a long poem which contains the vestiges of a transformation sequence. It is as though the two stories, the wild-man theme and the folk-tale of the Magician and his Helper (see Chapter One) have come together. The hag, unlike Ceridwen, has no specific reason for pursuing him. That she is called the Hag of the Mill, however, is not without its significance: the image of the Mill was a cosmological one widely recognised throughout the world. The Mill ground out the stars, and sometimes the very stuff of Creation, so that it here stands for much the same kind of symbology as the Cauldron – though this part of the old myth has been lost. These stories bring us back to Taliesin's own experience, and to the story of Ceridwen herself, which we must now consider in more depths.

The Crooked Woman

The name Ceridwen is usually taken to mean 'fair and loved', which, Professor Ifor Williams pointed out (13), seems unsuitable for one of her disposition. His own suggestion is that the name derives from an earlier version **Cyrridfen**, composed of **cyrrid**, 'hooked' or 'crooked' and **ben**, as in **benyw**, 'woman'. This would make her 'The Crooked Woman', a reasonable enough name for a hag. We may also remember the title **Gwythaint** 'The Angry One', discussed above. But the meaning is yet subtler than this. It is a well-attested fact that Otherworldly personages considered particularly dangerous or spiteful are always referred to by such names as 'The Good People' or 'The Kindly Ones'. Very often this describes one *aspect* only of the figure or figures in question. Ceridwen, then, could easily be seen as either fair or foul (cf. 187 the figure of Ragnall in later Arthurian Romance), or indeed, as both.

The Hag is only one aspect of the Triple Goddess, who is also Mother and Maiden, and shows all of her faces at various times. If the various authorities consulted are correct in assigning the title 'Goddess of Nature' to Ceridwen (a statement which requires some qualification) then this could be easily seen as a reference to the many faces shown by the elements.

In fact, none of the texts call Ceridwen a Goddess, although her possession of the Cauldron of Inspiration, along with her ability to change shape at will and to give birth to Taliesin, all point to her status as such. The word most usually applied to Ceridwen (casually translated as 'witch') is **wrach**. T. Gwynne Jones points out (148) that the word should properly be read as **gwrach** 'sorceress', but that the words for rainbow (often seen as a doorway to the Otherworld) in Old Welsh are **Bwa'r Crach**, 'The Hag's Bow', so that once again we are back at the idea of Ceridwen as the Hag – or perhaps as the 'gwyddan' discussed above. (We have already seen, in Chapter One, how her family present themselves as a probable pantheon of native gods and goddesses.)

That Ceridwen is also sometimes associated with pigs, and has been described as a Sow Goddess by more than one commentator, may lead us a step further. In the *Trioedd Ynys Prydein* (334) we find the following story, contained in Triad 26, 'The Three Powerful Swine-Herds of the Island of Britain'. The first two need not concern us, but the third is more important. It tells of:

> Coll son of Collfrewi who guarded Henwen, Dallweir Dallben's sow, which went burrowing as far as the Headland of Awstin in Cernyw and then took to the sea. It was at Aber Torogi in Gwent Is-coed that she came to land, with Coll keeping his grip upon her bristles wherever she went by sea or land. Now in Maes Gwenith 'Wheat Field', in Gwent she dropped a grain of wheat and a bee, and thenceforth has that place been the best place for wheat. Then she went as far as Llonwen in Penfro and there dropped a grain of barley and a bee, and thenceforth Llonwen has been the best place for barley. Then she proceeded to Rhiw Gyferthwch in Eryri and dropped a wolf-cub and an eagle-chick . . . Then the sow went as far as the Maen Du at Llanfair in Arfon, and there she dropped a kitten, and that kitten Coll cast into the Menai: that later came to be known as Cath Paluc 'Palug's Cat'.
>
> Trans. John Rhys, 259

This strange-seeming myth is clearly a fragment of a much earlier creation story. 'Hen-wen' means literally 'Old White One', and all animals which were white in body were considered to originate in the Otherworld. The sequence of objects and creatures dropped by the White Sow are nearly all crucial items within the Celtic culture. Wheat and barley were staple foods (as indeed was the flesh of the pig itself) and were thus sacred to the Goddess of Harvest. This was, we may remember, none other than Ceridwen herself, so that we may see her appearing in this story in two guises, as both Sow and Harvest Goddess. Possibly in the original story she herself transformed into the various creatures described, dropping them on the land. We may also note the reference in another of Taliesin's poems, **The Defence of the Chair** (translated on pages 294–6) to:

> The Chair and Cauldron of Ceridwen,
> Are they without defence?
> I remain tongue-tied in her enclosure,
> Where, to her glory,
> Milk, dew, and acorns are offered.

We may also notice, in passing, the similarity between the names of the old man who watches the Cauldron with Gwion – Dalban or Morda – and that of the owner of the pigs – Dallben – a further link in the chain of coincidences which surround this set of characters.

Finally, to complete this portion of evidence, we may note that in parts of Scotland and Ireland numerous folk-tales exist in which the 'Mountain Mother', also called sometimes 'The Great Old One' or 'Cailleach', striding across the land, lets fall from her skirts (a euphemism for giving birth) various natural features such as mountains, hills and rocks, or various creatures which then populate the land. Transformations to either hag or bird are aspects of the fearsome Celtic Battle Goddesses, described by Anne Ross as 'Divine Hags' (269). Whether Ceridwen was once such a Goddess we cannot be certain, but there are sufficient elements in her character to at least suggest this.

Highland folk-lore describes her as a venomous old hag who: 'When . . . the grass, upborne by the warm sun, the gentle dew and the fragrant rain, overcomes the Cailleach she flies into a terrible temper, and, throwing away her wand into the root of a whin bush, she disappears in a whirling cloud of angry passion.' (173)

This may seem to take us a long way from the 'Witch' Ceridwen, boiling up her Cauldron to give wisdom to her monstrous son; but the evidence all points to her identification with the great Mountain Mother, or Harvest Goddess of the Celts, who sometimes appears as the Great Sow, littering the land with a variety of creaturely life; and that this identification is wholly at one with that of the katabolic Goddess discussed in Chapter One.

The Giver of Wisdom

It is far easier to trace the image of Ceridwen as a giver of inspiration. Taliesin's poems are laced with references such as:

> I obtained my inspiration
> From the Cauldron of Ceridwen.
> **(History of Taliesin)**

and

> Conspicuous when came from the Cauldron
> The Three Inspirations of Ogyrwen ...
> Mine is the splendid Chair,
> The inspiration of my ardent song.
> **(The Royal Chair)**

A complex orthography establishes Ceridwen as the Goddess of Inspiration. Another poem of Taliesin's, the **Hostile Confederacy** refers to the 'Seven score **Ogyrwens**' who 'have shares in inspiration. But of these scores, only one truly.' (See pages 312–19 for full translation.) **Ogyrwens** is sometimes translated as 'goddesses', but a strong tradition exists to these being in some way connected with **awen** itself. This has led some authorities to identify **Ogyrwen** as a personality, possibly a 'God of Poetry' (260). However, it is more likely that the word is really a title, and was applied specifically to Ceridwen as a Goddess of Inspiration.

Traditions which relate to the Goddess as a giver of poetic or shamanic gifts is widespread. In Irish mythology, the Otherworldly well of wisdom, called the Well of Segais or Conla's Well, is the ultimate source of wisdom. It is also the source of the river Boyne, so called after the goddess, Boann. According to the **Dindsenchas**, she went to test the well's power, and challenged it by walking three times widdershins about it. Three waves from the well rose up and drowned her (59). While in another story, **The Adventures of Cormac in the Land of Promise** (184), when King Cormac went to the Otherworldly palace of Manannan, he discovered:

78

A shining fountain, with five streams flowing out of it, and the hosts in turn drinking its water. Nine hazels of Buan grew over the well. The purple hazels dropped their nuts into the fountain, and five salmon which were in the fountain severed them and sent their husks floating down the streams. (59)

Manannan explains this vision:

The fountain which thou sawest, with the five streams are the five senses through which knowledge is obtained. And no one will have knowledge who drinks not a draught out of the fountain itself and out of the streams. The folk of many arts are those who drink of them both. (ibid.)

The 'folk of many arts' are, of course the *aes dana*, the poets, and the origin of their wisdom is the fountain from which flowed the river Boyne.

For this reason the Boyne held a mystic place among Irish poets, and they often used images derived from this mythos to describe their craft. In the **Colloquy of the Two Sages** (295), which we shall discuss in detail in Chapter Four, when the youthful poet Nede asked the venerable Ferchertne: 'From where did you come?' Ferchertne replied:

> along the elfmound of Nechtan's wife,
> along the forearm of Nuadu's wife,
> along the land of the sun,
> along the dwelling of the moon,
> along the young one's navel string. (295)

These references are to the myth of Boann who lost a thigh, a forearm and an eye when the well overwhelmed her. 'The young one's navel string' refers to the god Oengus mac ind Og, the son of Boann.

Here we come back once more into the main arena of the myth, for it is the juxtaposition of great wisdom with extreme youth that is the supreme feature of both Taliesin's story, and that of Fionn Mac Cumhail when he eats the Salmon of Wisdom. Bound up in both myths, we find the common elements of the being of great wisdom who seeks to become even wiser, but who is destined to fail; and the refutation of malice.

Although Fionn's story does not directly link him with Boann, the goddess of the Boyne, she is nonetheless present in the salmon which is consumed; while Taliesin is directly pursued by Ceridwen, whom he serves, eaten by her and born of her womb. The way in which he is cast upon the waters of the river to land in a salmon-weir cannot be symbolically accidental. Both Boann and Ceridwen are preservers of wisdom, goddesses of the source of knowledge. The only difference between them is that, Boann's myth being more ancient, she has *become* the life-bearing waters, while Ceridwen is still an active deity in her own right. Both are frequently invoked as Goddesses of Poetry.

Among the many variant versions of the story of how Fionn came by his wisdom, two deserve mention here in that both relate the source of that wisdom to Otherworldly women. In the **Feis Tighe Chonain** (237) Fionn and two of his companions stumble onto the door of the **sidhe** of Carn Feradaig (Carnherry, near Limerick). The daughters of Bec Mac Buain (Mouth of the Boyne), who owned a wisdom-giving well, tried to shut the door against them. In the struggle a vessel filled with water from the well spilled its contents into the mouths of Fionn and his companions, from which *all* gained wisdom. In a variant version of the same story Fionn and four others followed a man and woman of the **sidhe** who are carrying a pig on a fork. A magical mist surrounds them and when they emerge from it they are close to the doorway of the **sidhe**. Entering, they experience several adventures, in one of which Fionn drinks from the water of two wells which are outside the palace of the Otherworldly king. This gives him wisdom.

As we shall see later, there are interesting parallels with the two wells mentioned in this second story and the wisdom they give forth, which may be of two very different kinds. (See Chapter Five.)

The Crane-Bag

In a line of the poem called **Hostile Confederacy**, Taliesin says: 'I have been a well-filled crane-bag, a sight to behold'. With this simple sentence we are at once in touch with a mysterious object of which records are to be found in other texts, none of which yield up their secrets easily, but which bridge the worlds of the poet and the shaman. For the crane-bag is nothing more than a repository for the Poetic Tradition itself, containing, like the shaman's pouch, the magical tools of Creation – and the secrets referred to by Taliesin throughout his works. It is discussed here rather than in the chapter dealing with inspiration (Chapter Four) because of its relevance to the main topic under consideration here, namely, the Cauldron or vessel of Inspiration.

According to a poem in the collection known as **Dunaire Fionn** (174) the crane-bag belonged to the ancient Sea-God Manannan Mac Lir, who made it to contain his most valuable treasures. In the poem, which is cast in the form of question and answer, Oisin asks why the bag was made and for more of its history. Caoilte, who is being asked the question, replies with the story of Aoife, who fell in love with Ilbhreac. This same hero was also loved by Iuchra, a powerful sorceress who, having persuaded Aoife to come swimming with her, turned her into the shape of a crane, so that she fled to the house of Manannan, where she remained for the rest of her life – fully two hundred years as the poem says. At the end of that time Manannan took her skin and made it into a bag in which he placed all his treasures.

> The shirt of Manannan and his knife,
> and Guibne's girdle, altogether:
> a smith's hook from the fierce man:
> were treasures that the Crane-Bag held.
>
> The King of Scotland's shears full sure,
> and the King of Lochlainn's helmet,
> these were in it to be told of,
> and the bones of Asal's swine.
>
> A girdle of the great whale's back
> was in the shapely Crane-Bag:
> I tell thee without harm,
> it used to be carried in it.
>
> When the sea was full,
> its treasures were visible in its middle;
> when the fierce sea was in ebb, the Crane-Bag
> in turn was empty.

It is evident from this, that the mysterious container was something not commonly spoken of. The fact that the Caoilte speaks of telling Oisin 'without harm', and that the things within the bag were 'to be told of' makes this clear. But of course, as is often the case, the description of the contents is far from obvious and gives up its meaning only after prolonged study.

For our first clues we must turn to the account of the crane-bag given by Ann Ross in her seminal book *Pagan Celtic Britain* (270). Dr Ross points out several interesting details concerning the lore and history of cranes. Midir, the powerful son of the Irish Father God the Dagda, possessed three cranes who lived with him on the Isle of Man (also known as Manannan's Isle). These birds kept all unwelcome visitors away by crying out 'Do not enter – keep away – pass by!' – clear enough indication that we are dealing with an Otherworldly place where some mystery not intended for the eyes of the uninitiated takes place. We note further that crane meat was considered unclean food among the Gaelic Western Highlands, suggesting that the bird was sacred, and that disagreeable or shrewish women were called 'cranes' in Ireland.

This tells us that cranes were considered sacred and that they guarded the gates of the Otherworld. Parallels from both Welsh and Irish literature are the Birds of Rhiannon, who sing men to sleep for seven years; and those owned by the Irish Goddess Cliodniu, who had three brightly coloured birds, sustained by everlasting apples (the fruit of the Otherworld) who also sang sick people to sleep.

Two more instances in which cranes play an important part in the poetic mysteries are found in stories relating to Fionn who, as we saw in Chapter One, later came to possess the crane-bag himself. In the first story, the folk-tale of **Bairne Mor** (The Great Child) (270), Fionn is saved from death by his grandmother who, in the shape of a crane, catches him when he is thrown over a cliff by his father's killers. (A later folk-tale 'The Birth of Fionn MacCumhail' (61) has him first sink into the lake, then rise to the surface again clutching a salmon. It is this which causes his grandmother to recognise him and to save his life.) In the second story, the **Cailleach an Teampuill** ('Hag of the Temple') (270), Fionn saves the hag's four sons who have been *turned into cranes*, by obtaining three drops of blood from the head of a sacred bull belonging to the Cailleach Bheara.

We may see, behind this, a story in which Fionn acquires the empowerment of the Cailleach. He later comes into the possession of the crane-bag, which had been in his father's hands until his death (at which time Fionn is saved by the Grandmother-Crane) and which comes to represent his recognition by Cumhail's loyal followers.

A further key to the magic of the crane-bag is to be found in these two carved reliefs, found respectively in Paris and Trier (see Figures 6 and 7). The Paris stone has on one of its four sides a powerful image of a bearded god cutting branches from a willow tree; while on the adjacent side is a bull with three cranes perched on its back. Above the bearded figure is the name Esus; above that of the bull the name **Tarvortigaranos** (The Bull With Three Cranes). The meaning of this is explored in detail by Miranda Green (103), who adds the following details on the significance of bulls within Celtic society, where they were associated with:

1 Fertility;
2 The Underworld;
3 Cranes;
4 The Solar Wheel;
5 The Celtic Apollo, God of Poetry and Healing.

On the Trier stone a similar scene is depicted, save that here the three cranes are standing on the tree which Esus is cutting down, while on one of the other faces of the stone are figures which have been identified with the Celtic Mercury and with the Goddess Rosmerta, who was also the guardian of a Cauldron.

Finally, our attention is drawn to a figurine, discovered at Maiden Castle in Dorset, of a bull with three horns, on whose back perch three women who appear to be half bird.

All of this adds up to something very curious indeed which, despite its complexity, makes a kind of sense. The birds – whether these are cranes or the birds of Rhiannon or Cliodnu – are all connected in various ways with the poetic mysteries. The cranes are protectors of the Otherworld; Rhiannon's and Cliodnu's birds are connected with either poetic trance or healing. The bull imagery clusters around the gods of poetry, healing and the underworld. Bull's hides are connected with poetic trance states (see Chapter Six).

The various Gods and Goddesses depicted on the stones are less easy to fit into the picture. Esus seems to have been a kind of woodland/harvester deity, worshipped, together with his consort, Rosmerta, in Gaul. Both the carvings are of Gallo-Roman origin and therefore corrupt, but there have

Figures 6 & 7 (left) Esus cutting the tree. Three cranes perch in the topmost branches. (right) Tauros Trigaranus (the bull with three cranes).

been suggestions that they form part of a very ancient tale also represented by the iconography of the famous Gundestrup Cauldron. There, also, we have reference to women turned into cranes, and to the ritual sacrifice of bulls (114). Others have, on admittedly slender evidence, identified Esus as a Druidic God, who cuts the Mistletoe from the Tree of Life, or the Poet's Wand from the Willow.

Finally, we should note that the poem which gives us the fullest account of the crane-bag, and which lists its various owners, ends with the hero Conaire, who 'slept on the side of Tara of the Plains; when the cunning, well-made man awoke, the Crane-Bag was found about his neck' (174). So that once again we have a story of someone who falls asleep and on waking finds the poetic mysteries have been vouchsafed to him.

All of this may seem to be taking us far from the point of the crane-bag and its contents, but the truth of the matter is that both the story and the carvings at Paris and Trier are a series of glyphs referring to the poetic/Druidic mysteries and to the magical arts of the shaman-poets.

Robert Graves suggests (100) that the meaning of the strange items within the bag are kenning references to certain letters of the Ogam alphabet (discussed more fully in Chapter Seven). He instances the belief, current among the Greek mythographers, that 'such letters of the alphabet as had not already been invented by the Triple Goddess', were discovered by Palamedes son of Nauplius ('Ancient Intelligence, Son of Navigator'). 'His inspiration came, it is said, from observing a flock of cranes, which make letters as they fly.' Graves goes on to suggest that the crane-bag was full when the tide was in and empty when it was out because the mysteries it contained were only known to 'The Sons of Manannan' – the shaman-priests who had brought the alphabet mysteries across the sea from Greece. The items described in the poem quoted above, then, stand for the five 'extra' letters added to the original Ogam alphabet (see page 214), which can all be represented in a form of sign language.

Now, one may believe this or not as one wishes. Certainly some of Graves' evidence is shaky (he is speaking poetically not rationally). There are admittedly seven items mentioned as being in the crane-bag, but only five letters. But what is important is the underlying message: that the crane-bag contained poetic secrets. Considering the evidence assembled by Ann Ross and Miranda Green there can be little doubt that this is indeed the bag's purpose. It is all a poetic/shamanic glyph. The three woman-cranes who perch on the bull-god's back; the three cranes in the tree which is being cut down by Esus; the presence of the Ogam letters in the crane-bag; the uses of the bull's hide for poetic incubation – all these are symbols of the shaman-poet's art. The cranes themselves do indeed 'make letters' – Ogam letters – as they fly; the bird-women recall the Birds of Rhiannon and Cliodniu, who sang men to sleep for seven years, during which time they learned the secrets of the inner realms. The stories of Fionn's rescue by his grandmother (surely, the Goddess herself) in the form of a crane, and his own task to restore the sons of the Cailleach *from* the shape of cranes with the blood of a sacred bull together form a recurring pattern in which, by looking *beyond* the obvious, we catch a glimpse of something more.

The Fionn stories clearly concern his empowerment by the Goddess herself, in the form of the Ancient Hag of the Land, whose nearest equivalent in Welsh mythology is Ceridwen, the initiator of Taliesin. It is possible, from the evidence presented here, to attempt a tentative reconstruction of the original initiation ceremony, as it might have been performed, long since, in both Britain and Ireland.

After imbibing a drink which contained some drops of blood from a sacrificial bull, the would-be aspirant had to leap over a cliff (perhaps blindfold) to show his faith in the Goddess he served. She, in her crane form, caught him, preventing him from falling to the ground and being severely hurt. If he was already in a drugged state, as a result of drinking the potion, and if the cliff were not too high, he could easily have jumped down without too much hurt and with all the sensations of flying. He was then vouchsafed a vision of some kind, probably involving the dancing of the Crane Dance. A similar kind of serpentine ritual dance was performed in Greece as an offering to Apollo (the God of Poetry and Healing). In this he may have danced with the Goddess herself and at the end was presented with the crane-bag as a symbol of his initiation, the contents of which represented the aspect of the poet's, or shaman's, art. Such a ceremony would have remained in the consciousness of the people long after it ceased to be performed, and this would explain the recurrent appearance of crane and bull symbolism in Celtic mythology, iconography, and folk-lore. It accounts for most, if not all, the elements described above, and provides us with a further important aspect of Celtic shamanism.

The Cauldron-Born

Looking at all the evidence assembled above, what can we say finally about the Cauldron? Apart from those discussed already, there are several other wondrous vessels in Celtic myth which will repay brief mention.

The most important aspect of these is their connection with the Otherworld. It is quite clear that no representation of the hidden realm was complete without such a vessel. Thus in a poem from the Fionn cycle, **Cael Praises Creide's House** (217). Here, in what is undoubtedly an Otherworld palace, where wounded men are described as being able to sleep 'to the music of fairy birds singing above the eyes of her bright bower', and where,

> There is a vat there of princely enamel
> into which flows the juice of pleasant malt,
> and an apple-tree above the vat with abundance
> of heavy fruit.
>
> When Creide's goblet is filled with the mead
> of that vehement vat, four apples fall
> simultaneously right into the goblet.

But of all the cauldrons in Celtic myth by far the most important of these must be that belonging to the Dagda, one of the four sacred treasures of the Tuatha de Danaan which is described in the **Cath Maige Turedh** (88) as follows:

> Out of Murias was brought the Dagda's Cauldron:
> No company ever went from it unthankful.

'Murias' here relates to the word **muir**, 'sea', and is properly seen as a name for the Land-Beneath-the-Waves. But, though the vessel is described as a Cauldron (**coirc**) in this text, in a poem from the **Dindsenchas** (297), very different terms are used. The text reads:

> Gabal Glas, son of Ethadon, son of Nuada Argatlainn, took away a bundle of twigs, which Ainge, the Dagda's daughter, had gathered to make a tub (**drochta**) thereof. For the tub which the Dagda used to make, would not cease from dripping while the sea was in flood, though not a drop came out of it during the ebb.

The same story, in the metrical version (107), is even more explicit:

> A tub was made for his [the Dagda's] daughter
> Above the breastwork of the high river mouth.
> It would not leak unless the tide were full . . .

This makes it clear that the Cauldron of the Dagda was in fact a kind of basket made of woven twigs, apparently for the god's daughter. It was full at high tide and empty at low tide, which immediately identifies it with the crane-bag. The 'breastwork of the high river mouth' seems to me to be another way of describing the famous weir of Gwyddno Garanhir, in which Taliesin, floating in a leather bag (or sometimes a coracle of plaited withies!) is discovered.

The final piece of evidence which connects all these wonder-working vessels is contained in the story of Gwyddno himself. It should come as no surprise to us to learn that, as well as the wondrous weir, from which so many salmon (the fish of knowledge) were removed every May Eve, Gwyddno also possessed a wondrous basket, called a **Mwys**, which held enough food for a hundred at a time. Thus when, in the *Hanes Taliesin*, the child poet is taken from the weir and is acclaimed as being of greater value, what is really being said is that poetic wisdom is of greater value than physical food (though, since salmon are the Fish of Wisdom this may well be a double meaning). Gwyddno's own title **Garanhir** almost certainly means 'Crane-Shanks', while Gwyddno itself means 'The Knowing One'. So that his full name is perhaps 'The Knowing One With Crane's Legs', a name very suitable to a guardian of the crane-bag itself. It seems more than likely that Gwyddno was at one time a God of the sea, and this association fits well with the idea, found in the *Hanes Taliesin*, that the waters which ran from the broken cauldron poisoned his horses; if they are taken to mean horses of the sea this would be an accurate description of the poisonous liquid flowing into the river which in turn poisoned the sea. Finally, the **mwys** is said to be one of the famous Thirteen Treasures of the Island of Britain (22), which, although tradition ascribes their guardianship to Merlin, are sometimes said to be guarded by Taliesin. He is thus truly described as one of the 'Cauldron-Born', having derived his wisdom first from that of Ceridwen, having later been set adrift in a cauldron-basket and having come to rest at last at the Weir, later inherits the shamanic crane-bag of poetic wisdom and understanding.

The diagram opposite, which includes several vessels not discussed here, makes the relationship clear.

Having established the provenance of the Cauldron and its function as a purveyor of inspiration, we must now look deeper into the methods by which this inspiration was obtained and what it meant to the Bards who experienced its effects.

Object	Owner/Guardian	Property	Place of Origin
Cauldron of Inspiration	Ceridwen/ Gwion/Taliesin	Dispensing Wisdom	Lake Tegid
Cauldron of Bran	Llasar Llaes Gwyfnewid and Matholwch/Bran	Dispensing Life and Food (?)	Lake of the Cauldron
Mwys/Weir of Gwyddno Garanhir	Gwyddno/ Elffin (?)	Food/ Wisdom?	The Sea
Cauldron/ Cup of Cormac	Manannan/ Cormac	Wisdom/ Food	The Sea
Cauldron of Curoi	Curoi Mac Daira	Food	The Sea
Crane-Bag	Manannan and many others Fionn	Wisdom	The Sea
Cauldron of Gerg	Gerg/Conchobar Mac Nessa	Food	A Lake
Basket/ Cauldron of Dagda	Dagda/Ainge	Food and Wisdom	The Sea (?)
Creide's Cauldron/ Cup	Creide	Food	The Otherworld?

Figure 8   The Cauldrons of Life, Inspiration and Plenty

Chapter Four

THE LIFE OF SONG: TALIESIN AND THE POETIC MYSTERIES

Seven years your right, under a flagstone, in a quagmire,
Without food, without taste, but the thirst you ever torturing,
The law of the judges your lesson, and prayer your language:
And if you like to return
You will be, for a time, a Druid, perhaps.

Ancient Irish Poem

The Songs of Taliesin

It is time that we looked a little more closely at the poems attributed to Taliesin. We have already discussed these briefly as they relate to the *Hanes Taliesin* and from this we can see that here is the main source of information relating to the inner life of the bard. However, they are far from easy to understand – at least at first glance.

To begin with, the versions that have come down to us are extremely corrupt. They have been copied, recopied, amended, added to and sometimes virtually rewritten by a succession of scribes from the moment they stopped being oral works and became written literature. It is also more than likely that even *before* this they underwent variations in the hands of other bards who thought they could improve the originals.

Certainly, at one time, manuscripts existed for many of the poems – probably of many more than we now possess. We know that the 16th Century bard Llewelyn Sion – who also probably wrote a version of the *Hanes* – made or had access to a collection at Raglan Castle. Indeed it seems as though he spearheaded something of a revival of interest in the works of the old poets, and that he helped institute a Bardic Chair in Gwynedd, at which poems and songs were recited, both old and new. Some of the poems in the *Book of Taliesin* may well date from no earlier than this, but they are usually not difficult to spot once one has become accustomed to the style and rhetoric of the original authors.

Another problem results from the fact that many of the copyists were Christian monks, who had a penchant for adding lines referring to God or Christ where there may originally have been none – or indeed, omitting lines or references to pagan deities or teachings of which they could not approve. This is not to say that Taliesin himself necessarily abjured Christianity – there are indications to the contrary that do not read as interpolations. If he was not actually a Christian himself, he certainly seems to have had respect for the 'new' religion which had established itself in Britain. In fact there are far too many assumptions within the picture that sets Pagans and Christians at each other's throats throughout the Dark Ages – there are indications that they managed to get along quite amicably most of the time, and that only later did real animosity break out, not before a certain amount of cross-fertilisation in *both* directions had taken place.

So on the one hand we have a legion of improvers, and on the other a number of dedicated 'cleaners-up' of the 'pagan' Bards. Which makes it all the more amazing that *anything* of the original work has survived at all. In fact, fortunately for us, quite a lot has. Once one has stripped away the obvious insertions, the references to historical events which happened long after the period of the original poems, we have a glimpse of what lies beneath. And very fascinating it is, being nothing less than the remains of a system of beliefs dating from long *before* the actual poems were composed. It is, unfortunately, only fragmentary, and we must be cautious of trying to fill in too many of the gaps from our personal knowledge – this was the problem which faced the 18th Century poet and antiquarian Iolo Morgannwg who sought to make a coherent system out of the bardic remains, and when he failed, as we shall see, did not hesitate to fill in the blanks from his own fertile brain. His work – though valuable in some ways – has made our own task more difficult.

At least one critic has suggested that the poems, sayings and other lore were invented by the bards of the 15th to 17th Centuries, though why they should do so is less easily explained. What seems more likely is that a much earlier body of material was *adapted* and *added to* by the medieval bards, in order to bring it in line with the times and with Christian teaching. And since the medieval bards seemed to regard Christianity as in some senses a fulfilment of Druidic teaching (the poet Wace attributed to Taliesin a prophecy of the Coming of Christ in his **Brut**, 313), it is not surprising to find a triad which claims that of the three religious impulses imbibed by the Cymry, Christianity was 'the best of the three'!

This meant, in effect, that anything unacceptable to the rather narrow minds of the medieval Christians, was either expunged or altered. In fact this does not disqualify the entire material; but it does present anyone concerned with its value with a considerable problem. Much can be immediately discarded as having no relationship to what we know of the times when the material was originally in circulation. Other aspects have to be looked at very closely to see whether, beneath the patina of medieval doctoring, we can still discern something of the original shape and form.

The third body of material is clearly original and exists virtually unchanged from the time it was written down. In the case of the Taliesin poems, a further complication arises from the very evident fact that the scribe responsible for the only extant manuscript of the *Book of Taliesin* was both clumsy and probably ignorant of the material he was copying, and also that his Christian prejudices prompted him to add references which were almost certainly not in the original.

Thus we have badly copied lines, often duplicating themselves; poems run together without titles, and additions inserted everywhere. One's first task, therefore, is to delete everything irrelevant. What remains can then be examined in a clearer light and sense made of the innermost meanings.

The Taliesin Tradition

'Tradition,' remarked Sir John Morris-Jones in his 1918 study of Taliesin (7), 'is ... one of our data, to be accounted for and interpreted ... where there is no other apparent reason for it, it may well be what it seems to be – a popular account of what once took place; and where more reliable data are scarce it may be of value in directing inquiry and confirming conclusions.'

It is in this light that we must regard the traditions attached to Taliesin and, in the same way, the poems which bear his name, and which, if not actually composed by him, retain a sense of what he stood for and the kind of work he is believed to have composed. Thus, whilst there is almost no textual evidence to support the belief that the Taliesin poems are any older than the 13th or 14th Centuries, we may treat them in the same way as the *Mabinogion* (144) which was itself written down at much the same time as the *Book of Taliesin* (10).

Few would now contest that these texts contain matter of an extremely ancient provenance, or that they are indeed the last remaining fragments of a once developed literature which reflected a tradition of considerable antiquity. In the same way, the poems of Taliesin, Aneurin and Myrddin, although some at least were in all probability composed by Welsh bards of the Middle Ages, draw upon, and in many cases contain, fragments of that same tradition. Whether or not we believe that there was an actual Welsh bard called Taliesin (there seems no reason to doubt it) is, finally, irrelevant to our present purpose. The figure of Taliesin who appears in the extant poems bears all the characteristics of myth. However, this in itself may be a reflection of the inspired nature of his work. It is often forgotten that Taliesin was a *poet*, and that poets can and do range as widely as their cultural inheritance permits. Taliesin's inspired works must have contained numerous references to genuine tradition and to real initiatory experience. To simply damn all his works as fiction because of their oblique vaticinatory and gnomic nature is equal to denying the reality of the modern Welsh poet Dylan Thomas on account of his unusual use of syntax and allusion which often make his works appear incomprehensible. Taliesin's works, when judged and examined in relationship to what is known of the times, the culture and the mythico-poetical background, often prove to be no less sensible than those of Dylan.

It is generally accepted that many of the poems as we have them could not have been written in the 6th Century because the word-endings used to give rhyme changed extensively during that period. However, since it is not known with any certainty *when* the language mutated, this does not necessarily follow. Obviously the change did not take place overnight, so that someone like Taliesin, writing at the *end* of the 6th Century could have been using a wholly different form of language to someone living at the *beginning* of that age. Gildas, himself writing at the latter end of the 9th Century, uses Latinate forms of the old British names in his list of the famous poets quoted in Chapter One. This is sometimes assumed to prove the later provenance of the poems; but since Gildas was writing in Latin, it is hardly surprising if the names appear in this form. They must derive from native forms, but there can be no specific proof that the language still retained its earlier form at this time.

The suggestion of Sir John Morris-Jones (10) that the development of the old British tongue into the forerunner of modern Welsh, took place before the separation of the Welsh and British strains, seems eminently satisfactory – and this means, of course, that the language in which the poems of the *Four Ancient Books* were written, *predates* the 6th Century. It is, therefore, possible that the poems as we have them today are much less changed *in their basic form* than has been supposed. It is with the various interpolations and fabrications that we must therefore deal, if we are to arrive at a basic picture of the original works of Taliesin, Aneurin, Myrddin and their like.

With all of these thoughts in mind, therefore, let us look first at a poem called the **Hostile Confederacy** – though in fact that title means very little, as do many of those given, somewhat arbitrarily, by various editors. It is a long poem – or miscellany of poems – and it ably illustrates both the problems which go with the Taliesin material, and the ways in which we have chosen to deal with them. It is given first in the translation by D. W. Nash, without glosses, followed by our own version and commentary.

The Hostile Confederacy

Is there a Bard here who has not sung an appropriate song?
When the song is finished,
If he is a learned person,
There will be from me
No denial of liberality.
according to the saying of Taliesin,
The day was waning,
When Kian finished
His numerous songs of praise.
Let my liquor by that which rightly belonged to
  Afaggdu.

94

Did he not skilfully bear away
The strains of knowledge?
Gwion, on whom it overflowed,
And he became profound.
He could restore the dead to life.
Though destitute of wealth,
They can make delicious things,
And boil without water;
They can make metals.

In ages of ages,
The day remains concealed,
For praising the profoundly eloquent one.
Not unlovely is concord,
To him who is accustomed to it.
Assembly of harmonious minstrels,
What has paralysed your tongues?
Why do you not recite a recitation?
Give us over the bright liquor
All your penillions?
I have sung without delay,
Before very long importunity.
There is a song on their coming,
A song on their going,
A song from a hundred minstrels;
And it is this they speak of,
The slaughter of the daughter of Lliant
Little was her pleasure in gold and silver,
What is the covering of the earth?
How many coverings has the earth?
How the breath is drawn?
Whence is the sward green?
What is the origin of trades?
Of trades what is the origin?
Do you know what is recorded,
Recorded in books?
How many winds, how many torrents,
How many torrents, how many winds?
How many rivers on the journey,
How many rivers there are?
What is the breadth of the earth,
Or what its thickness?
I know the . . . [names of the planets] [defective line]
Revolving round the earth;
I know the regulator
Between heaven and earth.

Whence the echo comes again,
And why its impulse dies away;
Whence the brightness of silver;
And why the valleys are dark;
What is the seat of the breath,
What is the best that has been;
Why the cattle have horns,
Why a woman is fond,
Why milk is white,
Why holly is green,
Why the kid is bearded,
Whence is the growth of cow-parsnip
In a multitude of places;
Why wine intoxicates,
Why the mallet is made sloping,
Why the little roebuck is spotted,
Why the sea is salt,
Whence is the briskness of ale,
Why the alder is of a purplish colour,
Why the linnet is green,
Why the berries of the dogrose are red,
Or what is the age of a woman;
Whence is the commencement of night,
What melting-pot must be used to liquefy gold.

No one knows what makes the sun red-coloured
On his first rising;
In an hour it goes away.
Why a harp string is white;
Why the salmon glitters,
What preserves it without fire;
What Garthan brought,
And Geraint and Garman;
What brings out the polish
On hard-worked stone,
Whence the sweetness of the balm,
When the green of young grass.
Talhaiarn is
the greatest of sages.
Who is deprived of life
With blood upon the breast.

A wonderful reciter,
A great singer of songs of praise,
Am I, Taliesin.

I compose songs in true measure,
Continuing to the end
To uphold Elphin.
Is there not a tribute
Of much gold to be paid?
When shall be hated and not loved,
Perjury and treachery?
I have no desire for benefits
By yielding imperfect praise
And salutations to the brotherhood.
Compared with me, no one knows anything.
I am learned in the principal sciences,
And the reasoning of astrologers
Concerning veins and solvents,
And the general nature of man.
I know the secret of composing songs of praise.
I have sung of the existence of God.
According to the saying of Talhaiarn,
For the gifted there shall be judgement,
And a judging of their qualities.
The poetic disposition
Is that which gives the secret virtue
Of a muse above mediocrity.
Seven score muses
There are in the inspiration of song;
Eight score in every score
In the great abyss of tranquillity,
In the great abyss of wrath,
In the depths below the earth,
In the air above the earth,
There is a recognition of it.
What sorrow there is,
That is better than joy.
I know the blessed gifts
Of the flowing muse;
To me it brings the rewards of skill,
To me happy days,
To me a peaceful life,
And a protection in age.
I am equal to kings, whatever their enjoyment,
I am equal with them through redemption.

[lacuna in manuscript]

[I know, or, Who knows, or, No one knows]
When the countenance will be animated,

When the sea will be pleasant,
When is the growth of the seed,
Whence it grows up high,
Or whence comes the sun?
What is it agitates the wood,
Or fashions the froth on the water?
I know good and evil,
The rising and motion of wreaths of smoke,
And many more [things] equally perfect;
Who it was emptied the bowl,
Where the dawn terminates;
What was preached by
Eli and Eneas.
I know the cuckoos in summer.
And where they will be in winter.
I will sing a song
Concerning the deep, I will bring it [to]
The common source of rivers.
I know its depth,
I know whence it diminishes,
I know whence it replenishes,
I know whence it overflows,
I know whence it shrinks,
I know whence [come/came] the creatures
That are in the sea;
I know all that are like them,
All in their assembly,
How many hours in a day,
How many days in a year,
How many spears in a battle,
How many drops in a shower,
Very delicate its separation.
Excessive praise infers reproach.
A mind with the learning of Gwydion
I know in nobody;
What caused the tide to flow
Over the people of Pharaoh;

Who carried the measuring line
In the presence of the Creator;
What ladder had he
When the heavens were lifted up;
What was the fork set up
from the earth to the sky.
How many peas there are in my pot
With one in my hand.

98

What is the name of the two shanks
Which cannot be wedged into one pot;
What is the cause of sea-sickness;
Whence is the fat of fishes:
Their flesh will be of sea-food
Until it is transformed,
While the fish contains it.
Why the white swan has black feet,
Why a sharp spear penetrates.
The region of heaven has no limits.
What are the four elements
Whose boundaries are unknown?
Is the pig or the stag of the most vagabond nature?
I ask of you, bigbellied bards,
Are the bones of man made of vapour?
Do the winds fall down in cataracts?
I am a reciter of information,
In Efrai, in Efroeg,
in Efroeg, in Efrai.
A second time in transformation,
I have been a blue salmon,
I have been a dog, I have been a stag,
I have been a roebuck in the mountain,
I have been a stump of a tree in a shovel,
I have been an axe in the hand,
I have been the pin of a pair of tongs
A year and a half;
I have been a spotted cock
Along with the hens;
I have been a stallion in stud,
I have been a fierce bull,
I have been a yellow buck,
Soft was my nourishment.
I have been a grain springing up;
The reaper came to me,
Thrusting me into a hole,
Rubbing me with a hand
In my afflictions.
A hen became pregnant of me,
With red claws and a cleft crest.
I was necessitated to be nine nights
In her womb as an infant.
I have been a possession of the meritorious,
I have been a gift for a king,
I have been dead, I have been alive;
Concealed in the ivy bush,

99

I have been carried about.
Before I received a gift I was poor.
Another welcome council
To me the red-fanged one gave,
A wonderful reciter,
A great composer of hymns,
Am I, Taliesin.
I compose songs in true measure,
Continuing to the end
To uphold Elphin.

On a first reading, much of this will seem nonsensical, confused, perhaps even meaningless. Yet, if we follow the precepts outlined above, we will begin to see light, and finally the work will reveal itself.

To begin with it is not one poem but several, a miscellany dealing with different, though related themes. It tells us a great deal more about Taliesin, about his mystical adventures and realisations, and about the shamanic and bardic mysteries in general. Lines 1–11 form a kind of prelude, in which a poet, possibly Kian or Kynon, is about to sing a song about (or by) Gwion-Taliesin. If he sings well he will be rewarded with 'the speech intended for Afagddu', i.e. with inspiration. But perhaps his song falls upon deaf ears since 'Not one heeds the words of Taliesin.' In our translation:

Behold a bard who has not chanted yet.
Soon he will sing
And by the end of his song,
He will know starry wisdom.

No recompense for my song –
Not one heeds the words of Taliesin.

The day dawns when
Kian will recite
A host of praises.
My reward will be the speech
Intended for Avagddu.

Next (lines 12–20) he sings about Gwion:

It was an ingenious exchange –
The lord's luck

Became Gwion's utterance –
His speech, a chance occurrence.
Gwion could make the dead alive –
A difficult endeavour.

Gwion kept the cauldron
Steadily boiling.
Gwion of small merit
Shall be until the ages of ages.

Here are related the mystery of the poet's transformation, of the cauldron which has given him eternal life and everlasting wisdom.

There follows a string of barbed insults, aimed at the foolish, drunken bards who understand nothing, who cannot even remember the words of their songs. Then the poet – now speaking in the 'voice' of Taliesin – sings of his own incarnation, of what he has seen and known in his present existence (lines 26–40).

The peace that you bring to me
Through the depth of your praises
Does it not rather resemble a hostile conspiracy?

What then is this custom?
Your tongue has recited
So many native songs
That you are no longer able to say
Words of blessing over the clear liquid
Or utter the theme of your eulogy.

I alone am your custom
An equal among judges.
Three score years
I have suffered earthly existence,
In the water . . .
In the element of earth.

Surrounded by a hundred servants
A hundred kings making oaths
A hundred forgetting them
A hundred returning to them.
A hundred bards chanting
And predicting all of this.

There follows an interpolated poem, (lines 41–59) referring to a now lost myth relating to 'Lladdon, daughter of the Wave', (possibly Latona?), into which has been inserted a four line reference to Elffin (48–51). There then follows an extended statement, in the 'voice' of Taliesin, cataloguing his wisdom and gifts (lines 60–238).

First he states his abilities:

> I am a wiseman of the primal knowledge,
> I am an experienced astrologer,
> I pronounce anger,
> I pronounce solutions,
> I speak to habitual sycophants,
> I continue to behold God.

Then follows a reference to Talhaiarn, the other great poet of the age, who may well have been Taliesin's own master. After which, in some crucial lines, he refers to the 'seven score **ogyrwen's**' (Goddesses) who give inspiration – though in truth there is only one who counts. This is a reference to Ceridwen as inspirer, as we saw in the previous chapter. It is followed by a prophetic statement, couched in oblique language, referring to the coming and going of 'anger in the earth'. Then begins one of the great catalogues of which there are so many within the Taliesin poems. Lines 90–95 return for a moment respectfully to Talhaiarn, then Taliesin is in full flood, describing all the things that he knows:

> I know the cuckoos of summer,
> I know where they go in winter.
> The inspiration that I sing
> I have brought it up from the depths.
>
> A river of wisdom flows.
> I know its length,
> I know when it disappears,
> I know when it refills,
> I know when it overflows,
> I know when it disappears,
> I know which foundation
> There is under the sea.
> I know its measure,
> I know everything that surrounds it.
> I know how numerous are the hours of the day,

> I know how numerous are the days in the year,
> How numerous are the spears,
> How numerous are the drops of a shower
> Gently dispersing . . .

He knows the craft of Gwydion, and all there is to know of seasons and times. He knows the very number of the winds, and the dimensions of the earth. Lines 157–193 are concerned with the essences of things: 'why a wife is loving, why milk is white' and so on. Then comes a brief salute to 'the bard of the border', perhaps he who is singing this song, and then a four line interpolation by a scribe attempting to put the whole catalogue into a Christian format.

There follows a long series of statements referring to the enduring things which Taliesin has experienced and felt so intimately that he is able to say that he has 'been' them. Finally he refers to his own incarnation through the womb of Ceridwen, 'the red hen with the double comb'. The poem ends with a restatement of lines 48–51, in which the poet again reaffirms his loyalty to Elffin, and with a final reference to the poet who is singing these very words, who may thus 'find it hard to be happy, but may find great glory in it.'

One poem or many? It is possible to read **Hostile Confederacy** in either way. We may, if we wish, subtract the interpolated lines, and arrive at a long and astonishing account of the poet's shamanic vision, the way in which it was acquired, and some of its innermost meanings. In the version which follows we have done just this, suppressing the interpolations and guiding the poem into a unified structure. There is no means of knowing how accurate this may be. The innate structure which comprises a poem gives one to suppose that it is at least one way in which the coded maze of lines may be interpreted. A full, 'unabridged' translation will be found on pages 312–19.

Angar Cyvyndawd
(The Hostile Conspiracy)

> I am a wiseman of the primal knowledge,
> I am an experienced astrologer,
> I pronounce anger, I pronounce solutions,
> I speak to habitual sycophants,
> I continue to behold God.

In the language of Talhaiarn,
initiation was the judgement,
whoever expounded to him the nature
and the power of poetry,
to him was wisdom bestowed,
and inspiration without fail.
Seven score **ogyrwen's**
have shares in this inspiration,
but of these scores, only one truly.

I know the law
of fertile inspiration
when it is skilfully tuned
to those happy days,
to a quiet life,
to the defence of the times,
to kings of whom long is the consolation
to the things which are on the face of the earth.

It is difficult to perform
such a task on a new instrument.
Why is the harp-string lamenting?
Why does the cuckoo lament?
why does it sing?
I know it as I know many pleasant things.
I know why Geraint and Arman
abandoned their camp,
I know when the spark
of hardness works from the stones,
I know why the honeysuckle smells good,
why crows are the colour of silence.

I know the cup
from which the wave has overflowed.
I know the end of the dawn.
I know who has preached
To Eli and Eneas.
I know the cuckoos of summer,
I know where they go in winter.
The inspiration that I sing
I have brought up from the depths.

Like a river it flows,
I know its length,
I know when it disappears,
I know when it refills,

I know when it overflows,
I know when it disappears,
I know which foundation
there is under the sea.
I know its measure,
I know everything that surrounds it.

I know how numerous are the hours of the day,
I know how numerous are the days in the year,
how numerous are the spears in battle,
how numerous are the drops of a shower
gently dispersing . . .

I know all the craft of Gwydion
who made great mockery and nearly a disgrace.
I know who it is
who fills the river . . .
I know who averts
the present questions.
I know with what enduring patience
the sky was raised.
When the great knowledge of the stars is imparted
then will be understood every high thing.

I know when the spirit is working,
when the sea is pleasant,
when the race is valiant,
when the most high is implored.
I know the extent over the earth
of the sun which shines upon us,
I know when the bird of anger goes to its rest –
the bird of anger goes to its nest
when the earth becomes green.

I know the number of the winds and streams,
I know the number of the streams and winds,
how many are its rivers.
I know the size of the earth
and its thickness.
I know the sound of blades
reddened on all sides under the sun,
I know the Regulator
of the Heavens and of the Earth.

I know why a hill resounds,
I know why devastators win land,

I know why the vault of silver is restored,
why breath is black,
why it is better so,
why the valley is radiant.

I know why the cow is horned,
why a wife is loving,
why milk is white,
why holly is green,
why the goat is bearded,
why the parsnip is crested,
why the wheel is round,
why the mallet is flat,
why the kid is speckled,
why salt is in brine,
why beer is a lively medium . . .

I know why the alder is purple coloured,
why the linnet is green,
why hips are red,
why a woman is never still,
why night comes,
I know the nature of the flood
but no-one knows why the interior of the sun is red.

I know who made the great pole
which connects earth and heaven,
I know the number of fingers in the cauldron.
I know what name of two words
will never be taken from the cauldron.
I know why the ocean rolls about us,
why fish are silent –
of sea food will their flesh be,
until the time when it will be transformed
when the fish will constrain the sea.

I know that the white swan's foot is black,
I know that the sharp spear is four-sided,
I know that the heavenly race are unfallen,
I know that there are four elements
(But their end is not known to me).
I know the wanderings of the boar and the deer.

I salute you, bard of the border,
how do you stand
beside he whose bones are of the fog

in a place where two cataracts of wind
come together in combat?

A second time was I created.
I have been a blue salmon,
I have been a dog, I have been a deer,
I have been a roebuck on the mountain,
I have been a trunk, I have been a beech,
I have been an axe in the hand,
I have been a pin in the tongs.

For a year and half,
I have been a white speckled cock,
among the hens of Eiddyn. [i.e. Edinburgh]
I have been a stallion at stud,
I have been a battling bull,
I have been a yellow goat.

Fecund and nourishing,
I have been a grain discovered
growing on a hill.
The Harvester took me
to free my essence
in a place full of smoke.

I have known great suffering;
a red hen took me,
she had red wings and a double comb;
I rested nine months
As a child in her belly.

I have been matured,
I have been offered to a king,
I have been dead, I have been alive,
I have possessed the ivy branch,
I have had an escort;
before God I have been poor.

The Protector has instructed me
between his red hands.
He who has spoken of me
will find it hard to be happy –
but may find great glory in it.

I am Taliesin
and I defend the true lineage

until the end of time
to the profit of Elffin.

It is evident from a close reading of this text that it constitutes a method of teaching by example. The seemingly innocent questions or statements (why is milk white etc.) are designed to make the reader (or listener) ask the question for themselves and evince a deeper answer than would normally be the case. There are references to so many things that we may indeed wonder at the vastness of Taliesin's knowledge, which extends to all of the major sciences then current. Taliesin's claim to know many things illustrates the universality of shamanic wisdom, and though we should be careful of describing this knowledge as 'Druidic', there is little doubt that understanding of this kind, the sheer *breadth* of wisdom expressed in these seemingly artless poems, is as clear an expression of the reality of Druidic teachings as we are ever likely to possess.

The rest of the major poems attributed to Taliesin are translated in full with commentary in Part Two of the present work. We need now to look in more detail at some of the themes found within them which throw further light on the mysteries of the shaman-poet.

Poetry and Madness

The Taliesin story, as we have seen, is very much concerned with the 'theft' of wisdom from the Gods. It is also, of course, concerned with the stealing of knowledge from the inner realm of the consciousness through meditation and ritual. Taliesin, as a pupil (initiate) of the Mysteries of Ceridwen, took his inner, shamanic journey at a sacred site and was gifted with supreme awareness. To this day in Wales it is said that anyone who spends the night in the rocky 'Chair' at the summit of Cader Idris in Merionethshire, will be found in the morning, dead or mad or a poet. It is not difficult to see echoes here of the ancient mantic fit which descended on the new poet after he had drunk the drink of wisdom, perhaps indeed on a mountaintop as Myrddin is believed to have done (308); or to recognise the Chair of Idris (Arthur) as parallel to the Bardic Chair or, indeed, to the Chair of Ceridwen referred to by Taliesin in more than one poem.

The borderline between poetry and madness has long been recognised as slight. The greatest poets all suffer from a divine exaltation which is akin to derangement. Frequently, their reports, on returning from the Otherworld, are found to be so utterly incomprehensible (requiring a different kind of understanding to that of the everyday world) that these are in themselves taken as the ravings of madmen. Myrddin, as we shall see in Chapter Seven, was at times believed mad, and gave out both poetry and prophecy at this time. Indeed it was said that after he was 'cured' of madness, by drinking from a sacred fountain, he never spoke mantically again.

Among those who suffered madness but were recognised as poets is the curiously named **Mac-da-cerda** ('Youth of Two Arts' – poetry and foolishness). His given name was Comgan, and he was the son of the King of Munster. He was the most superb athlete, and beat everyone in the games. But he had the misfortune to earn the hatred of a woman whose advances he had spurned, and who told an ill tale of him to a druid. This druid, waiting his opportunity, threw a **dlui fulla**, 'madman's wisp' over him. This had the effect first of bringing him out in boils and ulcers, and after of causing him to suffer terrible sickness:

> There he wasted away in body, his mind decayed, his hair fell off, and ever afterwards he wandered about the palace, a bald, drivelling idiot. But he had lucid intervals, and then he became an inspired poet, and uttered prophecies. (149)

One suspects that the 'wisp' may have had letters in Ogam, the mystical language of poets and druids (see Chapter Eight) carved on it, and it was this that caused the madness in Comgan who, like many other poets and prophets, was driven half-mad by his realisations, rather than, as in the story, that his inspiration derived from madness.

Others, such as the Irish Suibhne Geilt (see Chapter Three), the Scottish Lailoken, Tam Lin in the Border Ballads and the Rev. Robert Kirk in the 17th Century, all displayed signs of apparent madness, talking to trees and animals, living in trees with the birds, and undergoing strange transformations, in a way that we can easily recognise as the result of journeying shamanically to the Otherworld and returning with newly ancient wisdom.

The Laughter of Taliesin

A significant sign of the acquiring of such wisdom was the willingness with which the shaman-poets gave vent to sudden outbursts of laughter. The importance of this has long been recognised as an integral part of shamanic practice. The ability to laugh while in a state of detachment is a positive necessity in certain kinds of shamanic work. As Jose and Lena Stevens remark in their excellent book *Secrets of Shamanism* (287) 'Only the truly sane are able to laugh at the troubles humans get themselves into.'

Taliesin himself uses laughter in this way, as in the 'blerwm blerwm' episode, and there is a strong flavour of irony about much of his extant writings. Nor, as we saw from the **Hostile Confederacy**, was he above using that other old and well-tried method of teaching: the asking of seemingly nonsensical questions (Why is rain wet? Why is grass green?) which, when examined, prove to hold more than their seeming innocence would warrant. Further instances are to be found in the Irish **Vision of Mac Congline** where we find an immensely long list of such 'incongruities' (208), and the riddling exchange between the young poet Nede and the old poet Ferchertne, discussed in Chapter Five. That they are really a method of teaching is without question. The repeated asking of such seemingly obvious things sets up a chain reaction in the listener, who soon begins to see the world and nature with new eyes. It also presupposes that the poet has a ready succession of answers.

That this tradition was widespread is indicated by the following example from an account of the Gall priests of East Africa:

Priest: O wonder, O wonder!
People: What are the wonders?
Priest: The water runs without being urged; the earth is fixed without pegs; the heavens hold themselves up without support; in the firmament God has sown the stars.
(Quoted Chadwick 153)

Thus were great teachings propounded through the world. It is only with difficulty – or through inspiration – that we can recover the knowledge required to answer them in our own time.

The Coming of Awen

Awen – Inspiration – lies at the heart of Taliesin's world. All his works are clearly the product of received, or inspired, wisdom acquired, we are told, through the draught of the Cauldron. Elsewhere the poet makes other claims:

'I have been three periods in the Court of Arianrhod ...'
'In the Court of Ceridwen I have suffered for Wisdom ...'
'I am a genius of unbounded wisdom ...'

or, when he reviles Maelgwn's bards:

> Be silent, unwise bards
> Who speak only in rhyme,
> Who cannot judge
> Between truth and falsehood.
> If you are primary bards
> Formed in the Land of Promise
> Tell your king his fate.
> It is I, who am a diviner
> And an inspired bard,
> Who will do so.

All of these references are to the hidden knowledge of which Taliesin has been made aware by **Awen**; and it is **Awen** which enables him to be seemingly present at the greatest moments of recorded history: Alexander's conquest of the world, the building of the Tower of Babel, the Nativity and Crucifixion of Christ. In reality, it is his inspired, shamanic experience and training which enable him to enter an inner place where all these events – indeed the whole of mankind's history – are recorded; where he can experience them directly as if he had actually been present. Indeed, there is a sense in which he *was* present at these events – the **awen**-lifted spirit being capable of flights to which time or space form no boundary.

Calvert Watkins, in a recent article (316), has pointed out the kinship of certain words which have to do with the description of 'inspiration' and 'breath'. The Old Irish word **uath**, 'poetic art', is clearly of archaic origin. **Awen**, its Welsh cognate, is linked, in a text quoted by Watkins, with **seis**, 'musical art', **cluas**, 'hearing', and **anal**, 'breath'. Thus at least two of the primary senses, breath and hearing, are seen as forming an integral part in the experience of inspiration; the poet breathes in the **awen**, hears it and gives it forth in musical speech or song.

Knowledge of the Dead

In Irish mythology the shades of departed heroes were frequently summoned to give account of themselves. When King Mongan of Ulster was in dispute with the bard Forgoll, who had threatened to satirise the king's family over the question of the true account of certain events in the story of Fionn Mac Cumhail, the Fenian hero Caoilte returned from the Otherworld and substantiated Mongan's claim. On another occasion, when Senchan Torpeist, the Chief Poet of Ireland in about the year AD 598 called a meeting of bards and story-tellers to see if they could remember the whole of the great epic poem **Tain bo Cuailgne** (The Cattle-Raid of Cooley) (155), he found they could recall only fragments and forthwith sent two young poets forth in search of an ancient, long lost book said to contain the whole of the **Tain**, and which had apparently been given away in exchange for a copy of Isadore of Seville's **Culmen**.

On their way they reached the tomb of Fergus Mac Roith at Magh Aei in Roscommon, and there one of the young bards recited a poem of his own. At once he found himself enveloped in a thick mist, in which the figure of Mac Roith himself appeared and proceeded to recite the entire **Tain** over a period of three days and nights.

This is fairly clearly a reference to a kind of inspired shamanic trance in which the bard was able to communicate with the great dead and retrieve lost knowledge and understanding of his people's tradition. (That Taliesin apparently has access to *all* wisdom gives an idea of the respect in which he was held.)

Another, Christianised, version of the above story, tells how the assembled saints of Ireland prayed at the tomb of Mac Roith, and that he appeared to St. Ciaran of Clonmacnoise, who wrote the entire poem on vellum manufactured from the skin of his favourite dun cow. The book thus constructed was thereafter named **Leabhar na hUidre**, 'The Book of the Dun Cow', copies of which still exist today (59). What is interesting about this story is not only that it shows the Christian monks recognising the Otherworld as a source of knowledge unobtainable by any other method, but also because the idea of recording the epic on the skin of a cow recalls the method of the incubatory sleep which bards used to take **wrapped in a bull's hide** in order to receive messages from the Otherworld.

The best known example of this is found in the story of **The Dream of Rhonabwy** in the *Mabinogion* (144), where Rhonabwy, seeking shelter in the hut of an ancient crone (perhaps Ceridwen herself?) happens to fall asleep on a yellow bull's hide and dreams a long and fantastic dream of the warrior Arthur and his larger-than-life band of heroes. (See Chapter Seven for a more detailed discussion of this and other methods of inspired vision.)

Celtic literature abounds in such inspirational raids on the Otherworld, and a fuller exploration of these must wait for another occasion. For the moment we might mention the **Voyage of Bran Mac Febel to the Land of Promise** (209) where, having received the Silver Branch (which, as we shall see, is the sign of all poets), Bran sails off to a series of fantastic adventures which, on his return to the realm of mortals, he recounts in a series of Ogam quatrains. After which he bids them farewell, 'and from that hour his wanderings are not known.'

In Welsh tradition are the **Stanzas of the Graves**, a collection of memorials to great and famous warriors, most of whose deeds are now forgotten. Once, they must have formed part of the bard's inherited knowledge – and, of course, we find Taliesin making an appearance within the list:

> Truly did Elffin bring me
> To try my bardic lore
> Over an ancient chieftain –
> The grave of Rwfawn, too early departed. (146)

Since Taliesin had no other patron that we are aware of we may safely assume that it is he who is speaking here. Elffin seems to have brought him to an unmarked grave so that he could tell – in much the same way that Fionn did with the grave of Lomna – who was buried there. He was, of course, able to do so, and this leads one to believe that this aspect of shamanic lore may not have been attributed to Taliesin as well. Certainly, we know that the **Stanzas** are part of the great mnemonic system, together with the **Triads**, which formed the backbone of the bardic wisdom. Another poem, from the *Black Book of Carmarthen* (10) which begins in the voice of the Otherworldly figure of Gwyn ap Nudd, changes direction midway through, becoming a further catalogue of the great dead:

[1]
I have been where Bran was slain,
Son of Iwerydd, far famed,
Where ravens of battle screamed.

[2]
I have been where Llacheu fell,
The son of Arthur, extolled in song
Where ravens screamed for blood.

[3]
I have been where Meurig was slain,
Son of Carreian, an honoured man,
Where ravens screamed for flesh.

* * *

[4]
I have been where the men of Prydein fell,
From East to North
I am alive; they in their graves!

Sir Ifor Williams, speculating in one of his *Lectures on Early Welsh Poetry* (326), asked: 'Who is this survivor from the heroic age, who was present when they fell?' He points out the similarities between the anonymous speaker here, and in the **Stanzas**, and that of Caoilte, the Fenian warrior who returns from the Otherworld to inform Saint Columba of the real history of Fionn Mac Cumhail. If such a figure were to be sought for among the Welsh Bards, one would need to look no further than Taliesin for the most likely candidate.

The Inspiration of Fire and Water

As Professors Bloomfield and Dunn remark in their study of ancient poets and poetry:

> Besides tradition, the notion of truth is also closely connected with wisdom . . . The virtue of truth . . . was the highest royal virtue in Ancient Ireland. Why this elevation of truth? Truth is a quality which makes magic work and which enables a person to live up to his archetypes and his ancestors. (29)

Above all else, the shaman-poets recognised the importance of a true and living tradition. In the commentary on the Irish Law Tracts *Senchus Mor* (111), we find the following gloss on the idea of inherited knowledge.

> Tradition from ear to ear, i.e. the transmission of bright knowledge to preserve it, i.e. the lighted candle of bright knowledge, i.e. each preserving it, i.e. the conveyance of bright knowledge from one of them to the other ... it was they who had the other bright knowledge, i.e. the written law; or, the bright knowledge of one master to another, i.e. to the disciple; or, the repository in which is arranged to be stored up and preserved what is called **Senchus**, i.e. the storehouse in which this famous knowledge was arranged and treasured up for preservation; for hearing is conveying.

Here we begin to touch upon a profound mystery, for as well as the 'bright knowledge' mentioned here, there is a darker side. Amongst the varied information contained in the poems of **Dunaire Fionn** (174) is a long poem relating the history of the hero's shield.

> Scarce are they two on solid earth, unless there be some seer or sage, thou shield of the king of frosty Sigear, one that knows thy career.

> Scarce are they two on the same earth, man or woman, that can tell the reason why thy name abroad is called the Dripping Ancient Hazel ...

> 'Twas Balor that besought Lugh a short time before his beheading: 'Set my head on thy own comely head and earn my blessing.

> 'The triumph and the terror that the men of Inis Fail found in me, Will I wish henceforth they may be found in my daughter's son.'

> That blessing nevertheless Lugh Longarm did not earn: he set the head above an eastern wave in a fork of hazel before his face.

> A poisonous milk drips down out of the tree of strong hardness: through the drip of the bane of no slight stress, the tree splits right in two.

For the space of fifty full years the hazel remained unfelled, but ever bore a cause of tears, being an abode of vultures and ravens.

Manannan of the round eye went to the wilderness of the White Hazel Mountain, where he saw a leafless tree among the trees that view in beauty.

Manannan sets workmen at work on this tree without slackness: to dig it out of the firm earth: this were a mighty deed.

A poisonous vapour rises up incessantly from the root of that tree until it killed – perilous consequence – nine men of the working folk.

It killed nine others of them of the people of smooth Manannan – the story of the tree I well wot – and blinded a third nine. (174)

The language in which this is written is obscure in the extreme, but the sense is clear enough. The Irish death-god Balor is slain by his own son Lugh of the Long Arm, and his head severed. He asks of Lugh that his head should be preserved in his hall, from where it would give Lugh the benefit of Balor's wisdom (such I take to mean the reference to the setting of the head on his own head). But Lugh fails to honour his promise, instead having the head hung on a hazel tree on the White Hazel Mountain. From there the head drips poisonous blood, which causes much evil to the neighbouring trees and to anyone who comes near. Then, after many years, the God Manannan comes and orders the tree cut down. In the process, eighteen men are killed and a further nine blinded, but from the wood of the tree is made the shield which was later to be borne by Fionn, and which protected him from hurt for much of his life.

Behind this complex of mythic lore lies a deeper tale. Balor himself, nicknamed 'of the Evil Eye' is the most powerful of the Formori, the native gods of Ireland. His single eye is so baleful that it means death to anyone who meets its gaze. According to another story he lost the sight of the other eye whilst watching some Druids brewing up a Cauldron of Wisdom. Some of the liquid splashed into his eye and he was blinded. The other eye then became so baleful that it had to have nine shields always before it to prevent death and destruction coming upon Balor's own people. When the shields are raised Lugh, the god of Light, flings a spear into it. Balor is killed and his head hung on the tree. The tree becomes poisonous, but the God Manannan has a shield made from it which protects all who carry it.

Thus, in circular fashion, we may see that from the original Cauldron of Wisdom comes a pattern of good and evil, of light and dark. The parallel with Taliesin is interesting: he obtains wisdom from a Cauldron, the waters of which then become poisonous. His wisdom, as exemplified by his shining brow, is to do with light. Against him are set those who have acquired the baleful knowledge, Maelgwn's druids, or the foolish bards he attacks in poem after poem for having allowed their wisdom to become stultified.

What we are really seeing here is an underlying theme of the use and misuse of knowledge, or of two kinds of wisdom, the Bright Knowledge referred to in the **Senchus Mor** and the Baleful Knowledge which is the *second* gift of the Cauldron of Inspiration.

The association of fire (light) with water seems important in respect of **awen**, for heat boils water into steam and steam can bring about changes in consciousness. The nine maidens who guard the underworld cauldron of Pen Annwn, breathe upon the contents, each imparting a quality or gift which imbues the draught with inspirational variety. It is as though these nine sisters were indeed the muses of Celtic tradition. Traditions associated with Nechtan's Well in Irish mythology, which we shall examine later in the context of Prophetic inspiration, add to this picture, for here the Goddess Boand, one of the patronesses of Poetry in Ireland, is blinded by looking into the well, which then overflows and becomes the river Boyne, on the banks of which, we may remember, Fineces waited to catch the Salmon of Wisdom. Welsh folk-lore preserves the story of a fountain which overflowed to become Lake Bala (home of Ceridwen), drowning much of the land around it. From that lake came the Cauldron of Wisdom.

Are we, then, seeing a significant pattern in which a well or cauldron, associated with the giving of wisdom, overflows to become a river or lake in the waters of which are found both wisdom and death? One cannot help thinking of the famous quotation from Orphic literature which, once again, suggests an initiatory choice between light and dark – once again from the source of a well. The instruction on the Orphic tablet reads:

Thou shalt find on the left of the House of Hades a well-spring,
And by the side thereof standing a white cypress.
To this well spring approach not near.
But thou shalt find another by the Lake of Memory,
Cold water flowing forth, and there are guardians before it.
Say: 'I am a Child of Earth and of Starry Heaven;
But my race is of Heaven (alone).
This ye know yourselves.
And lo, I am parched with thirst and I perish.
Give me quickly the cold water flowing forth from
   the Lake of Memory.'
And of themselves they will give thee to drink from the holy
   well-spring
And thereafter among the other Heroes thou shalt have lordship.

(quoted in Merry 201)

This could have been written by Taliesin himself, and so nearly does it come to the idea of the choice between the Water of Light and the Water of Dark, that it must stand as an expression of this concept. Nor should we forget Taliesin's own poem **The Defence of the Chair** (translated in full on pages 294–5) in which the following significant lines appear:

My Chair is in Caer Siddi,
Where no-one is afflicted with age or illness.
Manawyd[dan] and Pryderi have known it well.
It is surrounded by three circles of fire.

To the borders of that place comes the ocean's flood,
A fruitful fountain plays before it,
Whose liquor is sweeter than the finest wine.

Once again we find the combination of fire and water, this time in the place from which all wisdom and **awen** originate, Caer Siddi, the turning fortress of the **sidhe** where Fionn also learned his skills, and from which Taliesin himself draws his own ultimate knowledge. It is clear from these texts that the elements of fire and water played a very considerable part in the acquiring of inspiration. In Chapter Seven we shall see how narrow are the lines between the inspiration of the poet

and that of the seer or visionary, and that both are subsumed
by the shaman.

Meanwhile we must look further at the question of the Bardic
mysteries, of what they consist, and the manner in which they
were taught.

Chapter Five

THE BARDIC SCHOOLS: TEACHING THE KNOWLEDGE OF THINGS

Hard is their toil when men of learning find not
the bright-threaded artistry of illustrious scholars,
to whom belonged the mystic import of words.
The Empty School, Trans. O. Bergin

The Field of Learning

We first hear of the famed Druidic 'schools' in the writings of the Classical authors whose legacy to us is their knowledge of the Celts. Caesar, in his *De Bello Gallico* (41), after a lengthy passage dealing with the manner and customs of the Druids (see Chapter Nine), speaks of people travelling from Gaul to Britain to study there. Elsewhere, Strabo, in his *Geographica* (Bk IV, vol. 4) comments that:

> Among the Gallic peoples, generally speaking, there are three sets of men who are held in exceptional honour: the Bards, the Vates, and the Druids. The Bards are singers and poets; the Vates, diviners and natural philosophers; while the Druids, in addition to natural philosophy, study also moral philosophy. (300)

We notice that the Bards come first in this list, though it is the Druids that we hear of most often at this early date. In the great Irish epic **The Tain**, as Queen Medb sets forth on an expedition, she meets a Druidess, and the following exchange takes place:

> 'What is your name?' Medb said to the girl.
> 'I am Fedelm, and I am a woman . . . of Connacht.'

120

'Where have you come from?' Medb said.
'From learning verse and vision in Alba', the girl said.
'Have you the **imbas forasnai**, the Light of Foresight?' Medb said.
'Yes I have', the girl said.
'Then look for me and see what will become of my army.' (155)

The girl looks and sees blood. She then gives forth a lengthy prophecy concerning the fate of the army of Connacht. The interesting fact we glean from this – aside from the reference to **imbas forasnai** which will be dealt with in Chapter Seven – is that Fedelm had been to Alba (Scotland) to study her skills, which included both poetry and magic.

Earlier in the same passage quoted above, Caesar elaborates on the Druidic schools.

Report says that in the schools ... the ... Druids learn by heart a great number of verses, and therefore some persons remain twenty years under training. (41)

Several hundred years later, in Christian Ireland, these schools were still flourishing, side by side with the monkish scriptoria, which had in all probability already begun to collect and record much of what the schools were teaching.

The basic curriculum of the Bardic schools (in Ireland anyway) has been assembled from various sources by Eugene O'Curry in *Manners and Customs of the Ancient Irish* (232) and Patrick Joyce in *A Social History of Ancient Ireland* (149). It consisted as follows:

1st Year: Fifty oghams or alphabets. Elementary grammar. Twenty tales.
2nd Year: Fifty oghams. Six easy lessons in Philosophy. Some specified poems. Thirty tales.
3rd Year: Fifty oghams. Six minor lessons of Philosophy. Certain specified poems. Grammar. Forty poems.
4th Year: The **Bretha Nemed** or Law of Privileges. Twenty poems of the species called **Eman**. Fifty tales.
5th Year: Grammar. Sixty tales.
6th Year: The Secret Language of the Poets. Forty-eight poems of the species called **Nuath**. Seventy or eighty tales.

7th Year:	**Brosnacha** (Miscellanies). The Laws of Bardism.
8th Year:	Prosody. Glosses (the meaning of obscure words) **Teinm Laeghdha. Imbas Forosnai. Dichetal Do Chennibh.** (See Chapter Seven.) **Dindsenchas** (Topographical stories).
9th Year:	A specified number of compositions of the kind called **Sennat, Luasca, Nena, Eochraid, Sruith,** and **Duili Feda.** To master 175 tales in this three year period.
10th Year:	A further number of the compositions listed above.
11th Year:	100 of the compositions known as **Anamuin.**
12th Year:	120 **Cetals** or orations. The Four Arts of Poetry. During the three years to master 175 tales in all, along with the 175 of the **Anruth,** 350 Tales in all.

The sheer scope of learning possible to someone following this discipline, or indeed that mentioned by Caesar, has been admirably assessed by R. A. S. Macalister, who writes:

> Suppose that the pupils were allowed two months' annual holiday, which is probably liberal: in other words, let us for arithmetical convenience keep them at school, 300 working days in a solar year. Then, if they learn no more than ten lines of poetry in a day, they will have acquired a total of 3,000 by the end of the year, and in twenty years they will be masters of 60,000 lines. This is considerably more than twice the length of the two Homeric epics. Even if they learned only one line **per diem**, they would have assimilated matter roughly equal in amount to the first ten books of the *Iliad*: if they enlarged their daily task to thirty-five or forty lines, they would in the end possess, stored in memory, matter equal in extent to the prodigious **Mahabarata**. (171)

Commenting further on the method of learning evolved, Dr Macalister gives a lively picture of the scene in a Bardic college:

> The master first repeated a line, or a quatrain, or whatever was regarded as the unit of verse. The students repeated it after him till they were perfect in pronunciation and intonation. The master then analysed it, explaining its grammatical structure word by word, and setting forth its meaning and the truths

... which it was intended to convey. When he was satisfied that the pupils had assimilated his teaching, he proceeded to the next section of the composition. In this slow, laborious way we may suppose the sacred canon to have passed from generation to generation. (ibid.)

But, for the fullest description of a Bardic school in operation we have to turn to a text written in 1722, **The Memoirs of the Marquis of Clanricarde** (23). Although the text is late, and concerns different aspects of the Bardic tradition, it has been recognised as carrying an authentic charge of that tradition.

It was ... necessary that the place should be in the solitary recess of a garden or within a sept or enclosure far out of the reach of any noise, which an intercourse of people might otherwise occasion. The structure was a snug, low hut, and beds in it at convenient distances, each within a small apartment without much furniture of any kind, save only a table, some seats, and a conveniency for clothes to hang upon. No windows to let in the day, nor any light at all used but that of candles, and these brought in at a proper season only ... The professors ... gave a subject suitable to the capacity of each class ... The said subject ... having been given over night, they worked it apart each by himself upon his own bed, the whole next day in the dark, till àt a certain hour in the night, lights being brought in, they committed it to writing ... The reason of laying the study aforesaid in the dark was doubtless to avoid the distraction which light and the variety of objects represented thereby ... This being prevented, the faculties of the soul occupied themselves solely upon the subject in hand ... Yet the course was long and tedious, as we find, and it was six or seven years before a mastery or the last degree was confirmed ...

The reference to the need for darkness in this passage has a bearing on the discussion of light and dark knowledge already mentioned in the previous chapter. The explanation is clearly an attempt to rationalise a tradition which was both ancient and sacred. Another valuable account, this time from Martin's *Description of the Western Islands of Scotland* (180), gives us more detail.

They [the poets] shut their doors and windows for a day's time, and lie on their backs with a stone upon their belly, and plaids about their heads, and their eyes being covered they pump their brains for rhetorical enconium or panegyric; and indeed they furnish such a style from this dark cell as is understood by very few . . .

This is very obviously an ancient shamanic practice, of which the most astonishing fact of all is that Martin's account dates from the 18th Century! That knowledge of such a practice had been allowed to slip through the net of Christianity is astonishing enough; that it was still practised is remarkable.

The Bardic Tradition

But the continuity of the Bardic tradition generally is itself astonishing. Throughout the Middle Ages and into the Renaissance, Celtic poets continued to compose works in praise of their masters – comparing them to heroes of old, to generous lords who would have listened to the songs of Taliesin himself, and using the same verse forms as their distant ancestors. Even in recent times, the Welsh Eisteddfod has seen heated discussion on metrical rules that were alive in the 6th Century and earlier. As Professor Bedwyr Lewis Jones has noted (142):

> The poet's function and authority remains the same. It was to maintain the existing social and political order by bestowing honour on individual rulers in whom the heroic values of society were seen to be incarnated.

The whole question of the poet's position within Celtic society is complex and difficult. His role overlapped that of both the other professional classes, the Druid and the Seer, so that it is sometimes difficult to decide which role a particular character is fulfilling. If we are correct in believing that all three professions developed out of the figure of the shaman, whose role was, so to speak, divided up amongst the Poets, Druids and Seers, then this is readily accounted for. Certainly, in the case of Taliesin, his deeds reflect the disciplines of all three orders, and within his poetry there is again reference to every kind of activity.

An early 17th Century tract in English called **Tri Chof Ynys Brydain**, 'Three Antiquities [or kinds of lore] of Britain', describes the Bardic system as follows:

124

The office and function of the British or Cambrian Bards was to keep and preserve **tri chof ynys Brydain**: that is the three records or memorials of Britain, or which otherwise is called the British antiquity which consists of three parts ... The one of the said three **cof** is the History of the notable Acts of the Kings and Princes of this land of Britain and Cambria; and the second of the three **cof** is the language of the Britons for which the bards ought to give account for every word and syllable therein when they are demanded thereof and to preserve the ancient tongue and not to intermix it with any foreign tongue ... And the third **cof** was, to keep the genealogies or descent of the nobility, their division of lands and their arms ... (323)

In other words the three chief concerns of the Bards were recognised as being the preservation of the language, the memorial of history and the knowledge of genealogy and heraldry. Professor Ford, discussing the role of the poets in an illuminating introduction to his edition and translation of the poetry of Llywarch Hen, a contemporary of Taliesin, remarks:

The seers, endowed with extrahuman capabilities, were the custodians of all the sacred tribal wisdom. Their office required frequent recitation from this store of wisdom for purely functional purposes within the society. (86)

This description could equally well be applied to the role of the Druid, as it is generally understood, and has a strong bearing on the role of the poet. Professor Ford goes on to outline the principal aspects of the poet's art within Celtic culture: to praise their rulers, satirise their enemies, and recite the genealogies which preserved the unity of the tribe. He concludes:

The corpus of institutionalised knowledge also included what may have been the corner-stone of early tribal lore, a fund of gnomic wisdom. (ibid.)

In fact this body of 'gnomic wisdom', need not have been all that large. We still possess an idea of what that store of knowledge consisted, in the form of the catalogues of materials such as the Welsh and Irish **Triads**, the **Twenty-Four Knights** of Arthur's Court, (143), the **Stanzas of the Graves**, (146), or the Irish **Dindschencas** (107), **Cormac's Glossary** (233) and so on. The Bards did not simply allow their knowledge to lie idle or to become static with the conclusion of their years of training. The Poets, Druids and Seers continued to seek new ways to refine their wisdom, to find deeper and deeper levels, new ways of applying the traditions they had learned. Endless combinations of words and thoughts were possible and must have been explored time upon time, always with differing results.

That the importance of this teaching was still recognised as late as the 17th Century, is indicated both by the continued existence of the Bardic schools, and by the words of the poet Giolla Brighde Mac ComMidhe, who stated that,

> If poetry were destroyed, men, and we without knowledge of history and old-poetry, without (knowledge) of anything but the name of every man's father, then none would have fame. (159)

A Wonderful Knowledge

In the **Trioedd Ynys Prydein** (334) it says:

> Three things that give amplitude to a poet:
> knowledge of histories,
> the poetic art, and old verse.

The **Triads** are undoubtedly the last remnants of the Bardic tradition, which received its death blow in 1567 with the publication of Gruffydd Roberts' *Grammar*, after which anyone could study the art of poetry without the necessity of a tutor. At one time, the bard and story-teller would have been expected to know the entire corpus of stories recorded in the **Triads**. But since these were transmitted orally we have lost a large number of the stories in question and can only hazard guesses at what they may once have been. The number mentioned exceeds 500. But not everything was lost. There is a suggestion that the native Bardic codes were taken over and Christianised by the monks of the Celtic church. If this is the case, it could well explain the extraordinary mixture of Pagan and

Christian elements in the Taliesin poems. The monks, finding an entire system of Bardic law, which codified the types of poetry, subject and metre, fit to be composed by the Bards, adapted them in such a way as to keep them alive but in line with theological thinking. Thus, instead of being destroyed, the tradition was reshaped to the needs of the time, just as it has been again and again since then – though probably never so radically.

Another factor is the significant overlap between the Druids, the Irish **Fili**, and the Welsh Bards. This is best resolved by saying that the Druids were most noticeably active in Gaul, less so in Britain and Ireland and scarcely at all in Scotland; the **Fili** formed the strongest element in Ireland. (R. A. S. Macalister (171) translates the Irish word **fili** – normally used to denote a poet – as 'Weaver of Spells', showing the awareness which must have existed of the magical power of the poets.) The Bards, who seem to have subsumed the office of Druids to some extent, are most pre-eminent in Wales. All three have strong links with the Indo-European shamanic tradition and we shall find that a great deal of what passes for either Bardic/Poetic or Druidic in the Celtic world, is usually synonymous with shamanism. Alwyn and Brynley Rees sum this up exactly in their brilliant study of Celtic culture and artistry:

> There is evidence from the Celtic countries and from India that the poets were also the official historians and the royal genealogists. The poet's praises confirmed and sustained the king in his kingship, while his satire could blast both the king and his kingdom . . . Such priestly functions as divination and prophecy also came within the province of these early . . . poets who, it may be added, wore cloaks of bright feathers as do the shamans of Siberia when, through ritual and trance, they conduct their audiences on journeys to another world. It was initiates with their power and authority who had the custody of the original tales, and they recited them on auspicious occasions, even as the priests of other religions recite the scriptures. (337)

Taliesin's own catalogues of Bardic Wisdom are many and varied. One such, sometimes called **Riddle Song**, sometimes **Taliesin's Bardic Lore** (translated in full on pages 301–4) has the following:

I am old, I am young, I am Gwion,
Universal, I am gifted with a perceiving spirit.
I am a bard, I do not vouchsafe my secrets to slaves.
I am a guide, I am a judge . . .

Have you seen the strong lord?
Do you know the master's prophecy
Concerning Uffern . . . ?

Whoever shall hear my bardic books,
Shall obtain sanctuary in the Otherworld.

We note that it is those who 'hear' the lore who will prosper, not those who read it. This dates still from the time when the wisdom was spoken aloud, chanted in the halls of kings and princes, or in the bardic schools. It is this wisdom which made the bards 'guides' and 'judges', which gave them the universality of spirit claimed by Taliesin in this poem.

The Dark Speech

That such richness was not always easily come by, and required special talents even after initiation, is shown by a story contained in various sources, including **The Book of Leinster**, **The Yellow Book of Lecan**, and the Irish Law tracts known as **Senchus Mor** (111). It illustrates both the complexity of the poetic art, and its shamanic qualities to the full. The story concerns a dispute between two **Fili**, Ferchertne and Nede, over who should succeed to the robe (and thereby the office) of the great Druid Adnae, whose son Nede was. He, in fact, was studying with the poet Eochu Echbel ('Horsemouth') when, walking by the sea, he heard a sound of lamentation in the waves, and putting a spell upon them, learned that his father had died and that the robe had been given to Ferchertne. Nede set off and, arriving at the court of Conchobar Mac Nessa, found his rival absent and donned the robe, together with a beard of grass to give him the semblance of age. When Ferchertne returned he demanded to know whom it was who had stolen the robe, and Nede's answer is the beginning of a fantastic riddling exchange which deals, among other things, with the origins of poetic inspiration. The **Senchus Mor** has it that they argued their case before the King, Conchobar

Mac Nessa, 'in a dark tongue', so that neither he, nor his chieftains, could understand them. 'These people,' the King's advisers declared, 'keep their judgements and their knowledge to themselves,' and Conchobar, agreeing, gave out that such a state of affairs should come to an end.

What is of interest here is the clear indication given in this story, that the **fili** possessed a language that was intelligible only to each other. We shall examine the evidence for this more fully in Chapter Six, but for the moment we might ask ourselves what *kind* of language it was. A glance at the text itself is enough to show that it was the speech of initiates, couched in riddling and symbolic terms which only they could have understood. That it may also have been in a more ancient form of Celtic language is also possible (see Chapter Six), but even if this were not the case, few would have been able to appreciate the subtle play on words and the intricate references contained in this poem.

The translation which follows is based on that of Dr Whitley Stokes (295); a shorter, much amended version appears in *The Poem Book of the Gael* by Eleanor Hull (130). A series of glosses is also to be found in Stokes' version. These derive from the medieval texts themselves, and show that to some at least of the scribes who copied the text in the 13th and 14th Centuries, the old learning was not dead.

Colloquy of the Two Sages

Ferchertne entered the house, and on seeing Nede, said:
'Who is this poet, wrapped in the splendid robe
Who shows himself before he has chanted poetry?
According to what I see, he is only a pupil,
His beard but an arrangement of grasses.
Who is this contentious poet?
I never heard any wisdom from Adnae's son!
I never heard him ready with knowledge!
A mistake it is, his sitting in this seat.'

And Nede answered Ferchertne honourably:
'O ancient one, every sage tries to correct another!
A sage may reproach any ignorant man,
But before he does so he should see what evil is in us.
Welcome is the piercing dart of wisdom.
Slight is the blemish to a youth until his art is questioned.

Step with care, O chieftain –
You belittle me with knowledge,
Though I have sucked the teat of a wise man.'

Said Ferchertne
'A question, wise lad, whence have you come?'

Nede answered
'Not hard: from the heel of a sage,
From a confluence of wisdom
From perfection of goodness,
From the brightness of the sunrise,
From the nine hazels of poetic art,
From splendid circuits, in a land
Where truth is measured by excellence,
Where there is no falsehood,
Where there are many colours,
Where poets are refreshed.

And thou, O my master, whence have you come?'

Ferchertne answered
'Not hard: down the columns of age,
Along the streams of Galion (Leinster),
From the elfmound of Nechtan's wife,
Down the forearm of Nuada's wife,
From the land of the sun,
From the dwelling of the moon,
Along Mac ind Oc's navel string.

A question, O wise lad, what is thy name?'

Nede answered
'Not hard: Very-small, Very-great, Very-bright, Very-hard.
Angriness of fire,
Fire of speech,
Noise of knowledge,
Well of wisdom,
Sword of song,
I sing straight from the heart of the fire.

And you, O aged one, what is your name?'

Ferchertne answered
'Not hard: Questioner, Declarer, Champion of Song,

Inquiry of science,
Weft of art,
Casket of poetry
Abundance from the sea of knowledge.

A question, O youthful instructor: what art do you practise?'

Nede answered
'Not hard: reddening of countenance,
Flesh-piercing satire,
Promoting bashfulness,
Disposing of shamelessness,
Fostering poetry,
Searching for fame,
Wooing science,
Art for every mouth,
Diffusing knowledge,
Stripping speech,
In a little room,
Making poems like a sage's cattle,
A stream of science,
Abundant teaching,
Polished tales, the delight of kings.

And you, O my elder, what art do you practise?'

Ferchertne answered
'Hunting for the treasure of knowledge,
Establishing peace,
Arranging words in ranks,
Celebrating art,
Sharing a pallet with a king,
Drinking the Boyne,
Making **briarmon smetrach** –
The shield of Athirne,
A tribulation to all men,
A share of wisdom from the stream of science.
Fury of inspiration,
Structure of mind,
Art of small poems,
Clear arrangement of words,
Warrior tales,
Walking the great road,
Like a pearl in its setting,
Giving strength to science through the poetic art.'

131

Ferchertne said
'A question, O youthful instructor, what are your tasks?'

Nede answered
'Not hard: to go to the plain of age,
To the mountain of youth,
To the hunting of age.
To follow a king
Into an abode of clay,
Between candle and fire
Between battle and its horrors
Among the people of Fomor,
Among streams of knowledge.

And you, O sage, what are your tasks?'

Ferchertne answered
'To go into the mountain of rank,
The communion of sciences,
The lands of knowledgeable men,
Into the breast of poetic vision,
The estuary of bountiful wisdom,
To the fair of the Great Boar.
To find respect among men,
To go into death's hills
Where I may find great honour.

A question, O knowledgeable lad, by what path have you come?'

Nede answered
'Not hard: on the white plain of knowledge,
On a king's beard,
On a wood of age,
On the back of a ploughing ox,
On the light of a summer's moon,
On rich mast and food,
On the corn and milk of a goddess
On thin corn,
On a narrow ford,
On my own strong thighs.

And you, O sage, by what path have you come?'

Ferchertne answered
'Not hard: on Lugh's horserod,

On the breasts of soft women,
On a line of wood,
On the head of a spear,
On a gown of silver,
On a chariot without a wheelrim,
On a wheelrim without a chariot,
On the threefold ignorance of Mac ind Oc.

And you, O knowledgeable lad, whose son are you?'

Nede answered
'Not hard: I am the son of Poetry,
Poetry son of scrutiny
Scrutiny son of meditation,
Meditation son of lore,
Lore son of enquiry,
Enquiry son of investigation,
Investigation son of great knowledge,
Great knowledge son of great sense,
Great sense son of understanding,
Understanding son of wisdom.
Wisdom son of the triple gods of poetry.

And you, O sage, whose son are you?'

Ferchertne answered
'Not hard: I am the son of the man without a father,
Who was buried in his mother's womb,
Who was blessed after his death.
Indeed, death betrothed him,
And he was the first utterance of every living one
The cry of every dead one:
Lofty Ailm is his name . . .'

Another hundred lines or so follow, in which Ferchertne and Nede vie with each other in prophetic utterance. Nede's prophecy is all of sunshine and burgeoning cornfields; Ferchertne's, by comparison, of doom and ruin and horror. At the end, he asked:

'Know you, O little in age but great in knowledge, who is greater than you?'

Nede answered
'Easy to say: God is known to me,

and the wisest of prophets.
I know the hazels of poetry –
And I know that Ferchertne is a great poet and prophet.'

The lad then knelt and flung to him the poet's robe ... and he rose out of the poet's seat ... and cast himself under Ferchertne's feet. Thereupon Ferchertne said:

'Stay, great poet, wise youth, son of Adnae!
May you receive glory and fame
In the sight of men and gods.
May you be a casket of poetry,
May you be a king's arm,
May you be a rock of ollaves,
May you be the glory of Emain Macha,
May you be higher than everyone!'

Said Nede
'May you be so, under the same titles!
Two trees springing from one root without destruction.
A casket of poetry, an expression of wisdom.
This is the perfect line of intellect:
Father from son, son from father.
Three fathers I have had:
A father in age,
A fleshly father,
A father of teaching.
My fleshly father remains not,
My father of teaching is not present,
You, Ferchertne, are my father in age!
You I acknowledge – may it be so!'

There is so much in this extraordinary text that it is not at all easy to analyse. It tells us a great deal about both the state of poetry in Ireland, and about the breadth of knowledge and understanding possessed by the poets themselves. Of course, it has been edited and tampered with, like all the pagan poetry of the time. But more has survived here than in most of the Welsh material.

Nede is presented in the same guise as we first meet Taliesin, as a kind of wondrous youth whose inspired utterances cause his critics to recognise him. Here, there is more friendship and humility in the contest between the two men, who call upon a wide range of knowledge to back up their claims. Small wonder that the King and his councillors were unable

Figure 9 Dialogue of the Poets *The top quarters of the slab depict two men, each one with his thumb in his mouth. Possibly they represent two poets in dialogue or dispute.*

to understand what was being said. But the text is far from non-sensical. Most of it reveals its meaning with a little thought.

In the first verse Ferchertne throws down the gauntlet, challenging Nede to show what wisdom he possesses. Nede replies, politely, that while any sage may criticise a younger poet he should at least hear what he has to say first, especially since, in this case, the youth has had the benefit of a wise teacher of his own. Then Ferchertne asks where Nede has come from and we have the first salvo of poetic answers. Nede has come from a conjunction of wisdom, he has eaten of the nine hazels of poetic art, which are said to grow about a stream which rises in the Otherworld. There, in that 'excellent land', are many colours each one, we are told in a gloss, denoting the power and quality of the people of that place. There, poets are refreshed.

Ferchertne, challenged in turn, replies that *he* has travelled down the 'columns of age', from the Otherworldly place where goddesses are to be found. He has come from the land where the sun and moon have their home, and he is a son of Oengus, (Mac ind Oic) the god of love and inspiration. He then demands Nede's name, meaning, of course, his poetic name. Nede's reply is full of crackling, kenning words: he is filled with the fire of poetic insight and wisdom.

Ferchertne's poetic name is about inquiry, art, deftness with words, abundant knowledge gleaned from questioning and long study. He demands to know what art his young opponent practises.

Nede speaks of satire, the most powerful weapon of the poet. He promotes 'bashfulness', causes cheeks to grow red. He also fosters the art of poetry itself, making 'polished tales' to delight kings, paring down speech to the bare bones, ordering his words like cattle, teaching and giving forth knowledge to all who will listen.

Ferchertne, too, speaks of hunting the 'treasure of knowledge', of the peacemaker's role, of celebrating the glory of a king, whose pallet he shares, meaning that he is as close to the king as it is possible to be. He orders his words like warriors, and he, too, practises the feared art of satire: **briarmon smetrach** of which it is said, in **Cormac's Glossary**:

> the name of an operation which poets perform on a person who refuses them [aught]. He [the poet] grinds the person's earlobe, between his two fingers, and the person dies on whom he performs (this) operation. (233)

The word **bri** itself means 'a malediction', from which we may see that the gloss really means to pierce the ear of the person satirised, in such a way that their inflated ego dies. Other instances of satire suggest that some poets were able to raise boils on the skin through the very invective of their words. Taliesin himself holds Maelgwn's court poets helpless with his simple 'blerwm blerwm'. Aithirne, referred to here, was famous for his satires. It was said of him that 'the lakes and rivers receded before him when he satirised them and rose up before him when he praised them' (77). He was also the foster-father of Amairgen, who has much in common with Taliesin (see Chapter One).

Nede's answer to all this is to speak of his own tasks as going to the plain of age, i.e. learning the wisdom which comes with advancing years. Yet he will remain youthful also, visiting the mountain of youth. He will follow a king into death itself, to the people of Fomor, the Otherworldly race who were the aboriginal inhabitants of Ireland.

Ferchertne then says that he will go into the place where knowledgeable men dwell, into the very 'breast of poetic wisdom' from which he will learn much. He, too, will face death, expecting to find great honour there.

The next exchange concerns the path by which the two poets have reached their current state of wisdom and enlightenment. Nede has crossed 'the white plain of knowledge' (another epithet for the Otherworld) 'on the back of a ploughing ox', which refers to the writing of lines of verse, eating of the mast, the favourite food of sacred pigs, and rich offerings of the Goddess, walking 'on my own strong thighs'.

Ferchertne has come 'on Lugh's horserod', a reference to the three inventions of the God, which are said to be: draughts, ballplay, and horsemanship (or sometimes a horsewhip, as in this text). He has come also in 'a chariot without a wheelrim, a wheelrim without a chariot', which refers to the chariot of poetry itself, which can be either gentle or rough, smooth paced or angry. The 'threefold ignorance of Mac ind Oic' is glossed thus: that 'he knew not when he would die, and what death would carry him off and on what sod he would lie'. Ferchertne seems to be applying this to himself, presumably in that all things and all futures are possible to the poet.

Nede's claims are equally modest. He is the son of poetry itself, he has the wisdom and lore that are born of knowledge, he is the child of the triple gods of poetry, glossed as 'three sons of Brigid the poetess, namely Brian and Iuchar and Uar.' Of this same goddess, who was later subsumed by the figure of St Brigit of Ireland, **Cormac's Glossary** says:

> Brigit the female sage, or woman of wisdom, i.e. Brigit the Goddess whom poets adored, because very great and famous was her protecting care. It is therefore they call her goddess of poets by this name. (233)

There is no evidence for Brigit's three sons being gods of poetry however. Brigit herself was a triple-aspected goddess, having authority for smithcraft and medicine as well as poetry.

Ferchertne's answer is more problematical. Most contributors have chosen to interpret this verse as a reference to Christian lore. **Ailm** is the name of the letter A in Irish and this has been assumed to refer either to Adam, who had no father, was buried in the womb of the earth (from which he was made) and who was blessed after his death, or to Christ as **Alpha**. Since the poem was copied by a Christian monk this is not surprising; possibly he substituted his own version for an originally pagan statement.

The last part of the poem takes the form of a series of prophecies, and with the final reconciliation of the two poets, who now seek to outdo each other in compliments, until finally Ferchertne yields his place and the robe to the younger man, who in turn acknowledges him as his 'father in age'.

What is particularly interesting about this poem is that the dispute is actually over the possession of Adnae's robe, as much as the office which (presumably) went with it. We know that the **pencerodd**, 'Chiefs of Song', won their Bardic chairs of office through disputation of this kind, though here we seem to have something more archetypal. The robe, which is described as being of three colours, 'to wit, a covering of bright birds' feathers in the middle: a showery specking of **findruine** (white-silver) on the lower half outside, and a golden colour on the upper half', is clearly the **tugen**, or Feathered Cloak, traditionally worn by all Irish poets. In **Cormac's Glossary** (233) another such garment is described as 'of the skins of birds, white and many-coloured . . . from the girdle downwards, and of mallards' necks and crests from the girdle upward to the neck.' This is clearly a shamanic garment, and like all such it was a garment of power, the wearing of which conferred wisdom and strength. Nede is already wearing it when he answers the elder poet's questions, which gives him the necessary skill to equal his adversary in the use of the poetic language. As an outward show of this he puts on a beard of grass so that he has the semblance of age.

The whole work tells us a great deal about the Bardic mysteries. The range of wisdom and the cunning use of words is considerable, as indeed is the case with the work of Taliesin. We also discover that the poets claim an Otherworldly origin for their inspiration, detailing the many different influences and skills necessary to practise the art. It has been suggested that this method of poetic contest was a regular practice by which Bards were chosen to occupy their Chair of Office. Competition would have been fierce, since poets were well treated, well paid and greatly honoured. In Taliesin's own work we see this reflected constantly.

In **The Fold of the Bards** (translated in full on pages 311–12) he says:

> With discretion I try
> The vain poems of the British bards,
> In contentious competitions,
> careful as the smith's skilled hammer.
>
> The enclosure of the Bards, who knows it not –
> fifteen thousand doors
> admit to its qualifications . . .

while in poems like **The Contention of the Bards** and **The Rebuke** of the Bards he attacks them with a professional regard to their skills in metre, rhyme and insight:

> If you are skilled bards
> of ardent **awen**,
> be not contentious
> in the court of your king.
> Unless you know the names of the verse-forms,
> be silent Heinin, unless you know
> the name of **rimiad**,
> the name of **ramiad**,
> the name of your forefather
> before his baptism . . .

The Power of Satire

There is, however, another aspect to all of this: a darker side to the wise and intricate exchanges described above. A poet could create magical changes in the landscape or in beasts, making both barren. His satires might be no worse than a fierce lampoon which would be gleefully spread by gossips and so work its eventual result: to hold up anyone who slighted him in a dishonourable and mocking light (267).

However, satires could be fatal. One of the most celebrated stories about an unjust satire is found in **Cormac's Glossary** (233). This concerns Nede at a later point in his career. Recognised as the adoptive son of his uncle, King Caier, he found himself tempted by the Queen, who conceived an adulterous love for Nede and offered him an apple of silver to lie with her. Nede refused her importuning until she offered to make him king after Caier's death. She bade him make a **Glam-Dichenn**, or satire, upon Caier, causing blisters to break out on his face. Since no blemished man might continue in the kingship, Caier would thus have to abdicate.

Nede pleaded the difficulty of this since, in order to create a **Glam-Dichenn** he would first have to have a request of his refused. The Queen already knew what to do; there was one thing which Caier would never give away, since it was **geas** (prohibited) for him to do so – it was a knife which had been sent to him from Alban. Nede then went and asked for the knife and on Caier's refusal to give it to him, he composed a satire:

> Evil, death and a short life to Caier;
> May spears of battle slay Caier;
> The rejected of the land and the earth is Caier;
> Beneath the mounds and the rocks be Caier.

The next morning when Caier went to wash in the fountain, he found that this final-sounding satire had had its effect. There were three blisters on his face, of crimson, green and white – 'disgrace, blemish, and defect', they were called. Caier immediately fled the land, dwelling as a stranger with Caichear of Dun Cearmna. Nede enjoyed the kingship for a whole year.

But Nede's heart knew the injustice of his satire and he set out to find Caier and speak with him. As his chariot approached the walls of Dun Cearmna, a watchman described the beautiful vehicle to those below. Immediately Caier rose up, crying, 'It is we that used to be driven in its champion's seat, in front of the driver's seat.' 'These are the words of a king,' said his host, who had not known his friend until that moment.

'Not so', said Caier, and rushed into the house and hid himself within the cleft of a rock. Nede followed him and Caier's greyhounds sniffed out their former master. Caier then dropped dead of shame at the sight of Nede. The rock boiled, blazed and burst at Caier's death and a splinter flew into Nede's eye and broke in his head. Whereupon Nede composed an expiatory poem before dying.

This story reveals several features central to an understanding of both the poet's and the king's role in Celtic society. The position of the king was that of a semi-sacral personage, chosen by a series of tribal and supernatural tests and examined as to his fitness to fill his office. Prime among these was his acceptance by the Goddess of the Land herself. Under the reign of a worthless king, the countryside was barren and its cows dry of milk. Any physical blemish was a serious rupture of the king's relationship with the land: hence Caier's extreme reaction in hiding himself among strangers and forsaking his kingship. Interestingly, it is the land which vindicates him at the last, since the rock strikes Nede in the eye. (182)

The role of poet was to uphold the truth and the natural laws, almost as a mirror of justice. His words reflected the essential goodness of his patron to all men and so he was intrinsically a light-bearer. Nede is quick to relinquish these duties. His lust for the Queen is outstripped by his desire for kingship, and he readily finds a loophole by which he can exercise the unjust satire upon his patron and adoptive father, thus compounding several crimes at once. But, as an upholder of natural justice, so he is eventually condemned as a regicide, a patricide and a dishonoured poet.

The form of satire referred to in this text as a **Glam-Dichenn** is given more substance in a little-known treatise on versification (232). There it is declared that the poet wishing to place the satire must go, with six other poets, at sunrise to a hilltop on the boundaries of seven lands,

> ... and the face of each one of them towards his own land, and the face of the ollave there towards the land of the king whom he would satirise, and the backs of them all towards a hawthorn which should be at the top of the hill, and the wind from the north, and a slingstone and a thorn of the hawthorn in every man's hand, and each of them to sing a stave in a prescribed metre into the slingstone and the thorn, the ollave singing his stave before the others, and they afterwards singing

141

their stave at once; and each was then to put his stone and his thorn at the butt of the hawthorn. And if it were they that were in the wrong, the earth of the hill would swallow them up. But if it were the King that was in the wrong, the earth would swallow him up and his wife and his son and his horse and his arms and his dress and his hound . . .

Clearly this would be a difficult set of conditions to reproduce! But the very detail of the instruction tells us something about the seriousness with which satire was regarded, and it is, of course, well known that where such elaborate conditions are required, a way will be found to fulfil every detail.

The Silver Branch

In various sources we hear of poets and their associates carrying a branch of either gold, silver or bronze. The most familiar, and undoubtedly the most important, of these was the Silver Branch which, besides being recognised as an emblem of the Poet's Craft, also had a deeper significance as a symbol of entry to the Otherworld. It is thus unlike the Golden Bough of Classical tradition, which is more specifically related to the mysteries of the cult of Nemea. In Celtic tradition, the Silver Branch is almost always given to a mortal either by the Queen of the Otherworld or one of her ladies. The most famous example of this is in the Irish story of *The Voyage of Bran mac Fabel to the Land of Faery* (209). The text begins mysteriously:

It was fifty quatrains that the woman from the unknown land sang on the floor of the house of Bran, son of Fabel, when the royal house was full of kings; they knew not whence the woman had come, for the ramparts were closed. This is the beginning of the story. One day in the neighbourhood of the stronghold Bran went about alone, when he heard music behind him. And often as he looked back it was still behind him the music was. At last he fell asleep at the sound of the music, such was its sweetness. When he awoke from his sleep he saw close by him a branch of silver with white blossoms, so that it was not easy to distinguish the blossoms from the branch. Then Bran took the branch in his hand to the royal house. When the hosts were in the royal house, they saw a woman in strange raiment on the floor of the house. 'Twas then she sang the fifty quatrains to Bran, the host listening, all beholding the woman. And she sang:

> A branch of the apple tree from Emain
> I bring, like those we know;
> Twigs of white silver are on it
> Crystal grows with blossoms . . .

Thereupon the woman went from them and they knew not whither she went. And she took her branch with her. The branch sprang from Bran's hand into the hand of the woman, nor was there strength in Bran's hand to hold the branch.

Bran follows the call of the Branch. It leads him into the Otherworld, where he again meets the Faery woman. There he remains for what seems to him no more than a year; yet when he returns to the land of men he finds that centuries have passed and that he himself is remembered only in legend and song.

Although the Silver Branch does not seem to have fruit upon it in this story, it does have blossom, and is said specifically to be of the apple tree. In other versions apples of silver are found upon the branch, and it is these which, chiming forth, intoxicate the poet, who is thus blessed by a vision of the Otherworld.

In **The Sickbed of Cuchulainn** (59) the Otherworld apple tree is described as growing in the midst of 'The Plain of Honey' (Mag Mell), another word for the Irish Elysium:

> There is a tree at the door of the Court,
> It cannot be matched in harmony,
> A tree of silver upon which the sun shines,
> Like unto gold is its splendid lustre.

> There are at the eastern door
> Three stately trees of crimson hue,
> From which the birds of perpetual bloom
> Sing to the youth from the kingly rath.

The idea of the apple as a fruit particular to the Otherworld is well documented. The following example, from a story called **Teigue, Son of Cian** (236), serves to show how it functioned.

Teigue arrived in the Otherworld, and crossed the Plain of Honey, to arrive at last in a fort with a silver rampart. Within it are a beautiful couple, with torques of gold about their necks:

> Now the youth held in his hand a fragrant apple having the hue of gold; a third part of it he would eat, and still, for all he consumed, never a whit would it be diminished. This fruit it was that supported the pair of them, and when once they had partaken of it, nor age nor dimness could affect them . . . Teigue looked away across the plain and saw a wide-spreading apple tree that bore both blossoms and fruit at once. 'What is that apple tree yonder?' he asked [. . . and was told]: 'That apple tree's fruit it is that shall serve for meat for all who come to this mansion . . .'

The Branch is a source of eternal life and of inspiration, another link between the poetic and magical arts and the inner realms visited by the shaman. And it was for this reason that it was carried by the shaman-poet who shook it when he was about to recite a poem. Just as the Otherworld Branch performed the function of bringing peace and silence to an assembly, or of offering entrance to the Otherworld, so the poet's branch, the **Craebh Ciuil**, could cause hostilities to cease or promise an Otherworldly experience through the eloquence of the Bard, which enabled his audience to share in his own knowledge of the inner realms.

These instances of the power of the fruit of a particular tree are widely attested to by those who have studied the shamanic tradition. In many cultures we find the idea of the fruit of the Otherworld and the tree that grows with its roots (or branches) in one world, and its branches (or roots) in the other. For the shaman-poet who traversed the way between the worlds, the silver branch, bearing the fruit of Elysium, could scarcely have been more appropriate.

Is it possible, also, that we have here an echo of the much attested ritual 'cutting of the mistletoe' by the Druid priesthood? It was said to be cut with a golden sickle, and the branch itself began with silvery, milky berries, gradually turning golden if it was kept for any length of time. Though its uses seem to have been quite different, there is clearly some degree of overlap between one custom and the other.

The Dream of Iolo Morgannwg

It is impossible to discuss the Bardic mysteries, or those of Taliesin, without reference to Iolo Morgannwg, the 18th Century scholar and poet, who probably did more to keep alive the heritage of Welsh literature than any other person before or since, but whose work offers numerous problems to the would-be commentator. Born Edward Williams in 1747, Iolo, as he called himself from 1785, was a wanderer and a poet in his own right, who became fascinated by the ancient Welsh poetic remains after he met the Bard Evan Evans, 'Ieuan Fardd', in 1784. A few years later while in Debtors Prison in Cardiff, he began to study the fragmentary materials to which he could get access, and to translate them, first into modern Welsh and later into English. Unfortunately, he was not content with this important and valuable contribution to scholarship. He hungered for something more, for a completeness that no longer existed. And so he began to add to the material from his own imagination, 'forging' literally hundreds of manuscripts, which he later claimed to have copied from works in the possession of various Welsh families. Unfortunately for those engaged in the deciphering of the original poems, he also really did copy certain documents, since lost, so that it is hard at times to tell what is real and what is the product of Iolo's fertile mind.

Another question we have to consider is that of a figure who stands behind Iolo – the 16th Century Bard Llewelyn Sion who, among other things, wrote a version of the life of Taliesin which differs radically from the better-known version published by Lady Charlotte Guest in her edition of the *Mabinogion*. Sion, according to the account given by Iolo in his book *Barddas* (335), copied the manuscripts relating to the Druidic mysteries from books in the library of Raglan Castle. It is on the authenticity of these that the value of Iolo's later 'versions' in part depend.

The vast and complex Bardic system described in Iolo's work is obviously to quite a large extent the invention of his brilliant mind – one may see this clearly enough once one has become sufficiently familiar with the material. One question we should also ask is: if the material is partly forged, who forged it? Not necessarily Iolo. It has been suggested that the Bardic system is purely the invention of the Bards of the 14th and 15th Centuries, and this has some credence – though one may well ask why they should have done so. Possibly the decline in the status of the Bard may have had something to do with it, as we see from even a brief glance at the changing social status of the poet.

The Decline of the Bards

We have already seen the extent of the training programme to which the Bards in Ireland (and almost certainly Britain) submitted themselves. Professor Ford sums this up admirably in his study of the early poets as story-tellers (85): '. . . the **fili** was expected to learn a tremendous amount of lore of all kinds, including laws, genealogies, place and personal-name lore. Both classical commentators and native Irish sources make it clear that much of the lore was versified and that the **filio** were expected to perform on request from that store of tradition.'

Despite this, the standing of the Bard was drastically reduced over the next two hundred years, to the extent that we hear of Rhys ap Tewdyr, who held sway over South Wales in 1100, bringing stories and Bardic lore from Brittany to teach to the Bards of Wales! And, despite a late flowing of poetic art in the 13th and 14th Centuries, there was less and less recourse to the ancient lore of the primary bards such as Taliesin, Aneurin and Myrddin.

In effect there evolved two distinct poetic schools: those of the Bards and those of the (much despised) Minstrels. A quotation from a medieval Welsh Bardic grammar contained in Peniarth 20 states that the work of the Bard had to be free of 'inferior minstrelry, without lies . . . and silencing inferior minstrels and ignorant story-tellers' (273).

Robert Graves, summarising the situation, writes:

> The two poetic schools did not at first come in contact, the 'big-bellied', well-dressed court-bards being forbidden to compose in the minstrel style and penalised if they visited any but the houses of princes or nobles; the lean and ragged minstrels not being privileged to perform at any court, nor trained to use the complicated verse-forms required of the court-bards. (101)

But the Welsh were ever deeply wedded to their traditions and, despite the fact that, under the harsh rule of their Norman masters, the native princes were forbidden to maintain bards of the court, or to have them compose valedictions in their own tongue, the traditions did survive – though in what fragmentary state we can only conjecture. It is indeed possible that this led to the forgery, or adaptation, of certain ancient lore to the times, and that when freedom to practise the old Bardic ways returned in the 16th and 17th Centuries, as well as an outside interest among antiquarians across the border, much was hastily 'restored' that might have benefited from a more considered attention.

Whatever the truth of this complex history, we owe to the Bardic tradition a debt of profound gratitude. It is the Bards who, through the centuries, have helped to preserve the traditions of these islands. That they have added to them (a fact which most scholars have decried) is, of course, inevitable, for these traditions are in no wise dead. The living form of the inner history of Britain and Ireland is to be found within the Bardic/shamanic remains which are the primary object of this book.

Chapter Six

THE ART OF TRANSFORMATION: HIDING THE FAMILIAR

'He had the mind of a fish
That moment. He knew the glitter of scale and fin.
He touched the pin of pivotal space, and he saw
One sandgrain balance the ages' cumulous cloud.'
Vernon Watkins: *Taliesin and the Spring of Vision*

Pictures in the Dark

The power of the dancing, shape-shifting shaman has been recognised from earliest times. His ability to assume the forms of hunted animals thus allied him with the continued existence of the tribe, and his communion with spirits in animal form gave him insights far above those of ordinary men and women.

In time of need, the shaman, the virtuoso dancer of the tribe, communes through ecstatic dances with his animal familiars in order to grasp the secrets of the tribe's gods. His animal helpers serve as vehicles to transport him to the pinnacle of ecstasy in dance, from which he climbs, in a state of trance, to divine heights ... Through his ecstatic prayer the dancer himself moves closer to immortality: in dancing the god he **becomes** him. (167)

The high preponderance of animal art and artefacts discovered throughout the ancient Celtic world suggests the importance attached to such representations. The archaeologist Charles Thomas, in his study of Pictish animal art, notes that these 'seldom served merely as animal ornaments' (306) adding that:

Each creature possessed obvious virtues, its own peculiar and widely known **mana** ... When we consider that, from an

148

early stage in almost all historically-documented societies, these virtues and special properties were generally expressed in terms of pantheistic religion, we have the real clue to the . . . animal-style art. (ibid.)

The current view, as expressed by authorities such as Dr Anne Ross (270), is that the animalistic iconography of Celtic art refers to theriomorphic deities – that is, Gods or Goddesses who either tend towards animal form or assume that shape for an indefinite period of time. It is my belief that this has been a mistaken reading from the start, and that what we are in fact seeing is a catalogue of the various totem animal helpers whose aid was summoned by the tribal shaman, or whose form he also, briefly, assumed, either during trance or by donning a costume created from the fur or feathers of the creature in question. This may, indeed, have led to the shaman figure becoming identified with the God or Goddess he served at a later period. This would certainly explain the reason why the Celts did not make representations of their gods until the influence of Roman and Greek art forms made itself felt. There would have been no need to do so if the shaman-priest regularly assumed the form of the particular animal, bird or fish.

Thus the glorious cave paintings as Lascaux, Altamira and elsewhere, depicting men in the act of hunting and killing a variety of creatures, not only represents the magical aspects of the hunt, but also the shaman's dream-magic, performed before the hunt sets forth. In this, the hunter (or his representative) entered into a symbiotic relationship with the beast in order to anticipate its every action and, perhaps more importantly, to make contact with its spirit-self in order to explain the need of the tribe for its flesh and fur. (This is still practised by the hunters of Lapland and the Far North.)

The fact that the majority of prehistoric cave paintings have been discovered in the very deepest and most inaccessible caves is not without significance. As we have seen, the shaman-poets sought out dark places in which to work their magic or experience their visions. There, in the dark, they left behind the only concrete symbols of that state – painted on the walls, perhaps while still in the altered state of being to which their ecstatic trance had brought them. The famous dancing shaman of Les Trois Frères in France is not merely a representation of the magical action itself, it is also a picture of the *consciousness* of the shaman *in the act of assuming the animal form.*

The Animal Helpers

The importance of animals within everyday Celtic culture is considerable. We already know that a very great deal of the shaman's power was bound up with his animal 'helpers', spirits who took the form of beasts, birds or fish and were able to guide him through both their own particular element, and through the Otherworld. As well as this, the shaman sought to take on the natural abilities of the creature itself: the strength of the bear, the speed of the hare, the keen-sightedness of the eagle or the hawk. By adopting the shape and consciousness of the creature, the shaman projected himself outside the normal range of human awareness, into a world where everything was different: more balanced; less complicated; less bound by the laws and mores of his own world. From this position he could view the world of mortals and perceive it more clearly, with the kind of insights not generally available to him. These concepts are still common enough in modern occult and shamanic practice, and there is distinct evidence that it was especially important to the Celts.

An example of the kind of animal helper featured in the work of the shamans is illustrated by the following story from the **Yellow Book of Lecan** (241).

The White Boar of Marvan was, according to his master, 'a herdsman, a physician, a messenger and a musician.' When asked how this was possible, Marvan replied:

> When I return from the swine at night, and the skin is torn off my feet by the briars of Glen-a-Scail, he comes to me and rubs his tongue over my foot, and he goes after the swine ... He is a musician to me, for when I am anxious to sleep I give him a stroke with my foot and

he lies on his back with his belly uppermost and sings me a humming tune, and his music is more grateful to me than that of a sweet-toned harp in the hands of an accomplished minstrel.

True, the owner of the boar is a herdsman rather than a shaman, but the communion with the wondrous beast is the same. He is both servant and friend to Marvan.

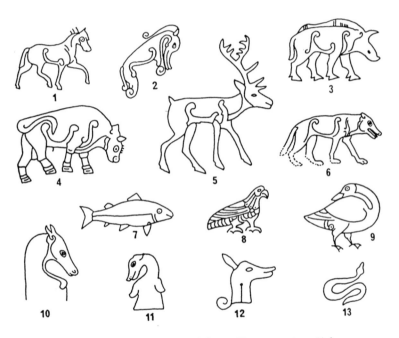

Figure 10   Pictish-Celtic Bestiary 1) horse 2) sea-creature 3) boar
4) bull 5) stag 6) wolf 7) salmon 8) eagle 9) goose
10) horse 11) seal or otter 12) wolfhound 13) snake.

Among the transformations listed by Taliesin, by which he clearly intends us to understand that he has metamorphosed, many are animals, birds or fish. We have already had occasion to comment on the importance of the crane to both the shamanic-poetic mysteries and to Taliesin in particular (see Chapter Three). Looking down the lists of creatures into which he has transformed himself we see that these are grouped as follows:

151

a) Animals	b) Birds	c) Vegetables	d) Others
Buck	Crane	Blossom	Axe
Bull	Eagle	Grain of	Bill-Hook
Cat		wheat	Bridge
Cockerel		Trees and	Coracle
Dog		Sedges	Crane-bag
Fox		Wood	Dust
Goat			Fire
Hare			Harpstring
Marten			Lanternlight
Roebuck			Mist
Salmon			Pin
Serpent			Raindrop
Snake			Road
Sow			Shield
Squirrel			Shout
Stallion			Spade
Wolf			Spear
			Sponge
			Star
			Stock
			Sword
			Torrent
			Wave
			Word

The prominence of such shape-changing, or of intimate relationships between men and animals, is marked in Celtic mythology. Numerous parallels exist from world-wide shamanic practice, the point being that:

> A corridor between earth and heaven, mortal and immortal, is maintained by servicing, magically, whatever is patent around them: rocks, roots, leaves, streams, wind, stars, and most commonly animals, which can serve as totems. (167)

This can be illustrated in a number of ways. On occasion the hero or heroine of the great Celtic myths is shown to be intimately connected with the life of a certain creature. In **The Destruction of Der Derga's Hostel** (59) for example, Mes Buachalla, the daughter of Cormac Mac Airt, is abandoned at birth and brought up by cowherds. Word reaches King Etersal of the mysterious girl and, since there was a prophecy that a woman of an unknown race would bear him a wondrous child, he sent men to fetch her to him. Before this could happen, a bird came to her and told her what would happen. Then, shedding his plumage, the bird took the form of a beautiful man and lay with her. Afterwards he told her that she would have a son called Conaire, who must never kill birds. The girl was then betrothed to Etersal, and it was generally believed that he was the father of her child.

Here the bird is clearly an Otherworldly personage who chooses this method to beget an heir of a human woman. Such stories are by no means unusual in Celtic mythology, where the parentage of heroes was continually attributed to the participation of deity. Among those who could claim supernatural parents were Mongan (whose father was Manannan Mac Lir), Cuchulainn (who was fathered by Lugh), and Owein (who was the offspring of Urien Rheged and the Goddess Modron).

Animals were frequently twinned with human births, so that the resulting offspring became closely allied in later life. (Either that or they were taboo, as in the case of Conaire's prohibition against killing birds.) In the *Mabinogion* Pwyll is stolen from his mother's side by a monster and left in a stable with a newborn colt which afterwards plays a significant part in his life. Cuchulainn's fate was linked with dogs (his name means 'Hound of Culainn'), and it was only after he had been tricked into eating dog-meat, and therefore breaking his **gaesa** (injunction), that he was finally killed. It was also said of Cuchulainn that a mare dropped twin foals on the night of his birth, and that these became famous as the Black Saighlenn and Macha's Grey, with whom Cuchulainn had an almost symbiotic connection, and which arose from the depths of a lake at his call.

Another story concerns Cairbre Cinn Cait, 'of the Cat's Head, since it was a cat's head that is the form or shape of a cat that was on his god' (270). This seems to me to be significant in a number of ways. 'Of the Cat's Head' suggests that Cairbre was 'of the tribe of the Cat', i.e. a tribe whose totem was the cat. Yet the wording, 'the form or shape of a cat *that was on his god*' (my italics) suggests something more – that Cairbre partook of the nature of the cat because the deity he worshipped also partook of that nature. From this I believe we may see further evidence of the assumption of animal form by the shaman of the tribe. Cairbre was a king rather than a shaman, it is true, but the principle is the same.

Figure 11   Romano-British Shaman's head *This Romano-British cast from Silchester depicts a male head with horns, both human and animal ears and a bird-like crest. Vestigial serpent shapes below the head indicate its owner's dedication to wisdom. This is very possibly the head of a shaman.*

Substance to this argument is added by the existence of parallels between certain forms of Celtic art and that of Siberia, specifically the Altaic region. This is important not only for the possibly shared cultural background which is suggested, but more especially for the very highly developed shamanistic practices of the latter area. While there is no desire here to suggest that the Celts were not capable of evolving their own tribal art forms, parallels between the two cultures suggest a similarity of growth in all areas, and hence the existence of shamanism among the Celts.

The Names of the People

The number of tribal names which have animal names hidden within them stresses the importance of animal symbolism even further. For example, there are the Epidii of Kintyre (Horse People), the Caerini and Lugi in Sutherland (People of the Sheep and People of the Raven), the Cornavii of Caithness (People of the Horn – as in horned animal), as well as the

154

Tochrad (Boar People), Cattraighe (Cat Folk), Gamanrad (Stirk People), Taurisci (Bull Folk), Brannovices (Raven Folk) and the Eburones (Boar People). These we must believe were the clan-totems, the power animals which guarded and guided the people of each group. Within the clan, individuals also would have possessed their own personal totem animals – chosen for them by the shamans or revealed in ordeals or initiations. Modern folk-lore records of Celtic families indicate that the association of a particular clan with its totem animal continued to be well-founded until quite recent times (96).

This is the origin of the heraldic devices worn by men and women in the Middle Ages and after, and which still consist largely of a veritable bestiary of animal symbolism. The early Celts must have displayed the head or pelt of their particular totem at the entrance to their settlement, whilst the warriors either painted their shields with devices of their own, or even had them tattooed on their bodies. In the case of the elite warrior group known as the Fianna, whose most famous leader, Fionn Mac Cumhail, we have met often throughout this book, there is actually a text which has preserved a description of the Banners of the Fianna (194). These were presented in visual form in the present author's study of Fionn (186) and need not be reproduced here. However the descriptions of the banners are themselves of interest:

> We raised Image of Sun, the great banner of Fionn of the Fian;
> [on many occasions] it caused a hot conflict around great
> Conan of Ceann Sleibhe . . .
> We raised Torch of Battle, the banner of [a particular] Faolan,
> the son of manly Fionn, the noble of the Fiana – a lad by whom
> a strenuous battle would be fought . . . (94)

Another, much longer, poem from the **Dunaire Fionn** (174) describes the shield of Fionn in terms which leave one in no doubt as to its magical properties (for text see Chapter Seven). Indeed, whilst there is no *exact* parallel in Celtic literature, there are indications that the idea of magical or powerful shields (familiar to students of North American shamanism) would have been recognised among the native shamans of these islands. Among the Amerindians the shield would have been painted with magical pictograms representing the spiritual estate of the person carrying it. Shields could also represent

155

the sacred directions (North, South, East, West, Above, Below) and the totem beasts of the tribe or the individual.

Two poems from the *Proceedings of the Great Bardic Institution* (56) illustrate this further. Here the poet, Dallan, requests **Dubh-Ghiolla**, the magical shield of the King of Oirgiall, and makes several poems about it. The shield was, indeed, made from one of the five sacred trees of Ireland, namely the Yew of Ross (see Chapter Eight). It is described as follows:

> Chasing is thy shield
> As the wave which runs its course . . .
> A speckled shield, the feeder of ravens,
> Wards off the foe from his borders.
> Surprising and beautiful shield
> Is with Hugh the son of Duach . . .

And again:

> Bright as the speckled salmon of the wave!
> Dubh-Ghiolla! panic of the banded brave . . .
> Fenced with its thorny mail the holly stands –
> So round the prince the guardian shield expands:
> The bull's strong hide the needle's point defies –
> Thus vainly round him baffled ranks arise . . . (56)

The idea even seems to continue into the time of St Patrick, whose famous **Breastplate** (130), though of late and Christian origin, suggests more than a little the notion of the protective shield.

The Oldest Animals

Another important role attributed to animals was their ability to provide inspiration, or to possess a knowledge of the past that far outstripped that of a human. The average lifespan of a bird or beast was probably unknown, which may account for this belief. Certainly some creatures were believed to live to very great ages, or were anyway of Otherworldly provenance and thus cognisant of wisdom more deep than that of mortals. In the story of **The Hawk of Achill** (128), we see this as part of a theme known as 'The Oldest Animals', in which a number of creatures are consulted about various things and refer the questioner to successively more ancient beings. A similar story appears in the Welsh saga of 'Culhwch and Olwen', in which the various animals: blackbird; stag; eagle and salmon, are consulted as to the whereabouts of the lost Child-God, Mabon, who is finally discovered, and rescued, by the warriors of Arthur, helped by various of the animals (183).

In **The Hawk of Achill** it is Fintan who addresses the bird in a way that makes his shamanic abilities apparent. It is remarkable for the clarity with which it presents the life of the ancient poet, who seems to have lived through most of history – though physically rather than in vision as with Taliesin – in the shapes into which he is cast. (The version given here is adapted from that of Eleanor Hull, much abridged.)

Fintan
Relate now, o bird of Achill,
The substance of your adventures;
For I am able finally
To converse in your tongue.

The Bird
Though you seem still young,
It is long since you became shrunken,
In Dun Tulera washed by the sea,
O Fintan, o wise man.

Fintan
O bird of Achill of the Fian,
Whom I have long desired to see,
Now that you are here indeed, tell me
Why you cleave to Achill?

The Bird
O Fintan, never was there
A single night in Achill,
When I failed to obtain by my strength
Fish, game and venison.

O son of Bochra, speak fair,
And, since we are able to converse . . .
Tell me of your life.

157

Fintan
Before the black flood
My life was more than two hundred years;
Afterwards I was given
A further five thousand five hundred.

O Hawk, out of cold Achill,
Blessing and success attend you!
From the time of your hatching
Tell me the number of your years?

The Bird
Equal is my life to yours
O Fintan, son of mild Bochra:
Exactly equal the period
From the time of the Deluge.

O Fintan, son of fair Bochra,
Since you are a poet and a prophet,
Tell me now without delay
The evils and wonders that befell you.

Fintan rehearses a catalogue of events to which he has been witness, then to his own misfortunes, and finally speaks his own transformations into the form of an eagle, a hawk and a salmon, in which shape he continued for long ages, following the course of the rivers of Ireland:

At the Slaney, and at the Liffey in the East,
The Maigue, and crystal Ethne,
The Moy, the Mourne and the Muir,
At the Solan, the Lee and the Laune.

At the Shannon, the Dael and the Dubh,
In the Sligo and the river Monad,
Until I came without trouble hither
To the waterfall of the estuary of the Erne.

I passed a night in the Northern wave,
And at Assaroe of the seals,
Never felt I a night like that
From the beginning of the world to its end.

I could not stay under the waterfall,
I took a leap, but it did not help me,

The ice came like clear blue glass
Between me and the falls of Mac Moduirn.

A crow came out of cold Achill,
Above the river-mouth of Assaroe;
I will not hide the fact, mysterious as it was,
He carried away with him one of my eyes . . .

The Bird
It was I who swallowed your eye,
O Fintan of bright nature;
I am the grey hawk . . .
Alone in the middle of Achill . . .

Fintan
Harsh is thy chant, o great wild bird,
Better it would have been, to wait a while.
Since it is I who am the gentler
I will speak of my own time.

For five hundred years have I been blind
As a long-sided heavy salmon,
On lochs, on diverse rivers,
On every rich clear-flowing sea.

For fifty years I was an eagle,
Few the birds that could fill my place;
A hundred years happily
I was a fierce blue-eyed falcon.

Till the King of the Sun thought it time
To put me in my own shape.
Where would I get anything worthier?
And yet, I am aged still today.

There is much more of the poem, with Fintan and the Hawk swapping stories and traditions until they finally reach a point of contemporary time and, having apparently nothing further to say, die on the same day. This text, which combines both the shamanic shape-shifting of the poet and a recital of the history to which he has gained access at first hand, is virtually unique in Celtic literature. In essence it is a summary of Irish mythological history, and there is a suggestion that Fintan's loss of an eye is a kind of fee for the acquiring of his great wisdom (as in the case of the Norse god Odin, who gave up his eye in return for the wisdom of Mimir). Since the Hawk itself admits to this act, in the shape of a crow, and later discusses the deaths of Fintan's sons, whose remains it seems to have picked over in the manner of a crow, we may assume that this was another of the bird's shapes.

In this case we may be able to identify it with the figure of the Battle Goddess Morrigan, who often assumed the shape of a raven and, since she is not far removed from Ceridwen in many of her attributes, we may draw a further parallel between Fintan and Taliesin, each of whom underwent changes of form at the hands of a Goddess after they had learned great wisdom. Certainly Fintan and the Hawk are closely connected, in that they both die at the same moment, and this in itself once again suggests a shamanic connection: the shaman and his 'familiar' spirit being thus intimately related to each other from the moment they discover each other to the day of the shaman's death.

The relationship of the stories is nowhere precise, but there are analogies which make it possible that both derived from a similar source which contained the record of a shamanic initiation. In Finece's case, there is no cauldron, no three drops of wisdom – but we know from the story of Fionn that he sought the flesh of the Salmon of Wisdom. There is a curious sense of rightness about this comparison. Gwion obtains the drops of wisdom by accident, as Fionn accidentally imbibes the wisdom of the salmon. Fintan, who had lived in the shape of a salmon for a thousand years, and sought that wisdom for his own, seems scarcely to need it. We seem to be witnessing a very ancient theme here, one which flows through both the *Hanes Taliesin* and **The Hawk of Achill** in a similar fashion. It is the age-old theme of the Quest for Knowledge, in which the shaman-poet or priest sought out the deep places of the inner realms and returned with riches beyond the dreams of mere men.

The Transformations of Tuan Mac Cairell

A story which parallels those of Taliesin and Fintan, and says much of the true nature of animal transformation, is that of the Irish seer Tuan Mac Cairell. He was discovered by the monk Finnian of Moville, and claimed to have been alive for several centuries, in several forms, during which time he had witnessed most of Ireland's early history. His story, in abbreviated form, is as follows.

> Then I was from hill to hill, and from cliff to cliff, guarding myself from wolves, for twenty-two years, during which Ireland was empty. At last old age came upon me, and I was on cliffs and in wastes, and was unable to move about, and I had special caves for myself. Then Nemed, son of Agnoman, my father's brother, invaded Ireland, and I saw them from the cliffs and kept avoiding them, and I hairy, clawed, withered, grey, naked, wretched, miserable. Then, as I was asleep one night, I saw myself passing into the shape of a stag. In that shape I was, and I young and glad of heart . . .

> > Then there grew upon my head
> > Two antlers with three score points,
> > So that I am rough and grey in shape
> > After my age has changed from feebleness.

> After this, from the time I was in the shape of a stag, I was the leader of the herds of Ireland, and wherever I went there was a large herd of stags about me . . .
> Then at last old age came upon me, and I fled from men and wolves. Once as I was in front of my cave – I still remember it – I knew that I was passing from one shape into another. Then I passed into the shape of a wild boar. Tis then I said:

> > A boar am I today among herds,
> > A mighty lord am I with great triumphs . . .

> In that shape . . . I was truly then, and I young and glad of mind. And I was king of the boar herds of Ireland, and I still went the round of my abode when I used to come into this land of Ulster at the time of my old age and wretchedness; for in the same place I changed into all these shapes. Therefore I always visited that place to await the renewal . . .
> Then [again] old age came upon me and my mind was sad, and I was unable to do all that I used to do before, but was alone in dark caves and in hidden cliffs.
> Then I went to my own dwelling always. I remembered every shape in which I had been before. I fasted my three days as I had always done. I had no strength left. Thereupon I went into the shape of a large hawk. Then my mind was again happy. I was able to do anything. I was eager and lusty. I would fly across Ireland; I would find out everything. Tis then I said:

> A hawk today, a boar yesterday,
> Wonderful . . . inconstancy!
>
> Among herds of boars I was,
> Though today I am among bird-flocks;
> I know what will come of it:
> I shall still be in another shape . . .

Then I was for a long time in the shape of that hawk, so that I outlived all those races who had invaded Ireland. However, the sons of Mil took this island by force from the Tuatha de Danann. Then I was in the shape of that hawk in which I had been, and was in the hollow of a tree on a river.

There I fasted for three days and three nights, when sleep fell upon me, and I passed into the shape of a river salmon there and then . . . Once more I felt happy and was vigorous and well-fed, and my swimming was good, and I used to escape from every danger and from every snare – to wit, from the hands of fishermen, and from the claws of hawks, and from fishing spears – so that the scars which each one of them left are still upon me.

Once, however . . . when the beasts were pursuing me and every fisherman in every pool knew me, the fisherman of Cairell, the king of that land, caught me and took me with him to Cairell's wife, who had desire for fish. Indeed I remember it, the man put me on a gridiron and roasted me. And the Queen desired me and ate me by herself, so that I was in her womb. Again, I remember the time that I was in her womb, and what each one said to her in the house, and what was done in Ireland during that time. I also remember when speech came to me, as it comes to any man, and I knew all that was being done in Ireland, and I was a seer; and a name was given to me – to wit, Tuan, son of Cairell . . . (209)

If we needed any further proof of the foundation of shamanism in Ireland this would surely provide it. Here, as in the story of Fintan, which it resembles in certain essential details, the seer is able to live through the long and magical history of Ireland, witnessing the waves of invasion by different peoples, while being continually renewed in different animal forms. He is quite specific about the way this happens. He always visits the same place to await his transformation, and there fasts for three days and nights, after which he 'sees' the change come upon him. This can only mean that he was practising a ritual of rebirth – apparently in a cave – and that although the transformations come upon him in the poem apparently without any agency of his own, we can be sure that at an earlier date this would not have been the case. At some point there must have existed, in oral memory, the story of a shaman who, at certain times, went into a trance state which enabled him to visit the past or future and see events which had occurred there. At such times, though aged, he was apparently renewed and became filled with vigour, drawing on the strengths of the totem beasts which were his especial helpers – the stag, the boar, the hawk and the salmon.

The end of the story, as we have it now, is analogous to that of Taliesin. Tuan is swallowed by the queen, carried in her womb and reborn in human shape, becoming a seer and poet. Although he is caught in the shape of a salmon, this is not so far removed from Taliesin's capture in the salmon weir, *after* his rebirth. We may conjecture that in some form the initiatory sequence identified above included the change to salmon shape – a sure sign of wisdom – after which the Goddess 'ate' the fish and gave birth to the new shaman.

Here the themes of rebirth and of the adoption of animal form come together. Like Taliesin, Tuan goes through a number of metamorphoses – though whether self-induced or not is unclear. In each case Tuan lives the full span of the creature in question, and is able to witness the changing history of Ireland. Finally, again like Taliesin, he is reborn, in human form, but with the accumulated knowledge of several hundred years in his consciousness. One of the manuscripts which contain the story says that Tuan was a hundred years in man shape, eighty years a stag, twenty as a boar, one hundred as an eagle (this should presumably read a hawk), twenty as a salmon, so that he lived a total of three hundred and twenty years before his rebirth as a man.

What is so fascinating about this story is the description of the changes, which read so much like the descriptions of shamanic operations in other parts of the world to make it seem certain that an actual ceremony of some kind is being recalled – though in a muddled way – and that Tuan actually undergoes a series of shamanic trance states in which he is able to perceive the past. Probably, at an earlier date in the transmission of the story, the period of each animal 'incarnation' would have been progressively longer, like those of the ancient animals in **The Hawk of Achill** and **Culhwch and Olwen**.

Figure 12   This gold bracteate from Lellinge, Denmark, possibly depicts a shaman, thumb in mouth, surrounded by animals, with star-signs in the background.

But the most important single factor in the stories of Taliesin, Tuan, and the Hawk of Achill is that the three protagonists, Taliesin, Tuan Mac Cairell and Fintan, are all carriers of tradition. It is not just the facts of history they relate, but the entire inner tradition of the land. Each is either vouchsafed total knowledge (Taliesin), or given extended lifetimes which enable them to witness the events they describe (Tuan and Fintan). Thus the tradition itself is kept alive and its representatives become living repositories of accumulated wisdom. The whole of what we have termed 'the Taliesin tradition' is of this kind, and the poems attributed to Taliesin himself are a great index to the traditions, rites and beliefs of the Celtic peoples.

The Pole of the Heavens

The following, medieval poem, attributed to John of Kentchurch, preserves a variant list and demonstrates the continuing tradition of the Oldest Animals (206):

164

The Age and Duration of Things

Triads of the ages in their complete progress	
Were formerly generally known.	
Three years is the duration of the alder pole.	3
Three times the duration of an alder pole	
Is the life of a dog in the green woodland.	9
And three times the age of the dog	
Is the age of a good and active horse.	27
Thrice the age of the horse	
Is that of a man – a short existence!	81
Thrice the age of man	
Is that of the bounding hart.	243
Thrice the age of the stag	
Is that of the melodious blackbird.	729
Thrice the age of the beautiful blackbird	
Is that of the earth-grown oak.	2187
Thrice the age of the oak	
Is judged to be that of the Earth itself . . .	6561

An interesting reference here is to the 'alder pole'. In almost every known case of shamanic activity the shaman possesses a pole (originally a tent pole) which represents the centre of the world. This he climbs, while in his ecstatic trance, pausing at various levels to describe what he sees. Each level represents a different stage in the long ascent to the Otherworld, all are depicted in the greatest detail (76). A story from the Fionn cycle seems to confirm the existence of such a pole in the Celtic belief system:

The story concerns the fortunes of one Derg Corra, who was so light of foot that he used to leap to and fro across the fire while he was serving food to the company. Because of this a woman who was Fionn's captive desired him, though he dared not respond because of Fionn's jealous nature. Because of this the woman turned against him and accused him of raping her. Fionn gave him three days to depart, and Derg fled. He lived in the forest where he used to 'go about on the shanks of a deer' so light was he, and came to live in a tree top. One day, as Fionn was searching the forest for Derg, he came upon a figure in a tree whom none knew because of a cloak of concealment he wore about him. But Fionn chewed his thumb of wisdom and knew at once that it was Derg. The description of the figure not only takes us firmly back to the cross-legged shaman of the Gundestrup Cauldron discussed in Chapter Two, but also adds to that figure in its detail.

> One morning as Finn was in the wood seeking [Derg] . . . he saw a man in the top of a tree, a blackbird on his right shoulder and in his left hand a white vessel of bronze, filled with water in which was a skittish trout and a stag at the foot of the tree. And this was the practice of the man: cracking nuts; and he would give half the kernel of a nut to the blackbird that was on his right shoulder while he would himself eat the other half; and he would take an apple out of the bronze vessel that was in his left hand, divide it in two, throw one half to the stag that was at the foot of the tree and then eat the other half himself. And on it he would drink a sip of the bronze vessel that was in his hand so that he and the trout and the blackbird drank together. And then his followers asked Finn who he in the tree was for they did not recognise him on account of the hood of disguise he wore. (270)

There is such a remarkable symmetry about this description that one is almost led to believe that the author is describing an actual icon. Though none that exactly mirrors this description has been found to date, there are many aspects which are echoed among the collections of carved reliefs from Celtic and Romano-Celtic sources. In particular the bird perched on the hooded man's shoulder and the bowl in his left hand are both familiar from such reliefs. Anne Ross notes a strong parallel with a relief from Donon, which may possibly represent the Gaulish God Vosegus. Her description reads as follows:

> The powerful deity, bearded and naked apart from a skin cloak about his shoulders, and wearing boots, has fruits suspended from his cloak (which bears an animal's head) amongst them pine cones, showing his connection with trees and their produce (Derg Corra has nuts and apples). To the right of the god and standing behind his legs is a stag on one of whose antlers the god rests his left hand. On the back of the stag a bird perches. (270)

The remainder of the iconography of this passage reads almost like a summary of many of the points raised throughout this book. The presence of the animals, the trout who stands in for the Salmon of Wisdom, the nuts which Derg cracks, and which recall the descriptions of **Imbas Forosnai** and **Dichetel do Chenaib**, the cracking open of the nuts of wisdom referred to in Chapter Seven. Even the apple is a sacred fruit, found most commonly in descriptions of the Otherworld.

The story is, admittedly, confused. 'The narrative has all the hallmarks of varying elements being jumbled together' remarks Daithi O'Hogain, in his commentary on the work (238). Yet the curious ritual of jumping to and fro across the fire before serving food calls to mind the idea of a ritual feast, while Derg's name itself derives from the Irish **daighre**, 'flame', suggesting that he may have been at one time a kind of fire-spirit.

Here, then, most clearly, we have a description of the shamanic lord of the beasts, the Otherworldly practitioner of flight who sits at the top of the cosmic tree and is disguised in a ceremonial hood which disguises him from all who have not (as has Fionn) undergone initiation. He alone is able to describe the man and to understand the meaning of his presence. Although the text of Finn and the man in the tree dates from no earlier than the 8th Century, we have no hesitation in ascribing it to a far earlier time, when such figures would have been common, as well as known and respected for their relationship to animals as for their numerous other skills.

It is this figure indeed, widely known as 'the Lord of the Beasts' who is described by Ann Ross:

> The Deity (i.e. most Celtic Gods) moreover, is never far removed from his cult animal. He may be encountered in the form of his sacred stag, dog, horse or bird as the case may be; he may, on the other hand, appear in fully anthropomorphic guise, accompanied by his choice of companion from the bird or animal world. (269)

In almost all of the versions assembled by Eleanor Hull in her study of the Oldest Animals theme the pole appears in one form or another, and although no two sequences of animal helpers are exactly the same, that listed in **Culhwch and Olwen** (144) is found in a similar form in the Irish **Book of Lismore** (128) which has:

> Three life-times of the stag for the blackbird;
> Three life-times of the blackbird for the eagle;

Three life-times of the eagle for the salmon;
Three life-times of the salmon for the yew.

It may be that here we are seeing traces of a sequence of related
bird-lore similar in many ways to the system of symbolic
references found in lists of Ogam (cf. Chapter Eight). In
The Hawk of Achill there is mention of the crane that lived
in Moy Leana, the eagle of Druim Seghsa, the stag known
as the Blackfoot of Slieve Fuaid. Welsh folk-lore records the
oldest living animals as the Eagle of Gwernabwy, the Stag of
Rhedynfre, the Salmon of Llyn Llifon, the Ousel of Cilgwri,
the Toad of Cors Fochno, and the Owl of Cwmcawlwyd.

The folklorist Douglas Hyde discovered the story of the
eagle-woman, Leithin who, in a dialogue with one of her
own nestlings, is asked if she could ever remember a night as
cold as the one just passed. Leithin answered that she did not,
but that there were those who did: 'Even Dubhchosach, the
Black-Footed one of Binn Gulban, the great stag who survived
the Deluge; or the white blackbird of Clonfert; or the blind
salmon of Assaroe (i.e. Fintan).' (135)

Elsewhere, in a late 17th Century manuscript, there is
mention of the Crane of Moy Leana, who had been turned
into a bird by her father who was jealous of her affections
for another man. Her name had been Miadhach the daughter
of Echdonn. This sounds like the story of Aoife, from whose
skin the crane bag was made (cf. Chapter Three).

Finally, we have a much defaced poem in the **Book of
Fermoy** (manuscript: Egerton 92) in which the story of the
White Blackbird is told (127). Enaccan, an old Bard, asked
a blackbird what had whitened its wings on one side, and
the bird replied that it was Christ who made him old, who
had whitened him. The bird then proceeded to relate certain
events it had witnessed in its long life.

He speaks of King Conchobar and the great gatherings of the
Ultonians in ancient days; of Queen Maeve and her expedition
on the Tain bo Cualnge. Far from him now was the vigour of
these gatherings, for he is older than Ross son of Ruadh [tutor
to Cuchulainn]. He has met with Oisin son of Fionn, a man of
wisdom; and with Caoilte with his Fianna; with Morgan, son
of Morann, blood pouring through his body. He had witnessed
the birth of Christ in the flesh. Sweet was his song from the

168

Wood of Cuan (taillte) when the host was destroying Troy (?).
Many had been his adventures since Bran went away on his
ship . . . (128)

All of this reads like a lost cycle of stories in which the
various animals were present at significant points in the
history of the world. If we assume for a moment that this
is so, and take the shamanic pole as the central point in a
series of shamanic experiences, we can express this with the
diagram in Figure 13.

Such a diagram, though purely hypothetical, fits the known
facts and provides us with a kind of glyph which illustrates
the way in which the Oldest Animals were understood – as
markers on the map of time which stretched back beyond the
memory of living men, but which gave them a convenient
extension of memory and a chart wherein they could identify
their own place in the endless stream of creation.

Transformation and Growth

Taliesin's transformations are all explorations of deeper and
deeper levels of the Otherworld, which he discovers through
the persons of the totem beasts and through the elements
which they represent. In the *Hanes Taliesin* the elemental
sequence through which he and Ceridwen pass is plain
to read:

Gwion	Ceridwen	Element
hare	greyhound	earth
fish	otter	water
bird	falcon	air
corn	hen	fire

This apportioning into the various elements of creation can
be taken on a number of levels:
1   Gwion has been in the Cauldron of Ceridwen's womb and
    therefore has been privy to the secrets of creation.
2   He has been through poetic initiation and is at one with
    all creation.
3   He has literally shapeshifted through many metamor-
    phoses, becoming acquainted with their natures.

169

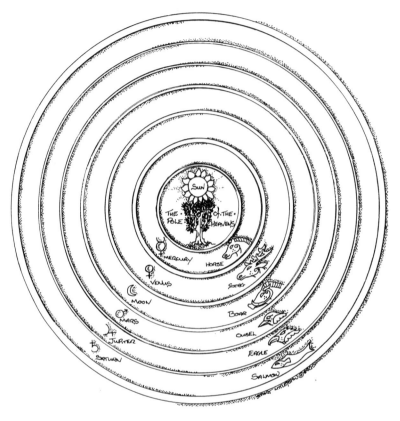

Figure 13   The Cycle of the Oldest Animals aligned with the planets.

The nine-month gestation period in the womb of Ceridwen is so that these cumulative experiences may be assimilated. When Gwion tastes the knowledge of the Cauldron, he receives a lightning flash of total knowing which he must process, mentally and physically. Finally, he is expelled from that realm, i.e. Ceridwen's womb, into the outer world again. Each transformation allows for growth, for change is itself a kind of growth. This is the experience of the initiate: to be saturated with information, then confined in seclusion and made to meditate upon the experience. Taliesin experiences his initiation through the medium of flesh as well as of spiritual understanding. He is brought into subtle relationship with all levels of creation: the elements; the mineral, animal and plant kingdoms. He becomes kindred of the kingdoms.

Among the many ways in which this idea is expressed among the Celts is through the concept of metempsychosis, rebirth in another form, often that of an animal. This is chiefly attributed to Classical authors, but may be presumed to have a foundation in reality. An example of this is to be found in a somewhat corrupt poem belonging to the Taliesin tradition, called **The Dialogue of Arthur and Eliwod** (338). In this the great warrior encounters his nephew Eliwod, who has been reborn in the shape of an eagle. The later part of the dialogue is a very generalised religious homily, but the opening stanzas betray more primitive qualities. The translation is that of Algernon Herbert, with some modifications.

Arthur
I behold a wonder, bardic,
Sitting high among oaken branches,
Is this the vision of an eagle, or an illusion?

Eagle
Arthur, of great fame,
Strength and power to your host.
This is an eagle that you see.

Arthur
I wonder at your being here,
And will ask you, in metre,
What is the vision of an eagle?

Eagle
Arthur, whose fame is widespread,
Whose host is of brilliant aspect,
This eagle have you seen before.

Arthur
Eagle, being on top of the oak,
If you are of the race of birds,
Are you domestic or tame?

Eagle
Arthur, great portent,
Before whose onset nothing stands,
I am the son of Madoc ap Uthyr.

171

Arthur
I know not this kind of eagle,
Frequenting the vales of Cornwall.
Madoc ap Uthyr is dead.

Eagle
Arthur of fierce and subtle speech,
Whose host is uncurtailed wrath,
I was called Eliwod.

Arthur
Eagle of blameless aspect
Whose discourse is sweet,
Are you Eliwod my nephew?

Eagle
Arthur, audacious in the onset,
If I am Eliwod
Am I welcome here?

Arthur
Eagle, true of speech,
If you are Eliwod
Was the slaughter good around you?

Eagle
Arthur, audacious of answer,
Before whom no enemy stands,
From death there is no escape.

To this we should add the following examples:

The Wooing of Etain

In this story, which may be seen as a variant on the theme of
the Oldest Animals discussed above, Etain was the beautiful
Otherworldly daughter of Ailill, King of the north-eastern part
of Eriu. She became the wife of the God Midir, who was
already married to the Druidess Fuamnach. So great was
Fuamnach's jealousy of the new wife that she made a great
spell which turned Etain into a pool of water. Everyone left
the house where this happened and, as the text says:

The heat of the fire and the air and the seething of the ground aided the water so that the pool that was in the middle of the house turned into a worm, and after that the worm became a purple fly [scarlet fly according to Gantz (89)]. It was as big as a man's head, the comeliest in the land. Sweeter than pipes and harps and horns was the sound of her voice and the hum of her wings. Her eyes would shine like precious stones in the dark. The fragrance and the bloom of her would turn away hunger and thirst from anyone around whom she would go. The spray of the drops she shed from her wings would cure all sickness and disease and plague in anyone round whom she would go. She used to attend Midir and go about his land with him, as he went. (25)

But Fuamnach's jealousy did not end here. She summoned a wind which blew the fly far away, so that it was unable to settle on any treetop or hillside for a further seven years. At the end of this time she found refuge with the God Mac ind Oic. But even here she was not finally safe from the vengeance of Fuamnach, who created another wind which blew Etain for another seven years throughout Ireland until at last, exhausted, she landed upon the roof tree of a house in Ulster and fell down into a golden beaker that was set before the wife of the Ultonian hero Etar. She drained the cup and with it the fly that was Etain, and in due time was delivered of a daughter. The text says: 'She was called Etain daughter of Etar. Now it was a thousand and twelve years from the first begetting of Etain by Ailill until her last begetting by Etar.'

Thus the semi-divine maiden had an extended life through being transformed into water, worm and fly, before being reborn as herself in a new body. While she was a fly she was able to make such beautiful sounds that she lulled Midir and his folk, and from the dew of her wings came healing.

Math Son of Mathonwy (144)

In this story from the *Mabinogion*, Math is depicted as the lord of Gwynedd. When not at war his feet were held by the virgin footholder, Goewin. Gilfaethwy, Math's nephew, lusted after her and was assisted by his brother Gwydion, who started a war to separate Math from his footholder. Gilfaethwy then raped Goewin. After the war, Math learned of the plot and insisted that his people give no shelter to his nephews. Calling them before him he struck them with his wand and turned them into hind and stag, in which form they lived for a year, returning with a young fawn which Math turned into a human child. He then struck the brothers again, this time turning them into a sow and a boar. For a year they lived in the woods, returning with a piglet which was also made human by Math. Finally, the enchanter turned them into a wolf and a bitch for a year, until they returned with a cub. All three children were later raised by Math. This ended their punishment, but later in the same story one of the nephews, Gwydion, helped his uncle to create a bride of flowers for their sister Arianrhod's child Llew. The bride was named Blodeuwedd (Owl or Flower Face) and subsequently proved treacherous, helping her lover Gronw to kill Llew. Gwydion later encountered a man whose sow could not be captured, and on following it found it feeding on rotten flesh which was falling from an eagle perched on top of a tree. By his magic Gwydion knew this was the spirit of Llew, and he called him down with three poetic verses, transforming him once again into human form. Blodeuwedd and Gronw were punished, the former by being turned into an owl which was condemned to wander forever in the night, the latter by death.

Thus, in brief, runs this strange and powerful tale of love, revenge and magic. Math ap Mathonwy is the primary Druid and shaman of the British tradition, endowed with tremendous powers (as his name, which means 'Bear son of Bearlike' indicates). As Taliesin remarks in the **Cad Goddeu**:

> There are few who know
> Where the magic wand of Mathonwy
> Grows in the grove.

Shapeshifting is an essential part of Gwydion's role in the story. He was second only to Math in magical abilities. In order to raise a war he engineered matters so that Math sent him to ask for the Otherworldly pigs brought out of Annwn by the hero Pryderi. By a spell Gwydion made twelve horses, greyhounds and their accoutrements, which he fraudulently exchanged for the pigs. Math had to go to war; Gwydion killed Pryderi by magic. Gilfaethwy raped Goewin. As a punishment, Math changed his nephews in the following sequence:

Gwydion	Gilfaethwy
stag	hind
sow	boar
wolf	bitch

After Llew's attempted assassination by Blodeuwedd's lover, he transformed into an eagle's shape. Gwydion found him and called him down from the tree with the following **englynion**:

> Oak that grows between the two banks;
> Darkened is the hill and sky!
> Shall I fail to tell him by his wounds:
> This is Llew!

> Oak that grows in upland ground,
> Does the rain not wet it? Have not
> Nine score tempests drenched it?
> Surely this is Llaw Llaw Gyffes!

> Oak that grows beneath the steep:
> Stately and majestic its aspect!
> Shall I not speak of it –
> Letting Llew come into my lap? (5)

Thus within the canvas of this single story, two generations are transformed: Gwydion and Gilfaethwy and Blodeuwedd and Llew. It is possible to read the poem of the **Cad Goddeu**, discussed at greater length in Chapter Seven, as a partial retelling of the story of Math and his nephews, cast in the form of a teaching poem, with a variety of other references. It shows the subtlety with which the shaman-poets could encode their thoughts whilst still keeping before them the artistic convention of the story.

Rennes Dindsenchas
Equally extraordinary is the following account from the **Rennes Dindsenchas** (241) of the birth of the magical bulls, Donn of Cuailnge and the Whitehorned Bull of Maeve, for which the great struggle between Connaught and Ulster, described in the epic **Tain**, was fought. According to this, Cronn son of Agnoman had two sons who were swineherds (ever a magical occupation in Celtic myth). And they were incarnate in seven

shapes for one year each and their names, when they were swineherds, were Rucht and Rucne.

> Ette and Engan (Wing and Talon) were their names when they were birds. Cu and Cethen were they when wolves. Bled and Blod were they when trout of the Boyne. Crunniuc and Dubmuc when they were worms.
>
> Then Crunniuc went to Glas Cruinn (Cronn's Stream) in Cualnge, and Dubmuc went and lay down in (the well called) Uran Garaid. A cow belonging to Daire mac Fiachna drank a drink out of Glas Cruinn, and the worm therein entered her womb and afterwards became a calf. A cow of (queen) Medb's went and drank a drink out of Garad's Well, and the other worm entered her, and afterwards became a calf in her womb.

If we compare these stories we find that:

Etain became a pool, a worm and a fly, but was reborn of Etar as Etain again. As the Otherworldly wife of Midir she is able to prolong her existence, despite Fuamnach's jealousy.

Tuan Mac Cairell became a stag, a boar, a hawk, and a salmon but was eaten by Cairell's wife to become a man again. He survived endless ages in various shapes, becoming ever wiser.

Gwydion and Gilfaethwy became deer, swine and wolves, before being restored to human shape by Math. They were punished by being thus transformed, and were made to couple as male and female in compensation for the rape of Goewin. This in fact caused them to learn deeper wisdom by way of their animal natures.

Rucht and Rucne became birds, wolves, fish, worms and finally bulls until they slew one another – their final transformation being into spirit form.

We are thus dealing with not one, but three different (though related), kinds of change:

metamorphosis or change of form;

metempsychosis or passing from one body to another after death;

reincarnation or becoming born again.

The most extraordinary thing about all of this is not that the humanity of the characters is changed, but that through their changes, Deity is changed as well. The descent of the initiate into the natures of each created species is an essential learning process. Divinity is implicit in all life – to discover and appreciate that divine nature is not accorded to many people. The initiate seer-poet goes into the hide, the feather, the scale, the atom, the DNA of all life-forms and reassembles them as a totality of knowledge:

> The divinity is by nature incorruptible and eternal, but it undergoes certain transformations under the influence of fate and of an ineluctable law. Sometimes it diversifies into all kinds of different forms, qualities and conditions as is the present case, and it then constitutes what we call world ... When the transformation of the gods ends in the ordering of the world ... wise men describe the changes undergone by innuendo as being **a tearing apart and a dismemberment** and they tell of certain divine deaths and disappearances, then of rebirths and regenerations, all mythological tales which merely obscure allusions in the changes of which I have been speaking. (339)

It is during such breaking down of the essential matter of the self that the shaman experiences his most profound visions – the subject of our next chapter.

Chapter Seven

THE ART OF PROPHECY:
REMEMBERING THE FUTURE

Taliesin, he was powerful in verse,
A Prophet's hope, he knew it.

Rhys Goch Eryri

Truth-Speaking

We have already discussed the importance of Taliesin's 'boasts'; his repeated claims to have been present at certain key points in history. That these are visionary statements is clear enough, but what are we to make of them in the light of the prophetic or divinatory material scattered throughout the whole canon of Taliesin's work? To answer this it is necessary to look at the whole question of prophecy and prediction as an essential part of bardic-shamanic tradition, and to see how this fits in with the other aspects of poetic inspiration (**awen**) elsewhere in this body of work.

Professor N. K. Chadwick, in her book *Poetry and Prophecy* (53), stated the truth simply and boldly:

> Among the early Celtic peoples the inculcation of poetic inspiration and the entire mantic art was developed and elaborated to a degree for which we know of no parallel.

She went on to define the concepts of both in words which can scarcely be bettered:

> Poetry and Prophecy are the expression of human thought at its most intense and concentrated moments, stimulated by excitement, and expressed in artistic form. Prophecy is the expression of thought, whether subjective or objective, and of knowledge, whether of the present, the future, or the past, which has been acquired by inspiration, and which is

178

uttered in a condition of exultation or trance, or couched in the traditional form of such utterances. Poetry, it has been said, is the record of the happiest and best moments of the best and happiest lives.

The element of prophecy within Taliesin's poetry is an important one – though less so than in the works attributed to Merlin and others. Most of Taliesin's prophetic utterances are limited to the 'I have been' kind, where he is said to have been present at various key points in history (or to have participated in various mythological events). Indeed, it may perhaps be more accurate to speak of Taliesin's prophecies as more in the nature of visions. However, prophecy remains one of the key aspects of the shaman's work and, as such, requires some investigation.

Essentially, we know of several methods of obtaining prophetic insight or access to inner wisdom, which was, from the beginning, one of the primary aims of the shaman. Within the Celtic traditions, the three most prominent, as well as the most mysterious, of these methods are known as **Imbas Forosnai**, **Tenm Laida** and **Dichetal do Chennaib**. There are numerous references to these three disciplines throughout Irish mythology, though within these sources they are nowhere defined with any clarity. For a definition of sorts we have to turn to the vast collection of texts known as **Senchus Mor** (111). Here we find listed the three things required of the Ollam-Poet:

> 'Teinm laegda', that is to say, 'teinm', means shining and 'teinm' means to understand . . . through his poem ['laid'] the things which he wishes to say . . .
>   'Imus forosnad', i.e. the abundant knowledge of the learning *given* by the tutor to the pupil . . .
>   'Dichedal do chennaib', i.e. there goes at once from the head of his art the common headship . . .

This is all fairly obscure, but can be explicated somewhat. **Teinm Laida** appears to mean that the poet understands or receives meaning through his poem or, to put it simply, that he experiences inspiration. **Imbas Forosnai** is described as wisdom imbibed directly from master to pupil, as it were 'by word of mouth'. **Dichetal do Chennaib** concerns 'headship', the acquiring of wisdom directly and without contemplation, i.e. in an inspired manner. All three, then, have to do with inspired knowledge or teaching.

Cormac's Glossary (233) to which we have referred as an authoritative source before, reiterates the catalogue of the **Ancient Irish Laws** with significant additions:

> Imbas Forosna, 'Manifestation that Enlightens': (it) discovers what thing soever the poet likes and which he desires to reveal . . . The poet chews a piece of the red [raw] flesh of a pig, or a dog, or a cat, and puts it then on a flagstone behind the door-valve, and chants an incantation over it, and offers it to idol gods, and calls them to him, and leaves them not on the morrow, and then chants over his two palms, and calls again idol gods to him, that his sleep may not be disturbed. Then he puts his two palms on his cheeks and sleeps. And men are watching him that he may not turn over and that no one may disturb him. And then it is revealed to him that for which he was (engaged) till the end of a **nomad** (three days and nights) . . . And therefore it is called **Imm-bas**, to whit, a palm (**bas**) on this side and a palm on that around his head. [St] Patrick banished that and the **Tenm Laida**, 'illumination of song', and declared that no one shall belong to heaven or earth, for it is a denial of baptism. **Dichetal do Chennaib**, 'extempore incantation', however, *that* was left, in right of art, for it is science that causes it, and no offering to devils is necessary, but a declaration from the ends of his bones at once.
>
> (Trans. Whitley Stokes. Insertions in square brackets mine.)

This offers several problems as well as solutions. In the first place the author of the *Glossary* was a Christian who did not fully understand (or approve of) what he was writing about, hence the references to St Patrick and devils. He almost certainly had never seen any of the methods he described, but was relying on literary evidence or hearsay. Thus we have to be careful in trusting what he writes. Nonetheless, there is much here of interest and value.

The description, on the face of it, seems clear enough. The person seeking enlightenment on any subject he wishes through **Imbas Forosnai** first chews a piece of raw meat, then places it on a doorstep and invokes the gods. He then apparently puts his hands over his face and sleeps for two or three days (an alternative version of the *Glossary* says nine days), during which time he is watched over to see that he does not turn over and is not disturbed by anyone. On the face of it this describes a form of trance state quite common among shamans the world over.

The placing of the two palms over the cheeks indicates the covering of the eyes. This seems like a reference to the darkened chamber in which poets were said to seek inspiration – or indeed to a meditational habit in which the outer world is excluded as far as possible. In Norse mythology we hear of Old Kveldulfr, who is said to have been in the habit of wrapping his head in his mantle and remaining silent during the evenings in order to acquire supernatural knowledge. At such times he is said to have been **hamramr**, his soul wandering abroad in animal form.

Other translations of the meaning of the **Imbas Forosnai** are those by J. Loth ('that which closes the eyes but which also illumines'), J. Dunn in his 1914 translation of the **Tain Bo Cuailnge** ('illumination between the hands'), both of which suggest the laying of the hands on the cheeks with the fingers spread, so that one peers out as if between the bars of a cage. It is to be noted that the three animals mentioned in the *Glossary*, the pig, the dog and the cat, were significant totem animals. Also we notice that the text does not say that the subject *ate* the meat, only that he 'chewed' it, and afterwards laid it behind the door. This almost certainly refers to the ancient sanctity of the threshold, across which one could not pass unless invited, and to a possible altar stone set up near the door for offerings to the household gods.

Fionn's Wisdom Tooth

The question of chewing the raw meat leads us to examine the appearances of **Imbas Forosnai** in the literature relating to the Irish hero Fionn Mac Cumhail who, as we have already seen, is related to Taliesin at a number of levels. Fionn is several times referred to as a poet and magician – indeed, he could be said to be more correctly described in these terms than as a hero, despite his prodigious feats of strength and warlike demeanour. We have already heard how he came by his wisdom and knowledge in a manner similar to that of Taliesin – by either eating the flesh of the Salmon of Wisdom, drinking the water of the **sidhe** or trapping his thumb in the doorway to a **sidhe** mound.

181

Figure 14 The Wonderful Child with the Oracular Birds *The lower half of this carving shows a youth tending a fire on which he is roasting a heart. He has his thumb in his mouth. Above is a man in a tree with two stylised birds.*
Possibly both are references to the Taliesin-Fionn myth.

Unlike Taliesin, whose received knowledge remained with him, Fionn had to revive his memory by chewing his thumb. In the collection of tales known as the *Fiannagecht* (204) the phrase is 'Fionn put his thumb into his mouth; when he took it out again, his **imbas** enlightened him.' This suggests that **imbas** was akin to the **awen** received by Taliesin, and recalls the chewing of raw flesh in the above account. If Fionn at one time did the same it would account for the later addition of the Thumb of Wisdom theme, and, since chewing suggests teeth, of the still later development in which he acquired a Tooth of Wisdom.

In other texts relating to Fionn's career we find this to be so, in addition to some clear indications of the way in which **Imbas Forosnai**, as well as the other disciplines mentioned above, was put into operation. A story called **Finn and the Phantoms** (296) illustrates this.

Fionn and his companions arrived at a house occupied by strange phantoms whose leader was a giant. He slew Fionn's horse and made a pretence of cooking its flesh, which was then offered to the heroes. However, it is implicitly stated that the meat was uncooked, and Fionn refused it. A later poem, on the same theme, has him say:

Take away thy food, o giant!
For I have never devoured raw food.
I will never eat it from today till Doom.

Fionn and his companions were then separated, Fionn alone being left behind and apparently beaten (or shaken) by the phantoms. He placed his thumb under his tooth of wisdom and found both the reason for the phantoms' attack upon him, and the strength to remain through the night unharmed. In the morning the phantoms had fled and their house vanished.

The interesting point here is that we have the themes of eating raw flesh and the presence of **Imbas Forosnai** in a clearly associated way. The inference is, here as elsewhere, that the food of the Otherworld is *always* uncooked, hence perhaps the well-known prohibition of eating the food of Faery, those who do so being afflicted ever after or being forced to remain in the inner realm. Fionn himself should undoubtedly have remained within the **sidhe**, had he not been outside when he drank of its enchanted water or trapped his thumb in the door. Part of him, indeed, remained within, while his physical self walked abroad in the realm of men.

Nora Chadwick, commentating on this story (52), suggests that in an earlier version of the tale, Fionn probably did not refuse the meat, and that his final vision came about as a result of chewing the raw food. She notes also that in the text of *Cormac's Glossary*, quoted above, there is a suggestion that the sleeper had to be shaken awake by those who watched over him, and points out that Fionn was apparently shaken about, either by the phantoms, or by his own men when they came upon him next day. This in turn recalls another form of divinatory sleep, known as **Tarbh Feis**, 'Bull Feast', in which a bull, preferably white, is first slaughtered and then cooked. The man desiring illumination then eats of the flesh and broth and goes to sleep. Four Druids then chant **or firindi**, 'true speech', over him, and he sees a vision which answers his question. Nor should we forget that in the Welsh story **The Dream of Rhonabwy** (144) the hero falls asleep on a yellow cow's hide and dreams a long and complex dream of the heroic Arthur. To this may be compared the procedure of the Yakut shamans of Northern Siberia, who lay on a white mare's skin before beginning their visionary voyage to the Otherworld.

This confirms the opinion expressed in Chapter Two that the element of entranced sleep was an important aspect of Celtic divinatory rites.

The Treasure of Darkness

The **Senchus Mor**, referring again to **Teinm Laida** offers further explanation:

> The chief poet, i.e. the learned poet who explains or exhibits the great extent of his knowledge by composing a quatrain without thinking ... At this day it is by the ends of his bones he effects it ... And the way in which it is done is this: When the poet sees the person or thing before him he makes a verse at once with the ends of his fingers, or in his mind without studying, and he composes and repeats at the same time ... but this is not the way it was done before Patrick's time ... [then] the poet placed his staff upon the person's body or upon his head, and found out his name, and the name of his father and mother, and discovered every unknown thing that was proposed to him, in a minute or two or three; and this is **Teinm Laegha**, or **Imus Forosna**, for the same thing used to be revealed by means of them; but they were performed after a different manner, i.e. a different kind of offering was made at each. (111)

Despite the fact that the author here confuses **Teinm Laida** with **Imbas Forosnai**, what he says is of itself interesting. The introduction of the poet's staff at this juncture leads us into a completely different area. **Imbas Forosnai** itself is a wholly interior act; **Teinm Laida**, by this definition, requires a wand or staff of power. Two stories illustrate this, both from *Cormac's Glossary* (233). The first concerns the blind poet, Lugaid, who arrived one day in Bangor, was shown a skull and asked whose head it was. Lugaid told them to put the end of the poet's wand upon it, whereat he said, 'The tempestuous water, the waters of the whirlpool destroyed Breccan. This is the head of Breccan's

184

dog; and . . . Breccan was drowned with his people in that whirlpool.'

Curiously enough, the second story also concerns the skull of a dog, which had been discovered by Connlae and taken to the poet Moen. 'Then the poet solved it by **tenm laido** (sic), "illumination of song", and said . . . "Thou wast dear in this house . . . This, says he, is the head of Mugh-eme, the first lapdog that was brought into Ireland." ' (111)

In the first story the method is described (the use of the poet's wand) while in the second the process is named without being described. This may lead us to suppose that the same method was used in both cases, and that we may deduce that **Teinm Laida** was in fact divination by wand. Other references to this staff suggest that it was carved with Ogam, and that it was regarded as a channel of the poet's power. Certainly, the following quotation, from a 17th Century *Description of the Western Isles of Scotland* by M. Martin, seems to bear out the reality of conveying visionary insights by touch alone.

> All those who have the second sight do not always see these visions at once, though they be together at the time. But if one who has this faculty designedly touch his fellow-seer at the instant of the vision's appearing then the second sees it as well as the first; and this is sometimes discerned by those that are near them on such occasions. (180)

In another story from *Cormac's Glossary* Fionn himself discovers the identity of a body from which the head had been taken. It was that of his Fool, Lomna the Coward, who had been murdered at the instigation of Fionn's wife. The body was brought to him to identify:

> Then Fionn put his thumb into his mouth, and he chanted by **tenm laido** (sic), 'illumination of song', and he said:
>
> > He has not been killed by people –
> > He has not been killed by the people of Laighne –
> > He has not been killed by a wild boar –
> > He has not been killed by a fall –
> > He has not died on his bed – Lomna!
>
> This is Lomna's body . . . His enemies have taken the head from him. (52)

185

Fionn next went in search of the murderer, Cairpre of the clan of Luaighne, and found him and his men in an otherwise empty house, cooking a fish and distributing it. Lomna's head was on a spit by the fire and was speaking in oracular verse. A special note is made that the head received none of the fish – as though this were an unusual omission. The head was then heard to say, 'You have divided a share . . . [but] a better division would be made by a drunken servant. I would like a piece of the stomach. The Fianna will hate the Luaighne for this!' Fionn then kills Cairpre.

This bizarre story is complemented by one which relates Fionn's own death. He was killed while crossing the Boyne river and his head cut off and placed on a spike by the fire. Then the man who had killed him proceeded to divide the fish he had caught into two portions. But every time he did so he found that somehow he had three portions instead of two. Finally the head announced that it required a portion of the fish for itself.

Nora Chadwick, who includes both these stories in her study of divinatory systems (52), makes the following comment:

> Can [. . . the] proximity [. . . of the heads] to the fire have anything to do with the term **tenm loida**, which is usually given to the songs chanted by such heads? The word **tenm** is generally regarded as derived from a root, **tep-**, 'heat'. Is it possible that in the first instance a **tenm** loida was the chant of a severed head beside the fire at a feast?

We may think here of the instance of Bendigeidfran, Bran the Blessed who, according to Welsh mythology, ordered his own head to be severed after he was wounded by a poisoned spear. The head then accompanied seven heroes, including Taliesin, to the Otherworldly island of Gwales, where the head entertained them in wisdom and song at a great ongoing feast. Again we have the theme of the oracular head by the fire and in the presence of food. It is tempting to believe that here we have a distant echo of a ritual in which the sacrifice was beheaded. (See the numerous stories of Beheading Games in Celtic mythology (187).) Then, when placed by the fire in the feasting hall, the head proceeded to give oracular advice – perhaps after the supplicant had chewed on some raw flesh?

The fact that fish is mentioned specifically in both instances reminds us of Fionn's partaking of the Salmon of Wisdom.

Two other stories are worth mentioning in this context. The first is once again from the Fionn cycle. In a story known as **Bruden Atha** (59) Fionn made peace with his enemy Fothad Canainne and invited him to a feast. Fothad, however, refused, on the unusual grounds that it was forbidden for him 'to drink ale without dead heads in his presence'. In the second grim little tale, the poet DonnBo was asked to recite before King Murchad Mac Briain on the evening before a battle. DonnBo replied that he was unable to do so that night, but that he would entertain them the next evening. In the battle he was killed, though his companions were victorious, and when they settled to their victory celebration, a warrior was dispatched to retrieve the poet's head. When the man came near to the body he heard sweet music and discovered the head in some rushes. It addressed him, 'I am DonnBo ... I have been pledged to make music tonight ...'. The warrior took the head back to the hall and placed it on a pillar. Then DonnBo 'turned his face to the wall of the house, so that it might be dark to him' and sang so sweetly and plaintively that the men were moved to tears and the warrior was soon ordered to return the head faithfully to the body.

In this story we not only have a further instance of an oracular head singing by a fire in a great hall but also, significantly, that the head turns its face to the wall in search of darkness – surely yet further evidence of the powerful connection between oracular utterance and the dark, or of the choice between light and dark wisdom discussed in Chapter Three.

What is so interesting about this in the context of both **Imbas Forosnai** and **Teinm Laida** is that they are also associated with light and fire – the fire of illumination itself. Both **forosna** and **teinm** have the element of burning, heat and brightness, suggesting that the definition of **Imbas Forosnai** as 'wisdom that illumines' refers to a literal illumination, such as the brilliant light which, in Irish tradition, is said to blast the eyes of all who drink from Nechtan's well (87). Patrick K. Ford, who has dealt with this material at length, points to similar instances from Iranian and Indian mythology of a brilliant light which illuminates at the same time as it blinds. It may be that here we have the seed from which sprang the later tradition that bards who had been blind from birth were the best; a tradition which was still operating as late as the 18th Century with the famous Irish harper O'Carolan. Such men were believed to have a special insight into the Otherworld since they could not see that in which they lived, and it is possible to believe that part of the initiation which resulted in an ability to prophesy included a ritual assumption of blindness.

This is the experience of the sun shining at midnight, which is common to the initiatory systems of many traditions, including that of Lucius Apuleius (19). The keeper of the secrets of Celtic tradition is the Dark Woman of Knowledge, the ancestral Mother, to whose presence the practitioner goes in vision, and from whom he is reborn. Nor should we forget that the very act of birth itself entails coming forth from a dark place into light!

It is notable that, in the case of the seeker after knowledge in *Cormac's Glossary*, he is able to deliver his oracular speech after sleeping in a darkened cave. To this we may add that Taliesin himself uttered his first song after he was released from within the confines of a dark bag and that his brow was so bright that he received the name which meant 'radiant brow'. A further story from the **Echta Cormaic** (59) seems to bear this out.

Here we are told that the poet Morann, who later became recognised as a great sage, was born with a caul over his head which was only removed when he was immersed in the sea, and the ninth wave (traditionally associated with poetic insight) washed it off. He at once delivered a song which began:

> Worship, ye mortals,
> God over the beautiful world!

which might indeed have come from the lips of Taliesin.

What we seem to be seeing here is a confused memory of a rite in which the bard or shaman sought illumination literally by first entering a darkened place or by covering his eyes with his hands and then, after a time, being brought forth into a brightly lit place – either fire or sunlight – at which point he gave forth his inspired utterance to all who were present. As is repeatedly the case in shamanic traditions, the physical manifesting of the inner experience assisted in the acquiring of the mantic fit. To this day, in modern magical practice, ritual and meditation perform the same function, externalising the mysteries so that they are confirmed both in the operants and in those who are looking on. Even the singing heads, of which there are sufficient within Celtic mythology to warrant a separate study, seem to bear out this theory. They are, after all, dead – at least nominally – and, unlike the Cauldron-Born warriors who are brought back to life in **The Story of Branwen** (see Chapter One), but who are unable to speak of their experience, they are able to return with messages after their shamanic ritual death.

The ethnologist Knud Rasmussen reported of Eskimo shamans that they often experience a mysterious light

> ... which the shaman suddenly feels in his body, inside his head, within the brain, an inexplicable searchlight, a luminous fire, which enables him to see in the dark, both literally and metaphorically speaking, for he can now, even with closed eyes, see through darkness and perceive things and coming events which are hidden from others. (120)

The Nuts of Wisdom

Much argument has raged over the exact meaning of **Dichetal do Chennaib**, the third of our Divinatory practices, though it is, indeed, closely aligned with both the others. Some would translate it as 'extempore recital', others 'extempore or inspired incantation', while others prefer 'incantation from the ends (of the fingers)' or even 'the ends of the bones', a description which is also applied to **Imbas Forosnai** by the author of *Cormac's Glossary*. It is evident that another kind of inspired utterance is being referred to here, whilst the actual meaning of the Irish words **dicetla**, according to O'Curry (232) is 'spells'. So we have 'inspired spells'. The fact that these are, somehow, conveyed from the ends of the fingers or bones poses a deeper problem. Does it mean that the poet made 'passes' with his hands, like a stage magician, or that he literally 'spelled out' words in Ogam to constitute the spell? Or could it also mean that the bones were the Ogam sticks discussed in Chapter Seven?

In the light of the evidence it seems probable that a kind of hypnotic mantra of power words might be inferred, which

189

could either enable the poet to enter an immediate trance or to cause some change in events. This is in line with shamanic practice, which is full of instances of self-induced trance brought about through chanting or drumming.

The fact that, alone among the methods of divination mentioned in *Cormac's Glossary* (233), **Dichetal do Chennaib** was allowed to be practised even after Patrick had put the other two disciplines under interdict, indicates that it was seen as a less primitive and, therefore, less 'dangerous' practice than the rest. It is possible that the Saint was convinced of this by some deliberate confusion. There seems little doubt that **Dichetal** is every bit as powerful a method of divination as the others and that it was used primarily by poets seeking inspiration which enabled them to compose and deliver their songs with astonishing readiness.

The variety of translations possible for each one of these disciplines has continued to confuse the issue. Quite clearly, the early commentators on **Dichetal do Chennaib**, as well as **Imbas Forosnai** and **Teinm Laida**, frequently confused the methods. However, 'meditation by finger ends' with its accompanying sense of 'the cracking open of the nut' makes it clear that **Dichetal** consisted of somehow imbibing the fruit of the hazel nut.

Several commentators have suggested (244, 52, 87) that **Teinm Laida** meant, literally, 'the chewing (or breaking open) of the pith'. Some assume that this refers to Fionn's thumb, which he is said to chew 'from the skin to the flesh, from the flesh to the bone, from the bone to the marrow, from the marrow to the juice' (Curtin: *Hero Tales of Ireland*). Yet in the context of the stories it would seem that what is actually being referred to is the eating of a nut – the sense of the word **teinm** being 'to crack open, or husk, (a nut)'. In this instance we may infer that the nut in question is one of the Nine Hazels of (Poetic) Wisdom referred to in various texts. The story of the origin of the River Shannon is contained in *The Dindsenchas* (107), a vast compilation of lore connected to physical sites in Ireland, and it tells us how:

Sinend daughter of Lodan Lucharglan ... went to Connla's Well which is under the sea, to behold it. That is a well at which are the hazels and inspirations of wisdom, that is the hazels of science and poetry, and in the same hour their fruit and their blossoms and their foliage break forth, and these fall on the well in the same shower, which raises on the water a royal surge of purple. Then the salmon chew the fruit, and the juice of the nuts is in their bellies. And seven streams of wisdom spring forth and turn there again.

Another text, a poetic tract on the subject of the getting of wisdom, says:

Into this spring [Segais] fell these nuts first of all, then out of the well every seven years or every year into the Boyne river, so that they – filled with **imus** (magical poetic quality) – come to certain persons. These drank the **imus** out of them, so that they then became master poets. (87)

The river Boyne, we may note, under the protection of the Goddess Boann, is considered to be the source of inspiration in Irish poetic tradition in much the same way that those who are reborn of Ceridwen's cauldron are likewise full of knowledge in British tradition. Not only Fionn went there, for as it is said elsewhere: 'the poets thought that the place where poetry was revealed always was on the brink of water.'

(Immacallum in da Thuarad, quoted by Ford, 86)

Thus the fruit of the tree of wisdom is carried downstream, to rise again in Nechtan's Well, or to be eaten by those in search of wisdom, like Fionn, in the flesh of the Salmon. Here we come as near as we can to a definition of **Dichetal do Chennaib**, the gaining of wisdom through the cracking open and eating of the fruit of the sacred Wisdom-Nuts, the hazels from the Otherworldly Well of Segais, which rises in the inner realms but sends forth its messages to the poets who seek to know.

A fourth method, of which almost nothing is known, is mentioned in the unpublished text of **Bretha Nemed** (316). This is **Anamain Cetharreach**, 'Anamain of the Four Intervals'. According to Calvert Watkins this is the name of an archaic metre, but also contains the sense of both inspiration and breath. We have already seen the links between **awen** and breathing; this further evidence suggests an even stronger link, pointing to the imbibing of wisdom from the element of air itself. Alternatively, there is a further sense of 'soul', *ana-monn, in the word aanamain, from which we may draw our own conclusions.

The Men Who Read Clouds

One final method of divination requires our attention before we move onward. This is **neladoracht**, 'divination by clouds'. An example from Manuscript Mat. 285 in Dublin refers to a certain king of Ireland named Dathi who happened to be at his residence on **Croc-na-Druad** (Druid's Hill) one Samhain Eve, and demanded of his druid to forecast the events of the next year.

> The druid went to the top of the hill, where he remained the night, returning at sunrise. He then addressed the king with these words: 'Are you asleep, O King of Erin and Alban [Scotland]?' 'Why the addition to my title' asked the King, 'I am not king of Alban'. To which the Druid answered: 'I have consulted the clouds of the men of Erin, and have discovered that you shall make a conquest of Alban, Britain and Gaul,' which accordingly he did soon afterwards. (149)

We have now looked at some length into the mysteries of poetic and shamanic inspiration among the Celts, drawing mostly upon the Irish traditions which are better preserved than those of Britain. We can be assured that identical or similar methods to those discussed above were practised in Wales and Scotland and the South. That these have not been preserved is due, to a considerable extent, to the accidents of history, which made it difficult to maintain the same continuity as we find in Ireland. At least one text, the **Itinerarum Cambriae** of Gerald the Welshman, though late by comparison with the Irish material, does more than merely suggest that parallel traditions existed in Britain. In Book One, Chapter Sixteen of his discourse Gerald writes of the 'Soothsayers' of the nation.

> There are certain persons in Cambria . . . called **Awenyddion**, or people inspired; when consulted upon any doubtful event, they roar out violently, are rendered beside themselves, and become, as it were, possessed by a spirit. They do not deliver the answer to what is required in a coherent manner; but the person who skilfully observes them will find, after many

preambles ... the desired explanation conveyed in some turn of a word: they are then roused from their ecstasy, as from a deep sleep, and, as it were, by violence compelled to return to their proper senses. After having answered the questions, they do not recover till violently shaken by other people; nor can they remember the replies they have given ... These gifts are usually conferred upon them in dreams: some seem to have sweet milk or honey poured on their lips; others fancy that a written schedule is applied to their lips, and on awakening they publicly declare that they have received this gift. (93)

Surely these **Awenyddion** – the word means 'inspired ones' and contains the root **awen** which we have encountered before – are not so very different from the Irish shaman-poets who had to be shaken before they would awake and who immediately delivered themselves of prophecies that were often hard to understand?

Apart from these fascinating accounts there also exists a vast collection of actual prophetic literature which, although it offers little in the way of clues to the methods involved in obtaining inner knowledge, does reflect the state of mind and situation of the people who sought it.

Thus, although the fate of the prophetic arts in Britain lies outside the scope of the present book, we must look at some of its manifestations, especially as they appear in the writings of Taliesin and Myrddin.

The Fate of Prophecy

The passing of Arthur in c. 555 seemed to signal an end to organised resistance on the part of the Britons against their Saxon invaders. In reality other chieftains, like Owein Gwynedd, continued to carry out sporadic raids on the enemy, and enclaves of native resistance existed across the country. Arthur's period as leader of the resistance had, in any case, blunted the force of the invasion to the extent that it became almost a semi-peaceful settlement. Added to this was the belief, which came into operation within months of his passing, that Arthur would one day return to lead his people to victory. Arthur returned to the Otherworld from which he had sprung, becoming a living legend in the souls of the British.

This situation created the need for a continuing Bardic tradition, above all for the art of prophecy. Taliesin, Myrddin and, to a lesser extent, Myrddin's sister Gwenddydd, all prophesied the return of Arthur (whom Taliesin at least outlived); in later times these prophecies were taken up, elaborated and added to, giving rise to a vast body of vaticinatory literature – much of it forged – which began to be applied to later political events.

As Margaret Griffiths pointed out in her study of early Welsh prophetic literature:

> During this period between the Sixth and Twelfth Centuries when the Britons were losing their lands and being gradually pushed westward till eventually they were confined to Wales, vaticination played an extremely important part in spurring on the hopes of the people from time to time. (340)

The Britons in Wales never ceased to fight the Saeson (English) and to hope for the appearance of a deliverer, whether in the shape of Arthur, Owein or Cadwaladyr, or of countless lesser figures. The prophetic literature of the period AD 600–1500 abounds with references to the strength of the Britons and their expected triumphs, to battles they have fought or will fight. To what extent this was recognised, and with what effect, is shown in the statute of Edward I against 'westours, Bards, Rhymers and others, idlers and vagabonds ... lest by their invectives and lies they lead the people to mischief and burden the common people with their impositions' (340). Henry IV was later even more specific in his condemnation of wandering minstrels who by their '*divinations*' (my italics) and lies were the causes of insurrection and rebellion in Wales'. (ibid.)

These factors played no small part in the way the ancient texts were handled, and the treatment they received at the hands of 'English' scribes. It is yet another reason why we have to treat the material which has come down to us with particular sensitivity.

The Great Prophecy

The best known of the prophetic poems found in *The Book of Taliesin* is known as **Armes Prydein Fawr**, 'The Great Prophecy of Britain' (324). It is generally supposed to have been written in the 9th Century and Sir Ifor Williams, the poem's editor, established that in its present form it was written about AD 930 and deals with historical events relating to the reign of King Athelstan. References to the English are clear; and a kind of pan-Celtic alliance between the Scots of Dal Riada, the Irish Gaeltacht and possibly the Danes settled around Dublin, is described in terms specific enough to add to the evidence. Many of the same details appear in the *Vita Merlini*, where this and other references indicate that Geoffrey of Monmouth knew the **Armes Prydein** and borrowed from it for Merlin's prophecies – as he may well have borrowed from other prophetic works in the *Book of Taliesin*.

Such, at least, is the argument put forward by Professor Williams (324). On the strength of this Taliesin could not possibly be the author of the work. However, there are other possibilities to consider.

First, if we consider the text of the poem as a whole, it will be seen at once that if the first verse and parts of the last two verses are deleted, what remains is an account of warfare against the Saxons which could very easily refer to Arthur. It was by no means unusual, as we have seen, for later heroes, such as Owein Gwynedd, to be substituted for earlier figures. Here we find Cynan and Cadwaladwyr referred to, although the substitution of Arthur's name would make the work an accurate, possibly even first-hand, account of the 6th Century wars against the Saxons, cast in a predictive mode by Taliesin himself.

Even Professor Williams suggests (324) that at one time the poem might have been called **Armes Taliesin** (The Prophecy of Taliesin) and that it had a more direct bearing on the poet's prophetic skills. This seems to be a strong possibility. Once again we have the situation where a cleric (the references to God and the Virgin make it clear that the copyist was a churchman) has taken an existing poem by Taliesin, probably referring to contemporary events in the 6th Century and, by interpolating material in the same style, formed a contemporary political statement about the harsh taxes levied by the English under Athelstan, and the battles which took place because of them.

We should also bear in mind that it is generally accepted that Geoffrey borrowed material from various sources dating from various periods, which he then placed in the mouth of Merlin (a fact which internal evidence supports). This indicates that the material in the **Armes** could also have been of an early date – one which Geoffrey saw, quite rightly, as belonging to his account of Arthurian Britain. Added to this it is also by no means impossible that the ancient British prophecies referred to by Gildas may indeed have been the **Armes Prydein**, in at least one of its many versions.

Searching for a shorter version of the prophecy, Professor Williams came across another poem in the *Book of Taliesin* which shows clear signs of being an earlier version of the **Armes**. It is given here in our version.

The Lesser Prophecy of Britain

My Awen foretells the coming of a multitude
Possessed of wealth and peace;
Of a generous sovereign, and eloquent princes –
But after this tranquillity, commotion in every place.

The seven sons of Beli will arise.
Caswallawn, Lludd, and Custennyn.
They will crack the heart of Prydein.
The country in uproar as far as Blathaon:
Exhausted warriors, tired mounts,
A country ravaged to its borders.
The Cymry will loose all their bounty,
And their servants seek new masters.

Lleminawg will come,
An ambitious man,
To subdue Mona,
To ruin Gwynedd.
From its borders to its heartland,
Its beginning to its end,
He will take its pledges.
Furious his face,
Submitting to no-one,
Cymry or Saeson.

Another will come from concealment
Bringing universal slaughter:
How extensive his armies,
A triumph to the Britons!

The reference here to a *lleminawg*, a 'predatory' or 'ambitious' man, who may have been from Ireland, recalls the figure of Llwch Lleminawg in the **Preiddeu Annwn** (168) who is described in similar terms as a fiery, powerful man with a flaming sword. That this may well be the first mention in literature of the character later known as Lancelot of the Lake is itself not without significance; for the argument for an earlier provenance for the **Armes Prydein** it is of particular importance, since this seems to establish the origin of Lancelot as a character and to push back the date of the Prophecy by three hundred years.

Apart from this the poem could be referring to the coming of Uther and Ambrosius who, according to various chronicles, were forced to flee into hiding in Brittany, from where they returned, lead by Ambrosius, to win back their lands. Reference to 'Blathaon' – possibly Bath, home of the bird-winged shaman Bladud (292) – which was known to have been the site of a famous battle of the Arthurian or pre-Arthurian period, seems to confirm this.

One could continue to speculate, but clearly the poem contains material from a much earlier period than the 9th Century, some of which may indeed relate to Arthur or to the time when he was active.

Taliesin and Virgil

There are a number of connections between Taliesin and the figure of Virgil who, like Taliesin, began as a historical poet and became widely celebrated as a magician in the medieval stories of his birth and deeds. In part this must stem from the sacredness and power of the word, especially the written word. Those who had the power of writing or composing words and music were especially gifted. The word 'shaman' itself means 'singer', thus poets like Taliesin and Virgil were attributed initially with prophetic and later with magical powers.

Just as Taliesin was born (or reborn) strangely, so Virgil is said to have been conceived after his mother drank a golden cordial, and when her son was born he had a golden star on his brows, just as Taliesin is named for the light emanating from his brow.

This makes sense of the curious reference in the *Hanes Taliesin* to Ceridwen consulting 'the books of Fferyllt' which, though it is sometimes translated as 'philosophers' or 'scientists', is really a Welsh attempt to form the name Virgil. Interestingly, the modern Welsh word *fferyllt* means chemist.

Elsewhere, in the poem **Cad Goddeu**, are the lines:

> Golden, gold-skinned, I shall deck myself in riches,
> And I shall be in luxury because of the prophecy of Virgil.
>
> > (trans. Ford, 2)

This may mean, simply, that Taliesin will live forever in glory because of the Resurrection of Christ (i.e. the 'Prophecy of Virgil' in the Fourth Eclogue). But in a poet as subtle as Taliesin we may look further. Virgil was himself famed and lauded by Christians for a poem in his **Eclogues** in which he seemed to prophesy the coming of Christ. Taliesin is said, by the Jersey poet Wace (313), to have made a similar prophecy (though here we are in mythic time again, since Taliesin lived long after the birth of Christ). Perhaps between these two ideas there is a kind of sense. Taliesin's prophetic utterances, his 'boasts' placed him at many of the great events of history, including the birth and crucifixion of Christ. Again, the reference to 'living in luxury' may possibly be a reference to the tradition found in some versions of the text which lists **The Thirteen Treasures of Britain** that Taliesin, rather than the more usually named Merlin, is said to have collected and became the guardian of these Hallows. This is also in line with what we know of him, since the chief of these Hallows was the Horn (substitute Cauldron) of Bran, as we know from the story of **Branwen Daughter of Llyr**, in the *Mabinogion*, that Taliesin did indeed go in search of this Cauldron (cf. Chapter One).

All of these stray pieces of information demonstrate how easily the two figures became associated, and how easy it would have been for one to lend aspects of this story to the other. Virgil was certainly known about at the time when the *Hanes Taliesin* was being first set down, and it is possible that aspects of Virgil's story became attached to that of the great Welsh bard (333).

Merlin and Taliesin

It is impossible to discuss the prophetic writings of Taliesin without dealing with those of Myrddin, who may well have been his contemporary and who certainly shares many of his archetypal attributes.

The history of Myrddin, or Merlin to give him his more familiar name, has been dealt with elsewhere and needs little repetition here. There is still some debate as to whether the Myrddin who wrote the poems which appear in the *Black Book of Carmarthen* (250) is the same character as Arthur's premier enchanter. There is also a third Merlin figure, Sylvestris, whom Count Tolstoy believes to have been the original, historical bard. Certainly, there are no direct references to Arthur or to events relating to the time in any of Myrddin's surviving works, and we may draw what conclusions we like from this.

The writings of the medieval pseudo-historian Geoffrey of Monmouth have provided us with both the identification of Myrddin with Merlin, and the fullest account of his prophetic utterances. Readers may recall the famous scene at the site of Vortigern's tower where Merlin, brought there as a child sacrifice, not only confounds the king's druids (in a scene strongly reminiscent of Taliesin's defeat of Maelgwn's druids) but gives out a lengthy series of prophecies which extend from Vortigern's imminent death to the end of time. These apocalyptic works have been recently explored by R. J. Stewart, whose commentaries and conclusions indicate not only that Geoffrey was in receipt of a profound array of original material, but that he was embodying ancient, traditional, prophetic works, much of which can be shown to have borne fruit.

If we look more closely at this tradition we find some striking points of reference which throw further light upon the whole prophetic tradition as it is contained in the Taliesin material.

Geoffrey himself claimed as his source for the whole of his *History of the Kings of Britain* (341) an ancient book in the British tongue, the existence of which has been debated ever since. Whether such a book really existed or not is, ultimately, not important. Geoffrey drew upon a still older work than any such physical manifestation – the living tradition of Britain. He was undoubtedly in receipt of authentic material, which dealt with the ancient past. Whether it was written on vellum or on the wind does not matter.

Another writer, roughly contemporary with Geoffrey of Monmouth and sometimes considered as only slightly more reliable, is Giraldus Cambrensis. His best known works are the *Topographica Hibernia*, 'History and Topography of Ireland' (92), the *Itinerarium Cambriae*, 'Journey Through Wales', and the *Descriptio Cambriae*, 'Description of Wales' (93). As we have already seen these contain much that is earlier than their date of composition in the 12th Century. But Giraldus wrote another book, *Expgunatio Hibernica*, 'The Exploration of Scotland', of which unfortunately we possess only the first two of the proposed three books, and a fragmentary introduction to the third, which was to have contained the prophecies of Merlin. However, although the prophecies themselves are missing, Giraldus' comments about his sources are revealing in the extreme.

He refers to them as **Liber Vaticiniorum**, 'Books of Prophecy', and talks of translating them from 'the barbarous garb of the British tongue' (340). He goes on to say that the prophecies were orally retained by many British bards, but that very few were actually committed to writing. Their publication, he adds, was much desired by King Henry II. Giraldus himself, being insufficiently skilled in the Welsh language, was assisted in his translations by native speakers. His next comment is even more illuminating. These prophecies are, he says, **much adulterated by modern additions, added by the bards**, all of which Giraldus has excluded, keeping only what seemed true to their rudeness and simplicity! (340)

Such a statement, coming from the pen of a writer himself given to degrees of exaggeration, is amusing. It is also significant, recognising as it does not only the existence of primitive material, but also the tendency in Medieval bards to augment the original material with current prophecies (and doubtless more besides).

Further evidence of the existence of original materials comes in the Merlin prophecies collected by John of Cornwall, a little after those of Geoffrey. He also claimed to have 'translated' them from the Welsh, though John speaks of 'our people' in a way that suggests he was Welsh himself.

The whole question of authenticity is thus brought into prominence. Geoffrey, John of Cornwall, and Giraldus, all testify to the existence of native materials – Giraldus in terms of Bardic wisdom and interpolation. From this it is surely not unreasonable to believe that manuscripts, copied during the early part of the Middle Ages, continued to circulate into the

17th Century, containing fragments of native lore; and that this was substantially embroidered by successive copyists and those studying the ancient history and lore of Britain.

William of Newburgh, a historian during the same century as Geoffrey of Monmouth, says of the earlier historian that he considerably added to the original prophecies while he was **translating** them into Latin.

The Converse of Wisemen

On examination the prophecies of Merlin and Taliesin prove to have many points of similarity. All seem to be largely made up of compilations based on much earlier genuine prophetic material, to which later generations have added stanzas in the style of the original bards. If these are successfully isolated and removed from the extant texts, we are left with a good idea of the originals.

The prophecies of Merlin are contained chiefly in long dialogues either between himself and Taliesin, or himself and his sister, Gwendydd, who was herself recognised as a prophet. Apart from these there are a number of curious poems addressed by Merlin to a pig, or to a particular apple tree beneath which he was accustomed to take shelter. All are set during a period of inspired madness, during which time Merlin lived as a wildman in the wilderness, and was visited by various people in search of wisdom. The **Afallanau**, is one of the most famous of these poems. It is given here in our own version.

Afallanau (Appletrees)

I

Sweet appletree, your branches delight me,
Luxuriantly budding, my pride and joy!
I will prophesy before the lord of Macreu,
That on Wednesday, in the valley of Machawy
Blood will flow.
Lloegyr's blades will shine.
But hear, O little pig! on Thursday
The Cymry will rejoice
In their defence of Cyminawd,
Furiously cutting and thrusting.

The Saesons will be slaughtered by our ashen spears,
And their heads used as footballs.
I prophesy the unvarnished truth –
The rising of a child in the secluded South.

II

Sweet and luxuriant appletree,
Great its branches, beautiful its form!
I predict a battle that fills me with fear.
At Pengwern, men drink mead,
But around Cyminawd is a deadly hewing
By a chieftain from Eryri – til only hatred remains.

III

Sweet, yellow appletree,
Growing in Tal Ardd,
I predict a battle at Prydyn,
In defence of frontiers.
Seven ships will come
Across a wide lake,
Seven hundred men come to conquer.
Of those who come, only seven will return
According to my prophecy.

IV

Sweet appletree of luxuriant growth!
I used to find food at its foot,
When, because of a maid,
I slept alone in the woods of Celyddon,
Shield on shoulder, sword on thigh.
Hear, O little pig! listen to my words,
As sweet as birds that sing on Monday –
When the sovereigns come across the sea,
Blessed be the Cymry, because of their strength.

V

Sweet appletree in the glade,
Trodden is the earth around its base.
The men of Rhydderch see me not.
Gwendydd no longer loves nor greets me,
I am hated by Rhydderch's strongest scion.
I have despoiled both his son and daughter:
Death visits them all – why not me?
After Gwenddoleu no one will honour me,
No diversions attend me,

Nor fair women visit me.
Though at Arderydd I wore a golden torque
The swan-white woman despises me now.

VI

Sweet appletree, growing by the river,
Who will thrive on its wondrous fruit?
When my reason was intact
I used to lie at its foot
With a fair wanton maid, of slender form.
Fifty years the plaything of lawless men
I have wandered in gloom among spirits.
After great wealth, and gregarious minstrels,
I have been here so long not even sprites
can lead me astray.
I never sleep, but tremble at the thought
Of my Lord Gwenddoleu, and my own native people.
Long have I suffered unease and longing –
May I be given freedom in the end.

VII

Sweet appletree, with delicate blossom,
Growing, concealed, in the wood!
At daybreak the tale was told me
That my words had offended the most powerful minister,
Not once, not twice, but thrice in a single day.
Christ! that my end had come
Before the killing of Gwendydd's son
Was upon my hands!

VIII

Sweet appletree with your delicate blossom,
Growing amid the thickets of trees!
Chwyfleian fortells,
A tale that will come to pass:
A staff of gold, signifying bravery
Will be given by the glorious Dragon Kings.
The graceful one will vanquish the profaner,
Before the child, bright and bold,
The Saesons shall fall, and bards will flourish.

IX

Sweet appletree of crimson colour,
Growing, concealed, in the wood of Celyddon;
Though men seek your fruit, their search is vain,

203

Until Cadwaladyr comes from Cadfaon's meeting
To Teiwi river and Tywi's lands,
Till anger and anguish come from Aranwynion,
And the long-hairs are tamed.

X

Sweet appletree of crimson colour,
Growing, concealed, in the wood of Celyddon:
Though men seek your fruit, their search is vain,
Till Cadwaladyr comes from Rhyd Rheon's meeting,
And with Cynon advances against the Saesons.
Victorious Cymry, glorious their leaders,
All shall have their rights again,
All Britons rejoice, sounding joyful horns,
Chanting songs of happiness and peace!

All of the prophecies contained herein are of a general kind,
referring to political events, battles and so forth – and to known
events and people. These are identifiable as separate from the
underlying matter of the poems, which is really the story
of Myrddin's madness, and of the period he spent in the
wilderness attended by a pig (a creature sacred to the Celts),
and remembering the terrible battle in which he lost his reason.
He thinks also of his sister Gwendydd, who has deserted him
because he (apparently) killed her son, and of his enemies, who
seek his destruction. Interspersed with this are prophecies of
events which took place long after – probably in the 8th or 9th
Centuries, when heroes like Cynan and Cadwaladyr had replaced
Arthur as the expected deliverer of the Cymry.

Of some interest is the use of the word **Chwyfleian**, which
has the meaning of Sibyl, or prophetess. This may be an oblique
reference to Gwendydd herself, who was reckoned a prophet in
her own right; but it clearly suggests that female prophetesses
were still recognised at this time. Phillip Legaloys, in a private
communication to the author, suggests that it may be related
to the colloquial **quim** (vagina), and that this would make the
meaning of **chwyfleian**, or its variant **hwimleian**, 'Votaress of the
Vagina'. Recalling the context in the life of Myrddin Wyllt, this
has strong possibilities. Especially as the word **cych** (a variant
of **cwch**) means both a boat or coracle, and a hole. The Welsh
Dictionary *Geiriadur Prifysgol Cymru* (81) suggests 'a wild man
of pallid countenance' for **chwifleian**, which may point to a
prudish monk's desire to obscure the real meaning – though

at the same time referring, quite correctly, to the pairing of Wild Man and Sheela-na-Gig. Thus we may well have an obscure reference to a deeper mystery, in which Myrddin the Wild is paired with Gwendydd as a Welsh Green Lady!

That some of the material relating to Myrddin has been suppressed is beyond question, so that we have little or no chance of establishing a full text either of this or of the remaining Myrddin poems. However, if one omits the first three and the last three verses, one arrives at a core of original material which can stand on its own. At one time this probably formed the verse interludes of a longer prose account of Myrddin's life – such a one as evidently formed the basis of Geoffrey of Monmouth's Latin poem *Vita Merlini* (54) which tells the story in full, and makes use of the above poem as well as others which belonged to the ancient saga of Myrddin.

In the versions which follow of Myrddin's other main poems an attempt has been made to provide diplomatic versions in which the obvious interpolations have been edited out, giving an idea of the quality of the original poems.

The Hoianau (Greetings)

Listen, little pig,
O happy little pig!
Do not go rooting
On top of the mountain,
But stay here,
Secluded in the wood,
Hidden from the dogs
Of Rhydderch the Faithful.

I will prophesy –
It will be truth!
From Aber Taradyr
The Cymry will be bound
Under one warlike leader
Of the line of Gwynedd.
Usurpers of the Prydein
He will overcome.

Listen, little pig,
We should hide

From the huntsmen of Mordei
Lest we be discovered.
If we escape –
I'll not complain of fatigue!
I shall predict,
From the back of the ninth wave,
The truth about the White One
Who rode Dyfed to exhaustion,
Who built a church
For those who only half
  believed.
Until Cynan comes
Nothing will be restored.

Listen, little pig!
I lack sleep,
Such a tumult of grief is within
  me.
Fifty years of pain I have
  endured.
Once I saw Gwenddoleu,

With the gift of Princes,
Garnering prey on every side;
Now, he's beneath the sod –
But still restless!
He was the chief of the North,
And the gentlest.

Listen, little pig,
Don't sleep yet!
Rumours reach me
Of perjured chieftains,
And tight-fisted farmers.
Soon, over the sea,
Shall come men in armour
Two-faced men,
On armoured horses,
With destroying spears.
When that happens,
War will come,
Fields will be ploughed
But never reaped.
Women will cuckold
The corpses of their men.
Mourning will come to Caer
  Sallawg.

Listen, little pig,
O pig of truth!
The Sibyl has told me
A wondrous tale.
I predict a Summer full of fury,
Treachery between brothers.
A pledge of peace will be required
From Gwynedd,
Seven hundred ships from Gynt
Blown in by the North wind.
In Aber Dyn they will confer.

Listen, little pig,
O blessed pig!
The Sibyl has told me
A frightful thing:
When Llogria encamps
In the lands of Eddlyn,
Making Deganwy a strong fort
Between Llogrian and Cymru,

A child will appear, leaping,
And the Franks will flee.
At Aber Dulas they will fall,
Sweating in bloody garments.

Listen, little pig,
Go to Gwynedd,
Seek a mate when you rest.
While Rhydderch Hael feasts in
  his hall
He does not know
What sleeplessness I bear
Every night –
Snow to my knees,
Ice in my hair –
Sad my fate!

Listen, little pig!
O blessed pig!
If you had seen
All I have seen
You would not sleep,
Nor root on the hill.
Listen, little pig,
Is not the mountain green?
In my thin cloak
I get no repose!
I grow pale because
Gwendydd comes not.

Listen, little pig,
O bit of brawn!
Don't bury your snout,
Love is neither pledge nor
  play.
This advice I give to
  Gwernabwy:
Don't be a wanton youth.
I'll predict now the battle of
  Machawy,
Where ruddy spears will shine in
  Rhiw Dymdwy,
From the work of contending
  chiefs.
Men will sit, breasts heaving, on
  their saddles,

206

And there will be mourning, and
  woeful mien.
A bear will arise in Deheubarth,
His men will infest Mynwy.
A blessed fate awaits Gwendydd
When Dyfed's prince comes to
  rule.

Listen, little pig!
Are not the thorn buds green
The mountain fair, the earth
  beautiful?
I will predict the battle of
Argoed Llewifain,
Bloody biers after Owein's assault.
When stewards dispute,
When children are perjured,
When Cadwaladyr conquers
  Mona –
Then the Saeson will be driven
  out!

Listen, little pig!
Wonders there will be
In Prydein – but I
Shall not care.
When the people of Mona
Ask questions of the Brython,
That will be a troublesome time!
A superior lord will appear:
Cynan, from the banks of the
  Teiwi.
Confusion will follow –
But he shall have the music of
  Bards to follow!

Listen, little pig –
Do you hear the birds at Caerlleon?
I wish I stood on Mynydd Maon
Watching the bright ones dance.
Instead I'll prophesy
Battle on battle:
At Machawy, on a river,
At Cors Fochno, at Minron,
At Cyminawd, at Caerlleon,
And the battle of Abergwaith,

And the battle of Ieithion . . .
And when this music shall end,
A child will come,
And the Brython will know better
  days.

Listen, little pig,
O little, spotted friend!
Can you hear the sea-birds crying?
A day will come when even
  minstrels
Will be sent away, without their
  portion,
Though they stand at the door,
No gift will come.
A far-flying seagull told me
That strangers will come:
Gwyddyl, Brython, Romans.
There will be confusion then!
And the names of the Gods
Will be taken in vain!
Fighting on both banks of the
  Tywi.

Listen, little pig,
O stout-legged, little one!
Listen to the voices of the
  sea-birds –
Great their clamour.
Minstrels will get no honour,
No fair portion theirs;
In a time when hospitality's
  repugnant,
A youth of strong feelings will
  come.
Then two Idrises will contend for
  land,
And their contention will be long.

Listen, little pig!
It's no use my hearing,
The scream of the gulls.
My hair is thin,
My covering likewise.
The vales are my barn –
Short on corn.

My summer harvest
Brings little relief.
Once, my passion was boundless;
Now I predict,
Before the world ends,
Shameless women,
Passionless men!

Listen little pig,
O little trembling one!

Under this thin blanket,
I find no repose.
Since the battle of Arderydd
I no longer care,
If the sky falls
Or the seas overflow.
But I predict that after many kings
With one bridge on the Taw
And another on the Tywi,
There will be an end to war.

Several verses are omitted here, as being later additions made after the coming of the Normans. As it is, verses 5 to 7 almost certainly belong in this category, though references to the Franks (Normans) may well have been inserted within the individual verses for those to the Saesons, Picts, or Scoti. Much of the poem still clearly refers to the story of Myrddin Wyllt which appears in the *Vita Merlini* – and to Myrddin's long sojourn in the wilderness, 'snow to my knees, ice in my beard'. The rest is a pitiless catalogue of battle and death: the final image, of the two bridges, somehow suggesting bridges of human bodies, which can almost never be sufficient until the end of time – a bleak prospect, as one might expect from the isolated spirit of Myrddin.

There is a distinct difference in tone between these poems and those attributed to Taliesin. In the following, which is a dialogue between him and Merlin, this becomes clearer. The poet who wrote this piece, whoever he may have been, clearly recognised the individuality of his characters. The prophecies are again of a general kind, with several interpolated references to medieval events.

The Dialogue of Myrddin and Taliesin

Myrddin
How sad with me, how sad,
Cedfyl and Cadfan are fallen!
The slaughter was terrible,
Shields shattered and bloody.

Taliesin
I saw Maelgwn battling –
The host acclaimed him.

Myrddin
Before two men in battles they
    gather,
Before Erith and Gwrith on pale
    horses.
Slender bay mounts will they
    bring,
Soon will come the host of
    Elgan.

Alas for his death, after a great
    journey!

Taliesin
Gap-toothed Rhys, his
    shield a span –
To him came battle's
    blessing.
Cyndur has fallen,
    deplorable beyond measure.
Generous men have been
    slain –
Three notable men,
    greatly esteemed by
    Elgan.

Myrddin
Again and again, in great
    throngs they came,
There came Bran and
    Melgan to meet me.
At the last, they slew
    Dyel,
The son of Erbin, with all his
    men.

Taliesin
Swiftly came Maelgwn's men,
Warriors ready for battle, for
    slaughter armed.
For this battle, Arderydd, they
    have made
A lifetime of preparation.

Myrddin
A host of spears fly high,
    drawing blood

From a host of vigorous
    warriors –
A host, fleeing; a host,
    wounded –
A host, bloody,
    retreating.

Taliesin
The seven sons of Elifer, seven
    heroes,
Will fail to avoid seven spears
    in the battle.

Myrddin
Seven fires, seven
    armies,
Cynfelyn in every seventh
    place.

Taliesin
Seven spears, seven rivers of
    blood
From seven chieftains,
    fallen.

Myrddin
Seven score heroes,
    maddened by battle,
To the forest of Celyddon they
    fled.
Since I, Myrddin, am
    second only to Taliesin,
Let my words be heard as truth.

The reiterated sevens, the stark images of war and battle
bear the weight of truth. The two great bards strike sparks
from each other as their **awen** lifts them into the realm where
they can see what has been and what will be.

209

All of this serves merely to illustrate the point from which we began this chapter, that the Celts were in love with prophecy, and that they possessed the abilities and understanding necessary to produce vaticinatory work of the highest order. In the next chapter we must look at other aspects of the shamanic arts, as borne out in the problematical subject of **Ogam**.

Chapter Eight

THE LANGUAGE OF TREES: OGAM AND THE CAD GODDEU

It is an excellent saying current among philosophers that they that have not learned to interpret rightly the sense of words are wont to bungle their actions.

Isis and Osiris, Plutarch

The Lost Language

The importance of language is stressed throughout the Taliesin material. Words themselves can be all powerful, as can song. One of the most important aspects of the bardic training was the learning of a secret language which could enable the initiated poets to converse with each other, if necessary in full view of a hall full of people, without anyone there being any the wiser.

This was done by means of Ogam, a linear alphabet found inscribed on stone or wood, apparently devised by the ancient Celts. It has been called 'the secret language of the poets' (171), and in its long and complex history many theories have been advanced to explain its origin and purpose. Before looking in detail at some of these we should begin with what is known about Ogam from early texts.

'Early' here means medieval rather than ancient, but we do have an enduring testimony of another kind, in the shape of the many inscriptions in Ogam found carved on menhirs and standing stones throughout Britain, Scotland and Ireland. The purpose to which these were erected has long been debated. It is assumed, generally, that they were grave markers: 'the stone of X', indicating where some great chieftain or hero was laid to rest. But there is at least one other possibility: that they were boundary markers, indicating the demarcation between one tribe's lands and another. This would explain the stones with more than one inscription, and is in line with the magical association of Ogam. A stone with the name of the tribe, its chieftain or clan mark would be as effective as a wire fence today – none would cross it without either permission or evil intent.

Many people have assumed that Ogam and Runic inscriptions must derive from each other, but this is not so. The former is a Celtic method, the latter a Scandinavian one, though both are concerned with arcane knowledge and under the patronage of gods of word-wisdom.

The main source of written knowledge about Ogam comes from a 14th Century Irish manuscript of *The Book of Ballymote* (42) in the Library of the Royal Irish Academy. Contained in this are some eight pages, generally referred to as **The Ogam Tract** (though its proper name is **Duil Feda**). This has been edited by George Calder with extensive commentaries, and need not be reproduced here (42). However, certain salient points are worthy of note. The account begins, as one might expect, with the creation of Ogam:

> What are the place, time, person, and cause of the invention of Ogham? (sic) Not hard. Its place **Hibernia insula quam nos Scoti habitamus**. In the time of Bres son of Elatha king of Ireland was it invented. Its person Ogma son of Elatha son of Delbaeth brother to Bres, for Bres, Ogma and Delbaeth are the three sons of Elatha son of Delbaeth there. Now Ogma, a man well skilled in speech and in poetry, invented the Ogham. The cause of its invention, as a proof of his ingenuity, and that his speech should belong to the learned apart, to the exclusion of rustics and herdsmen ... The father of Ogham is Ogma, the mother of Ogham is the hand or knife of Ogma ... This moreover is the first thing that was written by Ogham: ⊤ i.e. (the birch) **b** was written, and to convey a warning to Lug son of Ethliu it was written respecting his wife lest she be carried away from him into faeryland, to wit, seven b's in one switch of birch: Thy wife will be seven times carried away from thee into faeryland or into another country, unless birch guard her. On that account, moreover, **b**, birch, takes precedence, for it is in birch that Ogham was first written. (42)

This tells us several important things. Ogam was intended to be understood by the learned, noble class, i.e. the Druids, and not by the common people. Its first use seems to have been to inscribe a warning, and to have taken the form of a protective spell – if we are to understand the term 'unless birch guard her' in this way. Also we are told that the alphabet was invented by Ogma, whose rather complex pedigree is given. References to this same figure are found elsewhere, and it is clear from these that he was not a man at all, as in the **Ogham Tract**, but a god – Ogma **Cermait** (Honey-Mouthed), **Grian-aineach** (Sun-Faced), or **Trenfher** (Strongman, Champion), a son of the great god Dagda. He is usually described as a god of literature and of eloquence, as his alternative epithets suggest. In Gaul he was called Ogmios and worshipped as a god of light and learning. The Classical author Lucian wrote that he was the Celtic Heracles, and gives a description of a painting which depicted an ancient figure drawing a group of men chained by their ears to his tongue. Puzzling over this Lucian found a native Celt at his side who was willing to elucidate:

> We Celts do not agree with you Greeks in thinking that Hermes is Eloquence: we identify Heracles with it, because he is far more powerful than Hermes. And don't be surprised that he is represented as an old man, for eloquence . . . is wont to show its full vigour in old age . . . This being so, if old Heracles here drags men after him who are tethered by the ears to his tongue, don't be surprised at that either: you know the kinship between ears and tongue. (169)

Ogmios' title **Trenfher** (Strong Man) suggests an actual identification with Hercules/Heracles, whose Hellenized name means 'The Walker', and if we recall the original meaning of the word 'pedant' is derived from scholar, or 'one who walks up and down', we may see how this follows. Ogmios is clearly a God of Tradition, which binds men in chains of a kind, and which is shown to derive from the otherworldly realm of the Gods. In an inscription found at Richborough, Ogmios is depicted with rays of light coming from around his head and holding the whip of **Sol Invictus**, 'The Unconquered Sun'. He is thus in every way a suitable figure to be accredited with the invention of an alphabet which was to be associated with magical activities, with the transmission of secret knowledge, and with the writing of poetry.

The Secret Letters

The Ogam alphabet itself consists of various combinations of lines drawn across a vertical or horizontal stave, thus:

Figure 15   The Ogam Alphabet.

Each set of five letters has a name, as indicated, and the letters themselves have names, the most frequent being those of various trees. Thus Ogam is sometimes called 'The Tree Alphabet', or 'Beithe, Luis, Nion' after the first three names of the sequence (which occasionally varies from version to version. See below). The complete list is as follows, adapted from several different texts.

Ogam	*letter*	*tree*
Beithe	b	birch
Luis	l	elm/rowan
Fearn	f	alder
Saile	s	willow
Nuin	n	ash
(h)Uathe	h	whitethorn/hawthorn
Duir	d	oak
Tinne	t	holly/elderberry
Coll	c	hazel
Quert	q	quicken/aspen/apple
Muinn	m	vine/mulberry
Gort	g	fir/ivy [cornfield?]
(N)Getal	ng	broom/fern
Straif	str	willowbrake/blackthorn
Ruis	r	elder
Ailm	a	fir/pine
Ohn	o	furze/ash/gorse
Ur	u	thorn/heather
Edhadh	e	yew/aspen [white poplar]
Ido	i	service tree/yew
Ebadh	eba	elecampane/aspen

214

Oir	oi	spindle tree
Uilleand	ui	ivy/honeysuckle
Iphin	io	pine/gooseberry
Emancoll/Phagos	ae	witch hazel/beech

It will be seen from this that a number of variants exist as to the attribution of a particular tree or bush to a particular letter. Also the order has changed throughout its long period of development, so that we cannot always be sure of its original form. However, a series of poetic 'glosses' which explain, in riddling fashion, the meanings of the various tree names, adds to our understanding of the hidden meanings attached to them.

These may, just possibly, hold some more answers for us, both about the way Ogam was used by the shaman-poets, and about their application for us today. The first of these lists is as follows (26).

Word Ogam of Morann Mac Main

Feocus foltchain	Faded trunk and fair hair
Li sula	Delight of eye
Airinach Fian	Shield of warrior bands
Li n-aimbi	Hue of the lifeless
Corsdad sida	Checking of peace
Conal cuan	Pack of wolves
Ardam dossaibh	Highest of bushes
Trian	–
Cainiu fedaib	Fairest of trees
Clithar mbaiscaill	Shelter of a hind
Tresim fedma	Strongest of efforts
Millsiu feraib	Sweeter than grasses
Luth legha	A physician's strength
Tresim ruamna	Strongest of red
Tinnem ruccae	Most intense of blushes
Ardam iactadh	Loudest of groanings
Congnamaigh echraide	Helper of horses
Uaraib adbaib	In cold dwellings
Ergnaid fid	Distinguished wood
Siniu fedhaib	Oldest of woods
Snamchain fheda	Most buoyant of wood
Sruitem aicdi	Most venerable of structures

Tutmur fid uilleann   Juicy wood is woodbine
Millsim feda   Sweetest of wood
Luad saethaig   Expression of a weary one

The second list is attributed to the Irish love-god Aengus Mac ind Oic:

Alphabet of Word-Oghams of Mac ind Oic

Glaisium cnis	Most silvery of skin
Cara ceathra	Friend of cattle
Comet lachta	Guarding of milk
Luth bech	Activity of bees
Bag ban	Flight of women
Banadh gnuisi	Blanching of face
Gres sair	Carpenter's work
Smir guaili	Fires of coal
Cara bloisc	Friend of cracking
Brigh annum	Force of the man
Aruusc n-arrligh	Condition of slaughter
Mednercc	Ivy
[Etiud midach]	[Robe of physicians]
Moridrun	Increasing of secrets
Ruamna dreach	Redness of faces
Tosach fregra	Beginning of an answer
Feithim saire	Smoothest of work
Siladh clann	Growing of plants
Comainm carat	Synonym for a friend
Crinem feada	Most withered of wood
Cosc lobair	Corrective of a sick man
Li crotha	Beauty of form
Cubat n-oll	Great equal-length
Amram blais	Most wonderful of taste

A third list, attributed, interestingly, to Cuchulainn, has yet to be translated (26).

These lists suggest a complex series of riddling references which must have been known to the poets, and could be applied to extend the meanings of the Ogam letters in such a way as to make them comprehensible only to those proficient in Ogam. They seem, as do the kenning examples of the original Ogam lists, to be as important as the lists themselves, offering, through prolonged meditation, many answers to the way in which the alphabets were used.

216

Doubt, first expressed by Charles Graves as long ago as 1847 (99), and more recently explored by Howard Meroney (198), as to the authenticity of the Ogam Tree Alphabet, makes it clear that we must look again at the whole question of these identifications, which have been accepted quite literally by most commentators since the 1700s. The evidence points to them being copied and recopied until their *original* meanings became virtually lost, or so jumbled as to be virtually indecipherable. Meroney has reassigned some of the letters, using the various kenning lists printed above. These appear to have preserved earlier and more accurate glosses to the letters than those contained in the **Auraicept na N-Eces** (Scholar's Primer) or its variants. In these, quite often, the original glosses have duplications which suggest that the copyists themselves did not know how to decipher them (for example **pin** is glossed as 'a rowan, pine, or gooseberry'). What appears to have happened is that the *original* glosses for the Ogam alphabet (still quite late compared with the dating of the alphabet itself) were of a much more ordinary-seeming nature, and that these were changed at some unspecified time (probably between the 7th to the 9th Centuries) to fit a purely arbitrary system of tree and plant names.

By combining all the extant kennings, Meroney produces the following list:

Ogam letter name (After Calder)	Suggested original name (After Meroney)
beith	birch
luis	? flame (**luise**)
fern	alder
sail	willow
nin	fork
uath	fear(some)
duir	oak
tindi	bar of metal
coll	hazel
ce(i)rt	rag
muin	esteem
gort	field
(n)getal	charm (**cetal**)
sraiph	sulphur
ruis	redness
ailm	?

onn	wheel
ur	humus
edad	?
idad	?
ebad	?
oir	? gold (**or**)
uillend	elbow
emancoll	double C

It will be seen that this differs substantially from all previous lists, and indicates that the original letters may have had only a partial association with tree names, but that some copyist, noticing the preponderance of such names, forced the remainder into a complete (sic) alphabet of trees by wrenching the etymologies to fit his own scheme.

Lists of the various kinds of physically oriented Ogam (finger, nose, thigh, foot, etc) also exist, and were used in a similar fashion – touching the part of the body in a certain way would indicate to those in the know a word or letter which could be interpreted in this fashion. Other kinds of Ogam listed in **The Scholar's Primer** include Sow Ogham, River-Pool Ogham, Fortress Ogham, Bird Ogham, Colour Ogham, King Ogham, Water Ogham, Dog Ogham, Food Ogham.

The poet/druid/seer had thus to be familiar with a vast range of knowledge – not only of the general meaning of the Ogam character, but also of the many secret meanings which lay behind it. Thus the letter *///* meant not only **ng,** but also all that **ng** stood for tree, group of letters, phrase, part of the body and so on. The interpretation thus rested on a full spectrum of knowledge in which the relationship of the letter or letters to each other, to the remainder of the inscription, and to the context in which they were found, all had to be taken into account. Thus any one of the poetic epithets listed above could be interpreted differently according to their placement on the staves, and their relationship to each other.

R. A. S. Macalister notes (171) that all of the Ogam signs could be easily made with the fingers – hence their grouping in fives – and that the five 'extra' letters, which represent the vowel sounds and have often been suggested as late additions, are particularly appropriate for making with the fingers. From this he suggests that the earliest use of Ogam was as a sign language, and that only later was it adapted for use in the making of inscriptions. He also has some interesting perceptions on the possible origin of the alphabet, which he finds to be very nearly identical with a form of Greek known as the Formello-Cervetti alphabet. This was found inscribed on two vases dating from approximately 6th Century BC and from this, Calder believes they were borrowed by Gaulish Druids some time in the 5th Century BC and adapted to their own use.

Caesar remarks that the Druids used Greek letters to record their communications – though not their orally preserved religious teachings – which seems to bear out this idea. Certainly there was considerable interaction between the Celts and the Greeks for this curious borrowing to have come about. It establishes a date for Ogam of no earlier than 500 BC and lends weight to the belief that its original use was as a cryptographic system.

However, the story does not end here. An examination of the *language* of the Ogam inscriptions found in Ireland, Britain and Wales shows that they contain archaisms which point to an extremely primitive language still being enshrined in stone long after it had ceased to be spoken. Macalister, who deals with his linguistic evidence at some length (171), believes that it was Old Goidelic, the primitive language of the Celts, and from this infers that it continued to be spoken by the Druids, who taught it orally in their schools so that they were speaking a language no longer understood by their own people! References to 'the dark speech' found in contemporary literature, suggests this may well have been the case (but see also Chapter Five), and add not only to the antiquity of Ogam, but also to the Druids themselves. All of this leads Dr Macalister to suggest that a reasonable translation of the word **ogam** would be 'the language', thus indicating its primary place in Celtic understanding.

As well as all this, there is no doubt that the uses of Ogam are related very closely to the forms of divination discussed in Chapter Seven.

The Hidden Order

There is a great deal of disagreement over the order which the alphabet should follow, and over which tree or shrub belongs to which letter. The earliest lists we possess, and upon which the above examples are based, are those found in the **Ogham**

Tract and the **Auraicept N-Eces** (42), which differ only slightly. R. A. S. Macalister, in his brilliant exposition of Ogam (171) has given evidence to show that the order changed with phonetic requirements, so that the familiar Beith-Luis-Nion may well have been the earliest. After this there is a long gap in which various sources repeat the medieval lists more or less verbatim, until the 17th Century version by Charles O'Conor, quoted by Edward Ledwich in his 18th Century *Antiquities of Ireland* (161). This was derived in Roderic O'Flaherty's *Ogygia* (235), from whence it was redefined by the poet and mythographer Robert Graves. He included it in his 'grammar of poetic myth', *The White Goddess* (101), in which he recognised – correctly it would seem – that it formed the basis for 'a calendar of seasonal tree-magic'. Unfortunately he made certain amendments to the original order of the trees, in an endeavour to bring the system into line with the overall picture of the Muse Goddess he wished to describe.

This is not the place to argue the value of one system against another. Robert Graves' ordering of the Tree Alphabet is very much his own, and part of a much larger system. He almost certainly never intended it to be used, as has been the case, by those seeking a framework for Goddess worship. From this point of view the calendrical formulae worked out by Kaledon Naddair (221) are a better system to work with: he has extended the range of the Ogam alphabetic calendar to include colours, animals and objects, and has succeeded in establishing a remarkably coherent pattern. However, there remains much work yet to be done before the relationship between the shamanic calendar and the Tree Alphabet is fully established.

Plentiful examples are to be found throughout Celtic literature (especially Irish), indicating some of the other uses to which Ogam was put.

1 The Ulster hero Cuchulainn twice left challenges inscribed in Ogam before the army of Mebh of Connaught, one on a hoop of birch and a second in the fork of a tree (**The Tain**).

2 When Midir abducted Etain, the wife of Art Mac Conn, the Druid Dalan discovered her hiding place by cutting four wands of yew, on which he wrote Ogam inscriptions, thereby discovering the **eochra ecsi** (keys of divination) through which he found that she was being held in the **sidhe** of Breg Leith (**Tochmarc Etain**).

220

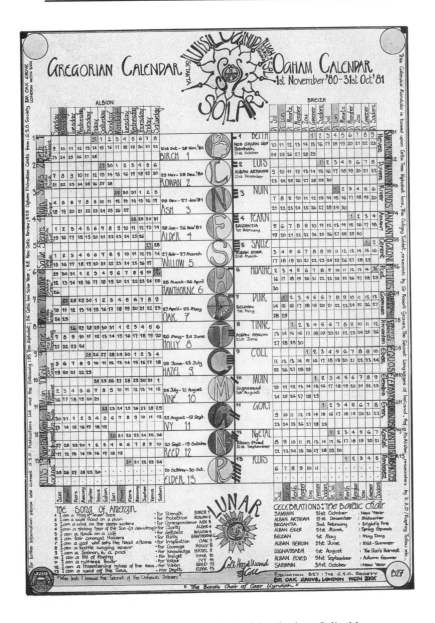

Figure 16   *The Ogam Calendar as devised by the late Colin Murray.*

3 When the Sovereignty of Ireland wished to offer her cup to the hero destined to reign over the land she asked to whom it should be given and was told that she must listen to the recital of all the sovereigns of Ireland from Conn to the end of time. The poet Cesarn managed to deliver an incantation (**dichetail**) using Ogam inscribed on four yew wands (**Baile in Scail**) (59).

4 Corc, the son of Lugaid, fled after spurning the advances of his step-mother. He arrived at the court of King Feradach and asked for shelter. The king's poet Gruibne Eces (poet or seer) saw that Corc had Ogam written on his shield requesting that the bearer should be beheaded. But Gruibne liked Corc and instead interpreted the Ogam to say that he should marry Feradach's daughter (**Book of Leinster**).

5 After the deaths of the lovers Aillinn and Baile an apple and a yew sprang from their graves. At the end of seven years the poets, seers and prophets of Ulster cut down the yew tree which was over the grave of Baile, and made it into a poet's tablet, 'and they wrote the visions, the espousals, and loves, and courtships of Ulster upon it.' The same was done with the apple tree growing on Aillinn's grave, and on that were written the courtships, loves and espousals of Leinster. Later, when King Conn of the Hundred Battles was looking at these famous tablets, they sprang together and could not be separated thereafter.

All of these instances have to do with magical or divinatory uses of Ogam. In the **Tochmarc Etain** (25) the woods are described as **eochra ecsi**, 'keys of knowledge'. This possibly refers to a passage from **Senchus Mor** concerning a method of judgement known as **crannchur** or 'casting the woods'. According to this, if there was doubt as to the identity of a murderer, thief or adulterer,

> The lots are cast in this manner: three lots are put in, a lot for guiltiness, a lot for innocence, and the lot for the Trinity. This is enough to criminate or acquit them. If it be the lot of the Trinity that came out, it is to be put back each time until another lot comes out. (111)

Despite the Christian gloss, there is an unmistakable ring of truth about this. The fact that three lots are placed within –

we may presume a bag – is in line with the Celtic obsession with that number. We may speculate that the method originally involved special woods, perhaps more than three, each of which was sacred to the gods; whichever was pulled forth would then have become the arbiter in the case, with possible further divinatory methods following on.

Apart from these uses, there were numerous other ways in which Ogam could be utilised. Whenever a hero was buried a slip of aspen was placed with him in his tomb with his name written in Ogam upon it. In one sense Ogam was indeed a library, but one which consisted of mnemonics, not unlike the *Welsh Triads* (334). It was concerned with people, places, and things, any number of which could be set against the Ogam stave. We may marvel at the complexity of learning necessary to those who used Ogam fluently. Depending on the kind of Ogam used (and there are no less than a hundred listed in the **Ogham Tract** and **The Scholar's Primer**) there must have been some kind of code to identify which one was being used. A river, a man or woman, colour, tree, hill, or whatever, could be identified and placed in context with local tradition. Thus an Ogam might refer to a certain hill which, in turn, referred to a legend or tradition concerning that place, and the outcome of that could be applied to the person giving or asking the question. The huge collection of **Dindsenchas** (Stories of Places) (107) still remains in Irish manuscripts; each one a story connected to the landscape, explaining and amplifying the meaning of the place-name in either riddling or punning form.

In the story of **The Wooing of Emer** (59) the hero Cuchulainn was tested by a series of riddling questions, all of which he answered. Then he was asked to describe his journey to the place where he found Emer. He did so in riddle, giving the kenning names of the places through which he had passed.

> From the Cover of the Sea, over the Great Secret of the Tuath De Danann, and the Foam of the Two Steeds of Emain Macha; over the Morrigu's Garden, and the Great Sow's Back; over the Glen of the Great Dam ... Over the Marrow of the Woman Fedelm ... over Great Crime and the Remnants of the Great Feast; between the Vat and the Little Vat, to the Gardens of Lug, to the daughters of Tethra's nephew, Forgall, king of the Fomorians.

Similar shamanic techniques exist in other parts of the world, as in the instance described by the poet Gary Snyder (284) who, when he visited Australia, was accompanied on a journey by a tribal shaman. As they rode together in the back of a lorry, the shaman began speaking with greater and greater speed, telling story after story of the landscape unfolding on either hand. Snyder realised that he was hearing a speeded-up version of the history of the land itself, kept in the minds of the shamans, like a recording, ready to be unfolded on journeys normally made on foot.

The Battle of the Trees

As we have seen, no precise evidence has yet been presented for the existence of a Celtic Tree Calendar. This does not, of course, mean that no such evidence exists. In the vast area of Celtic research new things are being discovered daily.

In the meantime, we may make the observation that if the ancient Ogam alphabet was in reality identified with various trees and shrubs (remembering that our only reference dates from the Middle Ages, and the fact that the modern Irish alphabet still draws on tree names for its letters) then there must have been a reason beyond, it is hoped, that of a simple **aide memoire** for their being so. It is possible, as Robert Graves and others have done with varying degrees of success, to arrange the trees in question around the wheel of the year. And if it is possible now, it was possible then.

Apart from this, a further important piece of evidence remains to be considered: the poem known as the **Cad Goddeu**, or 'Battle of the Trees', which is part of the main canon of the Taliesin material. The full text of this will be found on pages 296–301. What follows is a commentary based on that text in the light of the revised translation and the general shamanic nature of the work.

It is immediately apparent, on reading this poem, that it contains many of the so-called 'Ogam Trees'.

Tree	Ogam
Alder	fearn
Willow	saille
Rowan	luis

224

Blackthorn	straif
Dogwood	–
Rose	–
Raspberry	–
Honeysuckle	uill-eand
Ivy	gort
Poplar	–
Cherry	–
Birch	beith
Goldenrod	–
Fir	ailm
Ash	nuin
Elm	–
Hazel	coll
Privet	–
Beech	phagos
Holly	tinne
Hawthorn	huathe
Vine	muinn
Fern/Broom	ngetal
Gorse	onn
Heather	ur
Oak	duir
Chestnut	–
Yew	idho

This makes a total of nineteen Ogam trees and excludes the following six from the sequence:

quert	apple
ruis	elder
edhadh	aspen
eashadh	white poplar
oir	spindle
iphin	gooseberry

Nine others which appear in the poem are not normally associated with the usual Ogam lists. These are:

Dogwood	Goldenrod
Rose	Elm
Raspberry	Privet
Poplar	Chestnut
Cherry	

This constitutes a sufficient degree of similarity to suggest that the one may well be based on the other or, at least, that they are connected. It may even be that the *Cad Goddeu* preserves an earlier and more complete listing of the Ogams.

On the history of this mysterious battle there is little to tell save some cryptic references in the *Welsh Triads* (334), and an obscure fragment printed in the *Myfyrian Archaiology* (145). Triad 84 refers to:

> Three futile Battles of the Island of Britain;
> One of them was the Battle of Goddeu: it was brought about by the cause of the bitch, together with the roebuck and the plover.

The identity of these three beasts has exercised many minds. But it is possible that these are not beasts at all, but totemic identities from a mythological sequence which goes on throughout time. One of the major features of the British mysteries is the tendency for its mythic characters to fall into triads or eternal triangles of one woman over whom two men war. The characters mentioned within and surrounding this poem are all of this nature.

1 Pwyll received pigs from Annwn after having done Arawn, lord of the Underworld, a great favour. He changed places with Arawn for a year and slept chastely with Arawn's wife.

2 Pwyll subsequently wooed Rhiannon, the daughter of a lord of the Underworld. Her former suitor, Gwawl, caused considerable trouble for them both.

3 Math's footholder, Goewin, was loved by Gilfaethwy. In order to win her, Math had to be distracted, and Gwydion, by his magic, caused war between North and South Wales – between Pryderi of Dyfed, the son of Pwyll and Rhiannon and the possessor of the Underworldly pigs, and Math of Gwynedd.

4 Subsequently, Gwydion's nephew, Lleu was fated by his mother, Arianrhod, never to have a wife of mortal stock. To overcome this problem, Math and Gwydion magically created a woman, Blodeuwedd, out of flowers. She found a lover, Gronw, and with him planned Lleu's death. Lleu received the death-blow but did not die; he became an eagle and Gwydion found and restored him

once more, calling him down from the tree (see Chapter Seven).

These are merely four of the many similar triangular relationships and conflicts which cross-track this poem. The bitch, the roebuck and the plover probably stand, in this instance, for the eternal triangle of the woman and the two men who fight for her.

But there is one further triangle which must be spoken of. Bran the Blessed gave his sister Branwen to be wife to Matholwch, king of Ireland. When he mistreated Branwen, Bran was forced to bring war to Ireland and rescue her. Line 12 of the poem speaks of a royal maiden – both Branwen and Goewin suffer and make outcry in their different stories. This must be borne in mind when considering the following evidence.

The *Myfyrian Archaiology*, a compendium of bardic lore which was collected in the early 19th Century, says this in addition:

These are the englyns that were sung at the Cad Goddeu, or as others call it, the Battle of Achren, (trees) which was on account of a white roebuck, and a whelp; and they came from Annwn, and Amathaon ap Don brought them. And therefore, Amathaon ap Don, and Arawn, King of Annwn, fought. And there was a man in that battle, who unless his name were known could not be overcome, and there was on the other side a woman called Achren, and unless her name were known her party could not be overcome. And Gwydion ap Don guessed the name of the man, and sang the two englyns following:

> Sure-footed my steed, impelled by the spur;
> The high sprigs of alder are on thy shield;
> Bran are thou called, of the glittering branches.

> Sure-hoofed my steed, in the day of battle:
> The high sprigs of alder are in thy hand;
> Bran thou art, by the branch thou bearest –
> Amathaon the Good has prevailed.

Now, Bran's nephew was none other than Branwen's son, Gwern (Alder), and it was he who perished in the fire in Matholwch's hall. Amathaon was a son of the Goddess, Don, and he may represent the Wild Herdsman, the primordial, pre-Celtic deity who guards creation. The battle dispositions are thus as follows, according to this text: on one side were Amathaon, Gwydion, Llew and Achren, while on the other were Arawn and Bran – both noted gods of the Underworld. What we have is a battle between the Underworld and the immortals of the Earth. This has been seen as a combat between the retiring and incoming gods of the land, as is the story of Amairgen and the arrival of the Milesians in Ireland.

In modern Welsh the words for wisdom and trees are strongly interrelated: **gwydd** means 'trees'; **gwyddon** means 'magician'; and **gwyddor** means 'science'. The mutated form of this last word, (words lose or change their initial letter in Celtic languages according to their grammatical usage), **Yr Wyddor** means 'alphabet'. Significantly, Gwydion derives his name from the same root, **gwydd**. He is prominent in the Battle of the Trees, just as he is the instigator of the war between Dyfed and Gwynedd. His cunning and wisdom are much admired throughout the poems of Taliesin, who seems to have treated Gwydion as his inner, bardic mentor.

> I was a spark in fire,
> I was wood in a bonfire;
> I am not one who does not sing;
> I have sung since I was small.
> I sang in the army of the trees' branches
> Before the ruler of Britain.

Taliesin clearly means us to understand from this that he was present at the battle. Whether he was the author of **Cad Goddeu** or not, that he knew the secrets of the Tree Alphabet and the Ogam letters is beyond question. Although on the surface it appears to recount a battle in which the various trees, brought to life by the enchanter Gwydion, fight on his side, beneath the surface there is far more. In fact, once the various 'inserted' poems are removed, the picture is clear. There can be little or no doubt that, as with many other of the Taliesin poems, **Cad Goddeu** was intended as a teaching aid, concerned both with the mysterious nature of poetry itself, and with the way in which the multi-layered meanings of the Ogam letters could be used.

On another level, the poem must be seen as a major poetic prophecy of great importance, for Taliesin wrote the **Cad**

Goddeu in the manner of a Celtic Ragnarok, a scenario for the end of time.

The Lore of Trees

In Ireland there were five specifically named sacred trees: the Tree of Ross, the Tree of Mugna, the Tree of Dathi, the Tree of Usnach and the Tree of Tortu. They are listed in both *The Calendar of Oengus* (294) and the **Dindsenchas**, Metrical and Prose (107, 297). The former says of them:

> Eo Mugna, great was the fair tree,
> high its top above the rest:
> thirty cubits – it was no trifle –
> that was the measure of its girth.

> Three hundred cubits was the height of the
>   blameless tree,
> its shadow sheltered a thousand:
> in secrecy it remained in the north and east
> till the time of Conn of the Hundred Fights.

> A hundred score of warriors – no empty tale –
> along with ten hundred and forty
> would that tree shelter – it was a fierce struggle –
> till it was overthrown by the poets.

* * *

> How fell the bough of Dathi?
> it spent the strength of many a gentle hireling:
> an ash, the tree of the nimble hosts,
> its top bore no lasting yield.

> The ash in Tortu – take count thereof!
> the Ash of populous Usnach:
> their boughs fell – it was not amiss –
> in the time of the sons of Aed Slane.

> The Oak of Mugna, it was a hallowed treasure;
> nine hundred bushels was its bountiful yield:
> it fell in Dairbre southward,
> across Mag Ailbe of the cruel combats.

The Bole of Ross, a comely yew
with abundance of broad timber,
the tree without hollow or flaw,
the stately bole, how did it fall?

The **Prose Dindsenchas** (111) add:

Berries to the berries the Strong Upholder put upon his tree
[i.e. the Ash of Tortan]. Three fruits upon it, namely acorn,
apple and nut, and when the first fruit fell another fruit used
to grow. Now it was for a long while hidden until the birth of
Conn of the Hundred Battles (when it was revealed). Ninine the
Poet cast it down in the time of Domnall son of Murchad King
of Ireland (c. AD 500), who had refused a demand of Ninine's.
Equally broad were its top and the plain (in which it stood).
Or it may have been that in the time of Aed Slane that this tree
and the **Bile Tortan** fell together. Thirty cubits was its girth,
and its height was three hundred cubits, and its leaves were
on it always.

These are enigmatic references, clearly referring to cosmic
world-trees of the kind worshipped among the Norse as scions
of Yggdrasil, the World-Ash. (That three out of the five are in
fact ash cannot be without significance.) The fact that the
great Oak of Mugna is described as being 'overthrown by the
poets', is puzzling at first. That the poetic mysteries were intimately connected with tree-lore we have seen beyond doubt;
why, therefore, should the poets be described as destroying
the sacred trees? For a possible answer we must turn to another
text, **The Settling of the Manor of Tara** (27). Here we find the
following account:
The Chieftains of Ireland, having come together to discuss
the seemingly over-large dimensions of the Manor of Tara compared to their own lands, desired to learn of the original reasons
for the partitioning of the land. To this end they summoned
first of all two wise poets who, in turn, summoned five older
and wiser than they (including Tuan Mac Cairell who, as we
saw in Chapter Seven, underwent many changes of shape in
order to be present throughout much of the history of Ireland).
However, none of these were able to answer, and all agreed to
summon Fintan (the same who sought the Salmon of Wisdom)
who was agreed to be the wisest of them all. Fintan's discourse
is long and rambling. Much in the manner of Taliesin he gave

a poetic version of the history of Ireland, which he seemed to be able to remember personally. Curiously, in the light of our present line of inquiry, he mentioned another great tree:

> One day I passed through a wood in West Munster in the west. I took away with me a red yew berry and I planted it in the garden of my court, and it grew up there until it was as big as a man. Then I removed it from the garden and planted it on the lawn of my court even, and it grew up in the centre of that lawn so that I could sit with a hundred warriors under its foliage, and it protected me from wind and rain, and from cold and heat.

Fintan then went on to tell the story of an assembly of all the Kings and lords of Ireland, together with all their principal story-tellers, brought together on the day of Christ's crucifixion by a wonderful being called Trefuilngid Tre-ochair, the Strong Upholder mentioned in the **Prose Dindsenchas**. The text reads as follows:

> ... We beheld a great hero, fair and mighty, approaching us from the west at sunset. We wondered greatly at the magnitude of his form. As high as a wood was the top of his shoulders, the sky and the sun visible between his legs, by reason of his size and his comeliness. A shining crystal veil about him like unto raiment of precious linen. Sandals upon his feet, and it is not known of what material they were. Golden yellow hair upon him falling in curls to the middle of his thighs. Stone tablets in his left hand, a branch with three fruits in his right hand, and these are the three fruits which were on it, nuts and apples and acorns in May-time: and unripe was each fruit ... 'I have come indeed' he said, 'from the setting of the sun, and I am going unto the rising, and my name is Trefuilngid Tre-ochair.' 'Why has that name been given to thee?' said they. 'Easy to say,' said he. 'Because it is I who cause the rising of the sun and its setting.' 'And what has brought thee to the setting, if it is at the rising thou dost be?' 'Easy to say,' said he. 'A man who has been tortured – that is who has been crucified by the Jews today; for it [the sun] stepped past them [the Jews] after that deed, and has not shone upon them, and that is what has brought me to the setting to find out what ailed the sun; and then it was revealed to me, and when I knew the lands over which the sun set I came to Inis Gluairi off Irrus Domnann; and I found no land from that westwards, for that is the threshold over which the sun sets ...

Trefuilngid Tre-ochair then requested to know the history of the people of Ireland, and was given a much abbreviated version due to the fact that there were apparently no lore-masters who knew all the stories. Trefuilngid however, appeared already to know more than they, calling himself 'the truly learned witness who explains to all everything unknown'. Indeed, he summoned all the most learned men of the five provinces together and related *to them* the entire history of the island. He then drew Fintan aside and told him everything, since he was the oldest of all the wise, who had been alive since the coming of the first men. All this Fintan had remembered, and now related it to the assembly at Tara, detailing the reasons for the partitions, what they were best known for, and an extraordinary catalogue of the people who originated all the greatest works and deeds in the land.

The text continues:

> So Trefuilngid Tre-ochair left that ordinance with the men of Ireland for ever, and he left with Fintan son of Bochra some of the berries from the branch which was in his hand, so that he planted them in whatever places he thought it likely they would grow in Ireland. And these are the trees which grew up from those berries: the Ancient Tree of Tortu and the Tree of Ross, the Tree of Mugna and the Branching Tree of Dathee, and the Ancient Tree of Usnech . . . (ibid.)

Thereafter the Kings of Ireland were accorded, and Fintan set up a great pillar on the hill of Usnech in the centre of the land, marked with five ridges which showed the divisions of the land.

This is an extraordinary text, so full of lore and wisdom relating both to the ancient traditions and to the cosmological legends of the Celts. Essentially, there are three ways in which we can regard what it tells us. First, it is clearly a series of cosmological myths relating to the most distant past, when the world was created. Secondly, we may choose to view the references to the trees as relating to the great lineages of Ireland, which were 'cut down' or ended by time and circumstance conjoined. This is akin to the death of Tradition itself, the realm and responsibility of the shaman-poets and priests, and is suggested by the preponderance of names which translate as 'Son of Oak' (**Mac Dara**), 'Son of Rowan-Tree'

(**Mac Cairthin**), 'Son of Yew' (**Mac Ibair**), 'Son of Hazel' (**Mac Cuill**) – indicating, incidentally, that some tribes had trees as their totems rather than animals (see Chapter Six). Certainly many settlements were built beside, or derived their names from, the sites of ancient groves. Fintan's reference to the tree which he transplanted from his garden to 'the lawn of my court' reflects a reference to the nature of the ever-living tradition.

Thirdly, the idea of the cutting down of the ancient trees seems to have become synonymous with the spread of Christianity and the ending thereby of older ways. Perhaps the poets' deliberate cutting down of the trees of tradition can be seen in this light, as a desire to prevent their being felled by the axes of the monks! Certainly when we read in the *Calendar of Oengus* of 'a certain great tree which was in the world in the east' (294) and which was adored by the heathen until it was felled as a consequence of a Christian feast, we may feel this suggestion to be the case. Yet there is, to give the matter balance, a story of Columba which suggests that the sanctity of trees continued to be recognised.

When the Saint founded a church in Derry (which derives from **doire**, an oak wood) he burned the town and rath of the king in order to destroy utterly the works of men before reconsecrating the earth to God. 'So great was the fire and the blaze that it well-nigh burnt a grove of trees in that place' (127).

But Columba pronounced an invocation to protect the grove, and was so loath to fell so much as a single tree that he turned the oratory to face north and south instead of east and west. 'And he charged his successors to chop no tree that fell of itself or was blown down by the wind, till the end of nine days', after which time it was to be distributed to the poor. He was later reported to have said that while he feared death, he feared much more the sound of an axe in the woods of Derry!

This great respect for the power and sanctity of the trees, especially when they were part of a grove, is reflected throughout Irish history and tradition.

In historical times, each sept in Ireland had sacred tribal trees of great size and age, under which their princes were inaugurated. These trees, which represented and no doubt,

233

originally, were believed to contain, the essence of the royal and sacred functions of the chief, were held in great veneration. To hew down the tribal tree was the greatest offence that could be offered by any enemy, and was believed to indicate the downfall of the province. (127)

The Sacredness of Trees

The tradition of the sacred grove, or 'nemeton', was widespread throughout much of the western world. In central Asia Minor in about 280 BC the Gauls held a great council at a place called Drunemeton, 'the chief nemeton or sacred place', while later, in Caesar's time, the Druids were said to meet annually in the land of the Carnutes, believed to be the centre of Gaul (or of the world?) (268). Nearly every tribe in the country seems to have possessed a nemeton or sacred meeting place, marked either by a tree or a stone pillar, and we may imagine that this was the same in Britain and Ireland, and that the local shaman held sway there at all times. Certainly, as Tacitus says in the *Germania*:

> The grove is the centre of their whole religion. It is regarded as the cradle of the race and the dwelling-place of the supreme god to whom all things are subject and obedient. (303)

In Medieval Irish the word for sacred grove is translated as **fid-nemith** or **fid-neimid** which, in turn, derived from an older Celtic word **nemetos** meaning simply 'holy' or 'sacred'. This later became extended to mean a distinguished person or animal, or a poet, a king or a wise dignitary.

'Three noble, sacred things: groves or temples, filid or poets, rulers' say the *Triads of Ireland* (207), 'Three dead things that are paid for only with living things are an apple tree, a hazel bush, and a sacred grove.'

This is reflected in the harsh laws laid down for the damage caused to certain trees in the Law Tracts. In *Senchus Mor*, at the end of the tract entitled **Crith Gablach** (111), it is stated that the fines for cutting certain trees are as follows: For the 'Chieftain' trees: oak; hazel; holly; yew; ash; pine and apple, the fine is a cow for cutting the trunks, a heifer for either limbs or branches. For the 'Common' trees: alder; willow;

hawthorn; mountain ash; birch; elm and idha (possibly a species of pine), the fines are a cow for each whole tree and a heifer for the branches. For the 'Shrub' trees: blackthorn; elder; spindle-tree; white hazel; aspen; arbutus and test tree, the fine is a heifer for each tree. The 'Bramble Trees' are: fern; bog-myrtle; furze; briar; heath; ivy; broom and gooseberry. A sheep is the fine for each.

We can see from this that most of the trees are among those which fought at Cad Goddeu, and we may imagine, if we will, the kind of feelings which would have been evoked at the idea of taking swords to all of them! Each tree, like humankind, has its honour price or **dire**.

Two poetic grades mentioned in the *Senchus Mor* (111) indicate the connection of poets with trees. The first of these is the 'cli' poet.

> i.e. [he partakes of] the nature of the post (**cleith**) ... [which is] strong and straight, and it elevates and is elevated, it protects and is protected; it is powerful from the ridge to the floor. It is the same with this grade in the poetic house, i.e. his art is powerful, and his judgement is straight in the circuit of his profession ...

The second is the so-called 'dos' poet, so called,

> ... from his similitude to a tree ... i.e. it is through (under) the name of a tree they learn their art ...

Once again we glimpse the powerful shaman with his world-pole, protected and protecting, rising from earth to heaven, or being taught his mysterious powers beneath one of the magical trees which fought at Cad Goddeu, or formed the ranks of the Ogam staves which conveyed so much of mystery and wonder.

We have already noted, several times throughout this study, the significance in which trees were held (cf. the Silver Branch in Chapter Five, and the Otherworldly apple trees mentioned in Chapter Three and elsewhere). A further illustration, which seems to connect with the idea of the shaman climbing the world-tree and flying free, is illustrated by a poem attributed to the Irish 'madman' Suibhne Geilt, in which he praises certain trees (over which he presumably flies) in much the same way as Taliesin's reference in the poem **The Bright**

Trees (trans on pages 323–6) of which every verse begins with the line 'bright the tops of the noble . . .'

Suibhne Geilt Praises the Trees

Thou oak, bushy, leafy,
thou art high beyond trees;
O hazelet, little branching one,
O fragrance of hazel-nuts.

O alder, thou art not hostile
delightful is thy hue,
thou art not rending and
    prickling
in the gap wherein thou art.

O little blackthorn, little thorny
    one;
O little black sloe-tree;
O watercress, little-topped one
from the brink of the ousel
    spring.

O [vetches] of the pathway
thou art sweet beyond herbs,
O little green one, very green
    one,
O herb on which grows the
    strawberry.

O apple tree, little apple tree
much art thou shaken;
O quicken, little berried one,
delightful is thy bloom.

O briar, little arched one,
thou grantest no fair terms,

thou ceasest not to tear me,
till thou hast thy fill of blood.

O yew tree, little yew tree,
in church-yards thou art
    conspicuous;
O ivy, little ivy,
thou art familiar in the dusky
    wood.

O holly, little sheltering one,
thou door against the wind;
O ash tree, thou baleful one,
hand-weapon of a warrior.

O birch, smooth and blessed,
thou melodious, proud one,
delightful each entwining
    branch
in the top of thy crown.

The apern a-trembling;
by turns I hear
its leaves a-racing –
meseems 'tis the foray!

My aversion in woods –
I conceal it not from anyone –
is the leafy stirk of an oak'
swaying [always] swaying. (239)

This is somewhere between the **Afalannau** of Merlin and the **Cad Goddeu**. All three preserve the fragments of a once vast lore of trees, each of which had its own meaning, its associations, qualities, and a specific range of reference to aid the shaman-priest in his prognostications.

Chapter Nine

THE REGION OF THE SUMMER STARS: COSMOLOGIES AND COSMOGONIES

... the Bards of the Britons,
Liberal of wonders and the star-knowledge of the astrologers
Taliesin, To Gwallawg (Trans. D. W. Nash)

The single most famous line in the entire corpus of the poetry attributed to Taliesin must be that in which he refers to his 'original country' as 'the Region of the Summer Stars'. Whole books have been based around this statement, which has been taken to refer either to the 'Summer Country' (the Otherworld), or to an actual region in the cosmogony of the Heavens. Unfortunately, the usual text from which this line is derived does not easily bear out the interpretation put upon it. Depending upon which text one accepts as the least corrupt the line reads either **Am gwlad gynhefin/Iw bro Gerubin** (Nash), or **A'm gwlad gynnevin/Yw bro ser hevin** ('Idrisson'). The first translator to read the line in this way appears to have been 'Idrisson' (6), and his version appears in Lady Guest's edition of the *Mabinogion* (5). The correct translation of the first example would be 'the land of the Cherubim', which is, quite clearly, a later Christian gloss. The original sense of the lines was that Taliesin's original home was the Otherworld – a fact that we already know from *Hanes Taliesin*. The precise meaning of the words **ser hevin** is indeed 'Summer Stars' which Taliesin's role within Celtic tradition makes a far more apposite translation more apt altogether. It is so apposite, indeed, that we have no hesitation in retaining it in our own translation of the poem, as an example of the kind of accidental rightness which can arise out of a deep-rooted understanding of the material.

The amount of cosmological information in both this and
the remainder of the poems of Taliesin makes it clear that
a genuine tradition, albeit fragmentary, is being referred to.
Passages such as:

> I know the names of the stars
> From the North to the South . . .
> I was in the Hall of Don, [Cassiopeia]
> Before Gwydion was born . . . [Caer Gwydion = The Galaxy]
> I have been three times resident
> In the Castle of Arianrhod . . . [Northern Crown]
>
> *Hanes Taliesin*

have a meaning beyond more simplistic levels of perception.
They refer both to an actual cosmology and to an inner
worldscape which has its own 'stars in the earth'.

In an Irish poem written down in the Middle Ages, but once
again containing more primitive material, we catch a glimpse
of this inner cosmology, which holds within it all created
things, the heritage of a tradition as old as the land itself:

> Heaven, earth, sun, moon, and sea,
> fruits of earth and sea-stuff,
> mouths, ears, eyes, possessions,
> feet, hands, warriors' tongues.
>
> Horses, swords, chariots fair,
> spears, shields, and faces of men,
>
> dew, mast, sheen on leaf,
> day and night, ebb and flow

* * *

> Lore of Finn and the Fianna, a matter inexhaustible,
> Destructions, cattle-raids, wooings,
> tablets and wooden books,
> satires, keen riddles:
>
> Proverbs, maxims of might,
> and truthful teachings of Fithal,
> dark lays of the Dindsenchas for thee,

Teachings of Caipre and Cormac;
The great feast of Tara and other feasts,

the assembly of Emain and other assemblies,
annals there, it is true;
every division into which Ireland has been divided:

The story of the household of Tara, that is not scanty,
the knowledge of every cantred in Ireland,
the chronicle of women, tales of armies, conflicts,
Hostels, prohibitions, invasions:

* * *

so that all may listen . . . (337)

Maps of the Universe

Without doubt one of the most important functions of the
shaman-priest was a knowledge of the seasons, and of the
various influences, heavenly or terrestrial, which bore upon
them. To be able to recognise the stars shining from the vault
of the sky, to know which god or goddess ruled there was
essential, as was an understanding of the tides of the moon,
Arianrhod's Wheel, and the patterns of planetary influence
on all created matter. Judging by the significant number
of names, in both Irish and Welsh mythology which carry
the meaning of 'bright', 'fiery' (**Aine, Fainne, Grainne**) or
have to do with 'horses', or 'swift movement (through the
heavens)', (**Eochu, Eochaid, Echraide, Roach, March, Echbel**),
together with names relating to the Sun (**Grian, Rhiannon**) and
the Moon (**Arianrhod, Olwen**), there seems little doubt that
beneath the layers of material accumulated about the figures
of Celtic mythology, lies a considerable body of star-lore. This
became, in time, gradually overlaid with other meanings, and
names were given literal or corrupt interpretations, until the
original, cosmological meanings were lost or forgotten – as
indeed was the case in most cultures the world over. In
the end Goddesses who once represented the glory of the
sun were reduced to being depicted as wearing particularly
fine, circular golden brooches – the origin, perhaps, of

239

the many beautiful examples of 'annular' brooches discovered in Celtic burial mounds. (It is interesting to notice, also, that the word for ring in most Celtic languages is literally translated as 'thumb-tie' – perhaps an oblique reference to the divinatory thumb in the stories we have been examining?)

This all points to the fact that cosmological myths among the Celts must have been a reality which originated from the most distant past, perhaps from their original home. 'There is no time' remarks C. A. Burland in his study of folk-culture *Echoes of Magic* (39) 'of which we can state with confidence that the constellations of the Zodiac were unknown.' He continues:

> The precise astronomical alignments of Stonehenge and other great monuments testify to the skill and accuracy which our ancestors hid under the uncouth mass of the great stones. When trade came to Britain at the very beginning of the Bronze Age there was the likelihood of new knowledge about the starry hemisphere of heaven reaching the native population from the navigators of such ships as made their way there. One notes that the alignments at Stonehenge are set towards stars which were calendar markers in the days when Hammurabi ruled in Babylon [i.e. 6000 BC] ... All trade contacts would have brought new knowledge of the ways of the stars and moon.

Given the remarkable ability of the Celts to sail for thousands of miles across open seas without losing themselves, we may well believe that they possessed a considerable knowledge of the stars. This knowledge must have remained for a very long time in the consciousness of the Britons, and whether or not the Celts brought their own star-wisdom with them, or built upon that of their predecessors, there are sufficient memorials within Celtic tradition to indicate the existence of an ongoing cosmological tradition. The existence of a number of painted pebbles found at ancient sites in Scotland and the Orkneys (263) suggests that the shamans of Northern Britain may have carried charm-stones not unlike the **churingas** still borne by Australian aborigines. These serve not only as protective devices but as way-showers which enable the shamans to find their way across vast tracts of land.

The Taliesin material alone contains numerous references to star-lore and these, together with the addition of material from later, medieval sources – which frequently harks back to much earlier times – give a substantial, though fragmentary, idea of the extent of Celtic knowledge regarding the stars and planets and their influence, both magical and calendrical. These were their maps of the universe, both inner and outer, showing where the two overlapped, where the curtain between the worlds was thinnest, where it was easiest to move between the worlds.

The Shape of the Year

The existence of an extremely detailed calendrical system among the Celts was proved beyond doubt by the discovery of a number of bronze tablets, stamped with an intricate system of notation which has been interpreted as precise astronomical observance. The so-called Coligney calendar was discovered in 1897 near Bourg in France. Much work is still being done on its decipherment by experts such as Jacques Monard (200) and Garrett Olmstead (242), but there is no doubt that it represents a very sophisticated system of cosmological reference.

It is drawn up in sixteen columns of months covering a period of five years, each month being divided into two blocks of days by the word ATENOUX; in the first block are 15 days, and in the second block are either 14 or 15 days bearing a new, not a continued, enumeration. This is the regular use of the calendar in which the month is cut into two periods corresponding with the waxing and waning of the moon; but the important point about the Coligney calendar is that its real basis is not only lunar, but luni-solar, since an attempt has been made to square the system of lunar months with the solar year. The lunar term of the calendar had only 355 days, and the annual loss of 10 days from the true solar year of 365 days was restored by the insertion of an intercalary month of 30 days, occupying a double mensural space in the column, once in every two and a half years. This gives a total of 1835 days at the end of the 5 years, so that the table ends in excess of solar time, which should be just over 1826 days; but it is nonetheless a very creditable scheme ... (154)

The names of the months have been deciphered as follows, in our own translation. The precise meaning of the Gaulish words remains obscure.

Month	Name	Meaning	Festival
Oct/Nov	Samonios	Seed fall	Samhain
Nov/Dec	Duannios	The darkest depths	"
Dec/Jan	Riuros	Cold-time	"
Jan/Feb	Anagantios	Stay-home time	Imbolc
Feb/Mar	Ogronios	Time of ice	"
Mar/Apr	Cutios	Time of winds	"
Apr/May	Giamonios	Shoots-show	Beltain
May/Jun	Simivisonios	Time of brightness	"
Jun/Jul	Equos	Horse-time	"
Jul/Aug	Elembiuos	Claim-time	Lughnasadh
Aug/Sep	Edrinios	Arbitration-time	"
Sep/Oct	Cantlos	Song-time	"

It will be seen from this that the calendar is both seasonally and agriculturally oriented, with each month relating to the events of the natural year, and to the life of the tribe. It bears all the hallmarks of a shamanic calendar, designed to measure the turning seasons, and although in this form it is clearly late and possibly corrupt, in all probability it dates back to a very early period indeed. Placed upon the wheel of the year, it can be seen just how admirably workable it is (Figure 17).

We have seen that a number of attempts have been made to establish a Druidical, shamanistic calendar connected to the Great Year of the Celts and to the Ogam system of writing (see Chapter Eight). That something of this kind must have existed is beyond question – proving it, or delineating its shape, is less easy. Anthony Jackson, in his study of Pictish symbol stones (137), noticing firstly the number of triplicates in the Pictish Ogam inscriptions, and then the ease with which the most minor restoration to the many damaged carvings produced a high preponderance of the numbers five and seven, draws the conclusion that the Pictish Ogams (probably borrowed from the Irish system) consisted of calendrical markings to enable the working out of ritual dates for the year. He points out that the majority of these Ogams are to be found in areas where

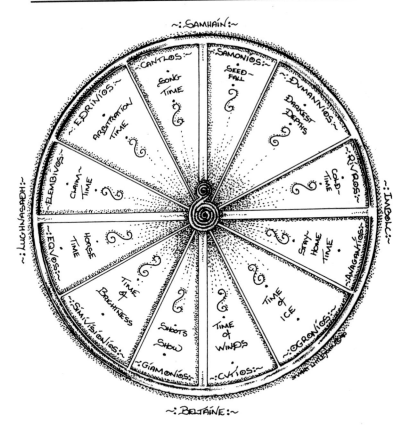

Figure 17   The Wheel of the Year.

Christianity came either late or hardly at all, and that as this
was a time and place when the magical potency of the symbol
stones was still widely recognised, this use is consistent with
the cultural background of the times.

A comparison with the Coligney calendar suggests that this
hypothesis is correct, and that we have a further indication of
the sophisticated use of astronomical observance among the
Celts. We may believe indeed that they had some method of
demarking the seasons, months and days of the year, based
upon direct observation. They were an agricultural people
and as such they required to know when to plant their
crops, when to harvest them and so on. The four great
festivals which divided the year: Imbolc, Beltain, Lugnasadh

243

and Samhain, together with the two Solstices and the two Equinoxes, provided a framework around which the year revolved.

Each of these festivals had cosmological myths attached to them. Imbolc was the time when the Cailleach transformed into the beautiful Maiden of Spring, who would not appear in her full glory until the Spring Equinox. A strange story contained in the **Book of Lismore** (312, 181) tells of an obscure game played by the boys of Rome: a board game with a hag at one end and a maiden at the other. The hag lets loose a dragon while the maiden releases a lamb; the lamb overcomes the dragon. When asked why they played this game the boys said it had been taught to them by the Sibyl. The truth behind this concerns a cosmological struggle in which the transformation of hag into maiden is seen as a battle.

Samhain, the great festival marking the beginning of winter, has many myths surrounding it. The mighty struggle between the Tuatha de Danaan and the Formorians, described in the **Battle of Mag Tuiread** (59), can be seen as a cosmic battle between the great powers of the Gods. A more human (though no less Otherworldly) story is told in **The Adventures of Nera** (337). Having accepted as a 'dare' to put a withy round the toe of a recently dead captive hanging outside the walls of the royal rath of Connaught, Nera finds that the moment he touches the body he experiences a vision of the Otherworld, and of his own future. He meets and encounters an Otherworld Goddess who gives him the fruits of summer to take back with him into the world of men, having extracted a promise from him that he should return to her when men came to conquer the **sidhe**, as they surely would when they heard Nera's description of it. All fell out as predicted, but Nera vanished into the Otherworld and the attempts to conquer it were, of course, a failure. Once again the underlying myth is cosmic, with the goddess of the **sidhe** transcending the seasons to show the reality of the summer at midwinter.

Beltain is the festival most nearly concerned with the myth of Taliesin, who is reborn (or rediscovered) in his leather bag at Gwyddno's weir on May Eve. His story reads like a cosmology – the birth of a star perhaps? – but above all his coming is an example of the kind of event which was always associated with this time of the year, a time when Otherworldly enchantments were overcome, when the soul of the initiate stood naked before the Gods and, if fortunate, passed their tests to emerge truly reborn.

Lughnasadh was a time of many Goddesses: Tailltiu, Macha, Carmen and Tea. Of the first two we learn that both died after a great struggle to accomplish a near-impossible task, Tailltiu the clearing of the entire country of Ireland for cultivation, Macha after racing on foot against a team of horses. Of Carmen, 'leader of an army in many battles' we learn that she bore three sons: the Fierce, the Black and the Wicked. In time, as we might expect from their names, the sons were banished, leaving Carmen behind in captivity. She died of sorrow, requesting beforehand that a feast be celebrated in her honour ever after. Tea also, patroness of the Feast of Tara, died in captivity after giving birth to three sons in the same night, each by different fathers. Thus the festival is associated with Goddesses who have to do with birth, cultivation, and trial by ordeal, each of which dates back to the most distant past of Ireland.

These four great seasonal festivals may be seen as revolving about a central point, the Centre, the World-Tree, the **Mundus**, or the Sacred Well. Celtic mythology abounds in descriptions which echo this concept. During a celebration held to mark the accession of Diarmait son of Cerbhall to the lordship of Uisnech, a great hail-storm occurred. And 'such was its greatness that the one shower left twelve chief streams in Ireland forever' (209).

On another occasion, recorded in **The Colloquy of the Ancients** (236), after Saint Patrick met the heroes Caoilte and Oisin, the latter went to the well of Uisnech to fetch water. This well had been invisible ever since the battle of Gabhra, where Fionn had fallen, but now it was revealed. There he saw 'eight beautiful salmon clothed in their diversely shaded hues', and took from the well eight sprigs of watercress and eight of brooklime. Then, dipping a pail into the well, he scooped out the eight salmon alive and leaping and took them back to Uisnach. There he set the vessel with the cresses and brooklime floating in it before the king. After that the night passed in feasting and merrymaking.

There is no explanation of this in the text, but it does not need much imagination to see the outlines of a cosmographic myth shining through. For here is a story akin to all those of mortals who steal something from the Gods, or from the Otherworld, and make off with them. The salmon are clearly

245

the salmon of wisdom, and the well probably Connla's Well of Segais, which had nine hazels growing above its rim, and from which came illumination and **awen**. Nines abound in Celtic myth: nine maidens/muses kindle the cauldron of Annwn; Blodeuwedd is created from the ninth wave; in both **Culhwch and Olwen** (144) and the **Cad Goddeu**, Caer Nefenhir, the Castle of the Highest Heaven or of the Nine Natures appears.

The pillar at the centre of the world, or the land, the well-head from which twelve rivers ran, the great trees which upheld the sky; these are all common factors in the cosmological myths of the Celts. They would have been very much part of the shaman's stock, the universal maps which enabled him to describe the indescribable and to find his way to the unreachable realms to hold converse with the spirits. Small wonder, then, if we find a deep understanding of the power inherent in the heavens within the lore and wisdom of Taliesin. We have already seen that there are traces of a 'family' of Gods in the figures of Ceridwen, Tegid Foel, Afagddu, and Taliesin himself (see Chapter Three). That this group, and the story contained in the *Hanes Taliesin*, may once have formed part of a native British cosmological myth, is something we should not rule out.

Games of the Gods

Several Irish and Welsh texts bear out this cosmological trend. In the **Fled Duin na Nged** (The Feast of Dun na Nged) from the Irish *Cycles of the Kings* (66) we learn how, when Dommnal son of Aed established a seat at Dun na nGed, close to the Boyne,

> he designed seven great ramparts about that fort after the manner of Tara of the Kings, and he designed even the houses of the fort after the manner of the houses of Tara: namely, the great Central Hall where the king himself used to abide, with kings and queens and ollams, and all that were best in every art; and the Hall of Munster and the Hall of Leinster and the Banquet-Hall of Connacht and the Assembly Hall of Ulster and the Prison of the Hostages and the Star of the Poets and the Palace of the Single Pillar . . . and all the other houses.

246

This tells us something about the nature of the original foundation at Tara, which must have been arranged in this way. It reads like a description of a cosmology, with its precise setting of houses within the great encircling walls. The seating plans which have survived from the great kingly raths of Ireland are well-documented. In a country where the sitting of a particular hero in the wrong place could give rise to a bloody feud or even a full-scale war, it was necessary to be careful of such things! The banqueting hall at Tara, like that at Dun na nGed or the Hall of Bricriu (59), recalls traditions from France (Charlemagne's twelve peers), Arthurian Tradition (the Knights of the Round Table), Norse Mythology (Odin's twelve councillors), Greek Myth (Odysseus and his twelve companions) and so on, all of which are recognised as cosmological groupings.

The division of the great raths themselves into fives, nines and twelves, reflecting the divisions of the land itself, takes this a step further. It has been expertly documented by Alwyn and Brynley Rees in their book *Celtic Heritage* (337), where are instanced parallels from places as far apart as China, India and Iceland. However, despite the Rees' statement that they 'know of no direct evidence connecting the divisions of Ireland and the court of the King of Tara, with the calendar' they give examples which indicate a strong possibility to the contrary.

> The account of the construction of Bricriu's Hall certainly embodies a calendrical symbolism. It took **seven** of the Ulster champions to carry every single lath, and **thirty** of the chief artificers of Ireland were employed in constructing and arranging the building. The hall contained the couches of the **twelve** heroes and it was built in the course of **one** year.

Conchobar Mac Nessa, the King who caused Tara to be built, had *twelve* foster fathers, was granted a nominal kingship of *one* year, and had *three hundred and sixty-five* people in his household. Apart from which 'seven prophets foretold his advent *seven* years before his birth, he attained the kingship at the end of his *seventh* year, and the feast he gave at Samhain lasted *seven* days . . . he was both the year and the week' (337, my italics).

It is evident from this, as well as other sources, that the Great Hall of Tara, along with those which were modelled upon it, represented a microcosmic structure, a mirror image of the macrocosm. Thus, in **Bricriu's Feast** (59), which provides the above information concerning seating arrangements, on the occasion of the feast of Samhain when the forces of the Otherworld were raging about the royal rath, the High King was seated inside surrounded by four client kings, four-square. This arrangement somehow keeps the earthly kingdom together, warding it from the forces of Otherworldly chaos.

Rees and Rees, noting this, draw attention to the symbolism of **brandhub**, a board-game played in Ireland from very early times. Though we know comparatively little about this, it is possible to reconstruct the game by analogies with the Welsh **gwyddbwyll** and **tawlbwrdd** and the Swedish **tablut** which, taken together, suggest that there was an arrangement of four pieces about a central 'king', and that opposing sets of eight were arranged along the sides of the board – the object being, as in chess, to capture the king and establish a presence at the centre.

Nigel Suckling has done much to reconstruct the original plan of the game (301) and has produced a trial board and sets of rules. The point being that once again there is a cosmological structure to the game which, in a poem composed sometime between the 13th and the 16th Centuries by Maoil Eoin Mac Raith (159), is extended to a comparison of Ireland itself with a **brandhub** board, and to human battles with the movement of its pieces:

> The centre of the plain of Fal is Tara's castle, delightful hill; out in the centre of the plain, like a mark on a parti-coloured **brandhub** (sic) board. Advance thither, it will be a profitable step: leap up on that square, which is fitting for the **branan**, the board is fittingly thine. I would draw thy attention, o white of tooth to the noble squares proper for the **branan** (Tara, Cashel, Croghan, Naas, Oileach), let them be occupied by thee. A golden **branan** with his band art thou with thy four provincials; thou, o king of Bregia, on yonder square and a man each side of thee.

We may see here the truth of the statement that 'Celtic stories are largely concerned with the intrusion upon the cosmos of strange chaotic beings . . .' (337)

All of this is reflected, though in a less detailed way, in the Welsh texts. There is some evidence of a fivefold division of Wales parallel to that of Ireland, with the mountain of Plynlymmon (Five-Peaks) at the centre. Once again, as in the case of the Irish **brandhub**, a story from the *Mabinogion* (144), in which Arthur and his nephew Owein play a game of **gwyddbwyll** which is really a symbolic battle between the world of men and that of Faery, suggests a cosmic framework (181).

The description of the game is so precise in its details that it can be easily expressed as a diagram:

Figure 18   The Cosmic Game.

Arthur sits on his great golden chair, which is placed on a sheet of ribbed, brocaded silk with a red-gold apple at each corner. Before him sits Owein with the gaming-board between them. It is tempting to believe that this represents a very ancient cosmological picture, depicting the shape and order of the universe. Although evidence is lacking to support such a theory, it is nonetheless worthy of consideration in the light of other stories.

In **The Second Battle of Mag Tured** (59), the God Lug Samildanach (Many-Gifted) defeats the Tuatha de Danaan at three games of **fidchell**, thus gaining the right to enter their fortress and earning for himself the position of **tanist** (successor) to Nuada Silver Hand. Once within he makes the **cro** of Lug, which is itself a kind of enclosure, suggesting that he created a secondary space, a **temenos** within the Hall of Tara. In a subsequent scene he returns the great central hearth-stone, flung through the wall by Ogma, casting it back 'so that it lay *at the centre* of the palace' (my italics).

Count Tolstoy has argued, persuasively, that this is a ritual act which was echoed at Hart Fell, in Scotland, by the shaman-priest and king of Britain. This consisted of a ritual game of **gwyddbwyll** in which:

> the King moved the pegs in their holes until the hostile, disruptive forces of the cosmos were check-mated and the mountain-top became once again Lug's enclosure; a micro-cosm of the mighty world whose Centre it was . . . (308)

The symbolism of the 'Mound of Adventure' in the *Mabinogion* and elsewhere, and of the several specific mounds outside raths in Ireland, suggests a further reference to the central **mundus** or axis point from which all adventures (especially those which took place in the Otherworld) began. The fact that the shamanic Lord of the Beasts was also found there directs us to recognise the potency of the symbol: from the top of the Mound, as from the mountain, one could see in all of the four sacred directions, seeing not only the actual world, but the inner realm as well, according to the ritual of the moment and the circumstance of being there.

Inner and Outer

The Otherworld in British myth is an inscape of or overlay upon Middle Earth. It has its specified gateways or crossing-places but it is not conceived of as being 'up or out there'.

Rather, it is contiguous with every part of life. In Taliesin's poems we find the Christianised, distanced stance of Classical cosmology, but the old Celtic Otherworld is ever present.

In the **Preiddeu Annwn** the underworld is reached by sea, just as in the Irish *immrama* to the Blessed Islands. However, Annwn is also reached by entry into the earth, through springs and by travelling overland to another valley, as well as by crossing a river and chasing a (usually white) beast. In the *Mabinogion* both Pwyll and later on Pryderi come there, as indeed the **Preiddeu Annwn** reminds us. It is time that we looked at this poem in more detail and recognised it as a cosmological myth.

Preiddeu Annwn
(The Spoils of Annwn)

1

The prison of Gwair was prepared in Caer Sidi
After the manner of the telling of Pwyll and Pryderi.
None before him was sent into it,
Into the heavy grey chains which bound the loyal
    youth.
And because of the spoils of Annwn he sang bitterly,
Until the Judgement, this eternal invocation of poets:
Three-shiploads of Prydwen sailed to Annwn,
Except seven, none returned from Caer Sidi.

2

I am the pre-eminent praiser; my song sounded
In the four-towered Caer, forever turning,
And of its Cauldron was my first song sung:
Nine maidens kindle the cauldron by their breathing.
Of what nature is the Lord of Annwn's Cauldron?
Enamelled iridescence and pearly white its rim
It will not boil the coward's portion – not so its destiny.
The flashing sword of Lleawg was thrust into it
And it was left in Llemeneawg's hand.
Before hell's gate, lights were lifted
And when we went with Arthur – splendid labour –
Except seven, none returned from the Caer of Honey-Mead.

3

I am the pre-emanant praiser: my song sounded
In the four-towered Caer, the Island of the Strong Door,

Where night is mixed with day.
Bright wine is set before the host.
Three shiploads of Prydwen we furrowed the flood,
Except seven, none returned from the Caer of the Royal Horn.

4

I merit better than makers of clerkly books
Who have not seen Arthur's might beyond the Glass Caer.
Six thousand men stood high upon its wall.
It was hard to speak with their sentinel.
Three shiploads of Prydwen went with Arthur,
Except seven, none returned from the Caer of Riches.

5

I merit better than the cowardly circuit-bards
Who do not know the day,
The hour or genesis of the chick,
Who did not journey to the Court of Heaven.
They do not know about the starry ox
With sevenscore linkings in his collar . . .
And when we went with Arthur – a sorrowful journey –
Except seven, none returned from Manawyddan's Caer.

6

I merit better than the weak-willed clerics
Who do not know which day our king was made,
What time his birth, what hour the owner's coming
Nor of the silver-headed beast they guard for him.
When we went with Arthur – a lamentable meeting –
Except seven, none returned from the Caer of Achren.

There is scarcely room to consider this in sufficient depth, so much detail is there to be found within it. Recently Marged Haycock (117) and Caitlín Matthews (181) have surveyed it with widely differing conclusions. R. S. Loomis' early rendition and commentary is still of value (168). But there can be little doubt that we have in this poem a considerable amount of information regarding Celtic cosmology.

At the centre, once again, is the theme of the theft of a great Otherworld treasure by a mortal – in this case Arthur. It is probably this, the earlier version of the theme, which has become familiar as the Quest for the Grail. Here it is the Cauldron of Life itself which, like the other Cauldrons discussed in Chapter Three, could give life, wealth, food and general plenty to all who possessed it. But to reach the Centre, the island of Caer Sidi where Arawn pen Annwn (Head of Annwn) ruled and where the Cauldron sat, watched over/warmed by nine muses, was a difficult thing, to be achieved only with great courage and after passing many tests.

Significantly, as with the **Cad Goddeu**, Taliesin is himself present – not simply relating the facts, but participating directly in them. The expedition moves through seven 'Caers':

Caer Sidi Also called **Caer Wydyr** (Glass Castle) in the text, and the place of Gweir's imprisonment. (Gweir is a type of Mabon, the Divine Child in Celtic Myth, who was taken from his mother's side when only two nights old and imprisoned until set free by Arthur in a raid not unlike that described in this poem. See this story in **Culhwch and Olwen** (144) and also the commentary in Caitlín Matthews' *Mabon and the Mysteries of Britain* (183).) Both Pwyll and Pryderi, as well as Little Gwion, can be said to have shared this 'imprisonment' in the Otherworld, which is analogous to the womb of Ceridwen. It is also the Caer of Arianrhod, or the Corona Borealis, the initiatory place of poets, where Taliesin has several times journeyed, and where Manawyddan has also been.

Caer Pedryfan The Four-Square or Four-Cornered Castle. It revolves four times, in common with Curoi Mac Daire's rath, of which it was said that whatever part of the world Curoi might be in, he sang a spell over his stronghold each night; it would then revolve as swiftly as a mill-wheel turns, so that its entrance was never found after sunset (89). The same concept is found in Anglo-Saxon astronomy, where the heavens are described thus: 'The heaven locketh up in its bosom all the world, and it turneth ever about us, swifter than any mill wheel ... It is all round and solid and painted with stars.' (55) The Four-Cornered Fortress may or may not be analogous to the Island of the Strong Door. In it are found the nine maidens/muses who guard the cauldron (cf. the *Vita Merlini* where Morgen and her nine sisters heal the wounded Arthur on the isle of Avalon). It seems to stand for the perfection of Middle Earth.

Caer Feddwyd Castle of Carousal, the mead-hall of the Otherworld, perhaps analogous to the hall on the island of Gwales where Bran the Blessed entertained the Company of the Noble Head to great feasting and drinking. 'And there was for them a fair and royal place above the ocean . . . And that night they were plentifully supplied and joyful. And all of the Sorrow that had been before their eyes . . . naught came to mind to them, either of that or of any mourning in the world . . . Nor did any of them know of the other that he was older . . . than when they came there.' (Trans. Loomis) This makes it clear that the Otherworld is being referred to. Here, perhaps, came heroes to dine and drink, and to forget their past lives of strife and trouble.

Caer Rigor Loomis suggests the Castle of the Royal Horn (**ri cor**) – a good name for a place of Otherworldly hospitality. Yet this is somehow different to the above Caer. Perhaps it suggests the Court of Joy, from Arthurian Romance, which is announced by the blowing of the horn. Haycock gives, as an alternative reading, 'Fortress of Inflexibility' (117).

Caer Goludd Loomis suggests Fortress of Frustration, which seems doubtful. Castle of Riches (Modern Welsh, **golut**) might prove more satisfactory in the light of the undoubted riches to be gained from the raid on the Otherworld. It must be admitted, however, that the line endings suggest that **goludd** is more likely. If this is the case, we may speculate that the 'frustration' was that of a difficult test or trial not easily overcome.

Caer Fandwy-Manddwy Marged Haycock believes this to be etymologically uncertain, but there is surely little doubt that it is Caer **Manawyddan**, who had a fortress in or upon the sea, and who fits into the pattern of deity represented by the poem.

Caer Ochren Perhaps the Fort of **Achren** from the **Cad Goddeu**? This might at one time have been Caer **Gogyrwen** (a pun on the modern Welsh **Gogrwn** to riddle, as in sieve), and might thus be seen as the Caer of Ceridwen herself.

That this represents, in part at least, a cosmological myth is evident from the presence of these references. Arthur, Taliesin and the Crew of Prydwen travel through the seven circles (levels) of the Otherworld in the same way as the shaman climbing his tree. The references to Gods like Manawyddan, Arianrhod, Ceridwen and of course Arawn himself, show that at one time the poem may have stood at the centre of a much larger cosmological myth in which Arthur, still a cosmic figure at this point in time (Nichols), sailed his sun-boat Prydwen through the heavens in search of the great Cauldron in which the elements of Creation were mixed.

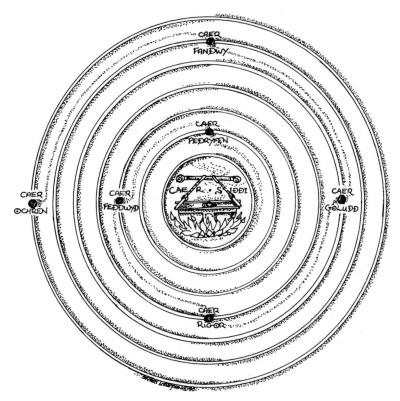

Figure 19   The Seven Circles of Annwn.

Two other sources which strengthen this supposition are to be found in another poem attributed to Taliesin, and in the story of **Culhwch and Olwen** from the *Mabinogion* (144). In the former, the poem entitled **The Defence of the Chair** (translated in full on pages 294–6), which we have already had occasion to quote, we read:

> My chair is in Caer Sidi
> where no one is afflicted with age or illness.
> Manawyd[den] and Pryderi have known it well.
> It is surrounded by three circles of fire

255

To the borders of that place come the ocean's flood,
A fruitful fountain plays before it,
Whose liquor is sweeter than the finest wine.

This description is so vivid that it can be expressed in a diagram:

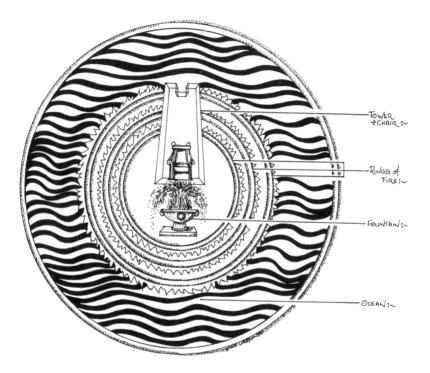

TOWER
+CHAIR :~

RINGS of
FIRE :~

FOUNTAIN :~

OCEAN :~

Figure 20   The Defence of the Chair.

The cosmological significance of this is clear. In the second example, from **Culhwch and Olwen**, it is less so, but nonetheless in the light of the remaining evidence presented here, we can be fairly certain that it represents another of the cosmological battles of the kind represented by **Cad Goddeu** and the Irish invasion myths.

In this story Culhwch, the nephew of Arthur, comes to the court to enlist his uncle's help in winning the hand of the daughter of the giant Yspaddaden Pencawr. To achieve this means obtaining several magic objects, including the Cauldron of another giant, Diwrnach.

'Arthur set out . . . and went on Prydwen his ship, and came to Ireland. And they set out for the house of Diwrnach . . . And after they had eaten and drunk their fill Arthur asked for the cauldron . . . When it was refused them, Bedwyr (Bedivere) arose and seized the cauldron and placed it upon the back of Hygwydd, Arthur's servant . . . Llenlleawc the Irishman grasped Kaledfwlch (Excalibur) and brandished it, and slew Diwrnach the Irishman and all his host . . . After putting the armies wholly to flight, Arthur and his men embarked in their presence in the ship, and the cauldron with them . . . (144)

This reads almost like a summary of the **Preiddeu Annwn**. All of the same elements are present, and surely Llenlleawc is the same as Lluch Lleminawc, brandishing a sword which flashed? In the end the raid is successful and the Cauldron carried off.

In the **Preiddeu Annwn**, as indeed elsewhere, Taliesin seems almost to tease us with his oblique references to things which are known to him but not to the 'foolish' or 'cowardly' bards. This has led one commentator (117) to remark on the 'braggadocio element' of the poem and its author; but in reality it is more in the nature of a challenge to all who heard (or later, read) the poem, to follow where the great bard had gone before and, in following, learn.

Taliesin and the Creation of the Worlds

It is perhaps no longer surprising to find the character of Taliesin attributed with knowledge beyond that of ordinary men. In Geoffrey of Monmouth's famous text we first hear of Taliesin (or as Geoffrey calls him Telgesinus) visiting Merlin at the latter's behest, to discuss weather-lore. He had, it would seem, recently come from Brittany where he had learned 'sweet philosophy' from Gildas the Wise. This is an interesting point because we know that Gildas did indeed settle in Brittany and that he lived contemporaneously with Taliesin. Once he had arrived the two wisemen settled down to a long cosmological discussion. Taliesin expounded at

257

length on the creation and the formation of matter 'under
the guidance of Minerva . . .'

> Out of nothing the Creator of the world produced four
> [elements] that they might be the prior cause as well as
> the material for creating all things when they were joined
> together in harmony: the heaven which He adorned with stars
> and which stands on high and embraces everything like the
> shell surrounding a nut; then He made the air, for forming
> sounds, through the medium of which day and night present
> the stars; the sea which girds the land in four circles, and
> with its mighty refluence so strikes the air as to generate the
> winds which are said to be four in number; as a foundation He
> placed the earth, standing by its own strength and not lightly
> moved, which is divided into five parts [sic], whereof the
> middle one is not habitable because of the heat and the two
> furthest are shunned because of their cold. To the last two He
> gave a moderate temperature and these are inhabited by men
> and birds and herds of wild beasts. He added clouds to the
> sky so that they might furnish sudden showers to make the
> fruits of the trees and of the ground grow with their gentle
> sprinkling. With the help of the season these are filled like
> water skins from the rivers by a hidden law, and then, rising
> through the upper air, they pour out the water they have taken
> up, driven by the force of the winds. (245)

Taliesin continued at length, describing the types of the
four winds, the outer realm of the fixed stars, the moon and
sun, and the spaces between which are filled with spirits,
both good and evil. He then discoursed upon the biology of
the seas which, like the land itself, have hot streams leading
down to the Underworld and cold streams nourished by the
rays of the planet Venus. Next he introduced more details
relating to the earth, with an account of certain islands, of
which Britain is said to be the most fair,

> for it bears crops which throughout the year give the noble
> gifts of fragrance for the use of man, and it has woods and
> glades with honey dripping in them, and lofty mountains and
> broad green fields, fountains and rivers, fishes and cattle and
> wild beasts, fruit trees, gems, precious metals, and whatever
> creative nature is in the habit of furnishing. Besides all
> these it has fountains healthful because of their hot waters
> which nourish the sick and provide pleasing baths, which

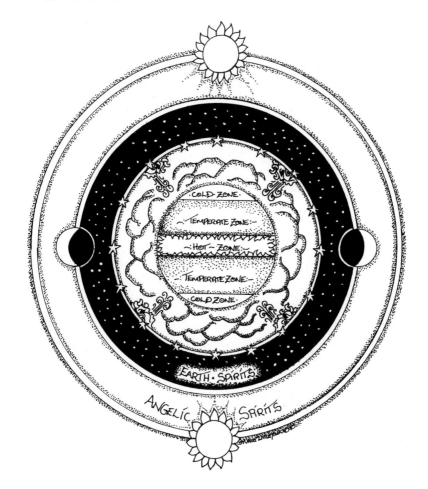

Figure 21   The Creation According to the Vita Merlini.

quickly send people away cured with their sickness driven
out. (ibid.)

This is obviously a description of a kind of earthly paradise
rather than an actual account of Britain, and from this Taliesin
goes on to describe the Otherworldly realm of the Fortunate
Isles, demonstrating exactly the kind of totally integrated cosmological vision of the shaman. R. J. Stewart has explored this

material at length and his interpretation can hardly be bettered (288). It can be expressed most simply in diagrammatic form (Figure 21).

Geoffrey clearly had access to a number of straightforward medieval accounts of Creation, such as Bede's *De Natura Rerum* or the *Cosmographia* of Bernard Sylvestris. However, much of his information seems to have come from the writings of Isidore of Seville (AD 560–636), a Spanish monk who was, curiously enough, roughly contemporary with Taliesin himself (37). Various arguments have been produced to prove that his works were, or were not, available as early as the late 6th or early 7th Centuries in Britain and Ireland, and certainly there are fragmentary manuscripts which seem to support this claim (283). Isidore was really an encyclopedist who collared a vast range of material from every possible source in a completely unsystematic way. He was also totally credulous, which means that much of what he wrote borders on the fantastic. There is little doubt that he was a major influence on the Celtic cosmographers, and that many of his ideas are reflected in the later Taliesin material.

Aside from these late sources which, nevertheless, themselves drew on earlier beliefs, especially in the case of Isidore of Seville, Geoffrey seems also to have had access to some of the material attributed to Taliesin. J. J. Parry, the work's earliest translator and editor, first drew attention to this and published versions of the poems in question in his edition of 1925 (245). He was, however, using Skene's unreliable translation. With the benefit of our own versions of the works, we can see even more clearly how much the account in the *Vita Merlini* owes to the Taliesin tradition.

Several poems relate to cosmological matter, of which the most powerful must be **The Song of the Microcosm** (sometimes called 'The Song of the Little World'), which contains the following verse:

> The good God made
> Five zones of the earth,
> For as long as it lasts:
> The first is formed cold,
> The second is formed cold,
> The third is formed hot,
> Injurious to flowers,
> Unpleasant and hurtful,

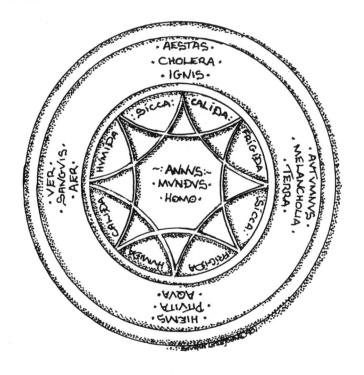

Figure 22a The Cosmology of Isidore of Seville.

> The fourth is paradise
> Which people shall enter.
> The fifth is temperate,
> The habitable part of the Universe.

This is close enough to the description contained in the *Vita Merlini* to have been a direct influence upon it. Of course it must be said that all of this could derive simply from late medieval sources, but it is equally possible that *their* sources derived from those of an earlier age. Certainly, within the context of the Taliesin material, everything is very much of a piece.

Another poem, not contained in the *Book of Taliesin*, adds to this. It was printed from several later versions in the *Myvyrian Archaiology* (145). Despite its lateness and obvious Christian overtones, we can see an older picture hidden below it. It

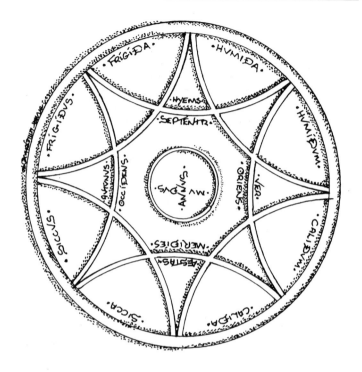

Figure 22b The Cosmology of Isidore of Seville.

is translated in full here, rather than in the main selection
of Taliesin poems, because it is of less clear origin. Our
translation owes something to that of D. W. Nash (8).

The first six and last four lines are an invocation to the
Judaeo-Christian God in Biblical terms and are therefore
omitted. After that the cosmological section begins proper.

> First there was a separation of the elements:
> The fire and water, the sea and the earth,
> (For not of one nature are fire and earth).
> A tangled chain from earth to sky –
> Who but the Skilful One connected them,
> With skill and artifice in all things;
> And who filled the sea with brine?
> (For not of one nature are heaven and earth).
> Neither stone nor iron make it strong,
> Nor reeds nor straw create for it a roof;

Nor heavy lead weighs upon it,
Nor metal worked with fire encircles it.
Has not the Skilful One clothed it in water and ice?
A pure prophet has proclaimed it:
Is it not the skill of the Ever Living One . . .
Has not the Skilful One adorned the heavens
With stars and signs, with sun and moon?
Daily the sun wheels around the earth,
Giving light from on high
To the five zones framed by the wonderful Creator.
The two furthest are bound by snow and ice,
On account of their cold no one goes near them.
The others are set off from these,
Filled with fire and burning heat.
The fifth lies in between – no one inhabits it,
Because of the sun's rays in their course.
The rest are temperate,
Receiving heat from one side, cold from the other.
God erected two fountains of perfect goodness:
A fountain of heated air, where the sun revolves;
A fountain of water from which comes the sea . . .

This reads almost like an earlier try or a variation on the themes of the **Song of the Microcosm**. The references to fountains, which appear both in this poem and in the *Vita Merlini*, recall one of Taliesin's most important works, **The Three Fountains**, the text of which will be found in full on pages 287–8 together with commentary. It is a difficult and obscure poem, but if our understanding of it is correct, it seems to offer a detailed cosmological map which owes nothing to either medieval or classical learning. Placed side by side with details from other works, a surprisingly homogeneous picture emerges:

There is an odious worm/from Caer Satanas
it has conquered all/between depths and shallows.

Its jaws are as wide/as the Alps.
Death cannot conquer it,/nor hand nor blade.

It weighs 900 stone/its two paws are hairy:
one eye in its head/green as the glacial ice.

There are three fountains/in its neck.

(The Three Fountains)

263

The dragon comes out/and crawls towards
the cups of song;/of the song of the cups of gold.
The golden cups are in his hand/his hand is on the knife
and the knife is/above my head.

(Protection of the Honey Isle)

There are three fountains/in (the worm's) neck . . .
The River of Gifts, the River of Blessing
is the name of the three fountains.

. . . one of grey brine . . . to restore the wave,
over the seas it vanishes.
The second, in perfection, strikes the hill-foot,
whence do we have rain . . .
The third is in the veins of the mountains,
like a sparkling feast.

(The Three Fountains)

There are three fountains/on the mountain of skill,
there is a citadel/over the oceans' wave.

(Riddle Song)

And three fountains there are
two above wind and one above the earth.

(Black Book of Carmarthen, Skene)

And of course, the poem on the inundation of Cantre'r
Gwaelod:

Accursed be the damsel,
Whom, after the wailing,
Let loose the Fountain of Venus, the raging deep.

Accursed be the maiden,
Who, after the conflict, let loose
The fountain of Venus, the desolating sea.

(Seithenin)

According to the Iolo manuscripts, perhaps to be trusted here,
the three names of the sea are **Maes Gwenhidwy, Llys Neifion,**
and **Ffynon Wenestr** (The Field of Gwenhidwy, The Court of
Neifion, and the Fountain of Venus), which may well be
alternative terms for parts of the heavens. For the rest we

seem to have the fragmentary remains of a cosmological myth concerning a great serpent. This is a theme which appears so widely in the creation myths of the world th/at it can scarcely be otherwise. The fountains which seem to spring from the great creature's neck and to become rivers recall again the central wells of Irish mythology. Nor should we forget, indeed, the great Dragon of the Heavens, the constellation of Draco, which turns about the central nail or Pole, holding together the fabric of the cosmos itself. Figure 23 combines some of these elements into a coherent whole.

Whilst on this subject it may be as well to list here the various names of the constellations found scattered through the vast wilderness of Celtic myth and folk-lore. Where possible, the constellations in question have been identified, though there are many gaps. The letters after certain entries refer to their appearance in either the *Hanes Taliesin* (HT), *The Book of Taliesin* (BT) or the *Welsh Triads* (TYP).

The Names of the Constellations

1	The Court of Arianrhod (Caer Arianrhod)	Corona Borealis HT
2	The White Throne	Spica in Virgo
3	Arthur's Harp (Telyn Idris)	Lyra
4	The Court of Gwydion (Caer Gwydion)	The Galaxy/The Milky Way
5	Arthur's Plough-Tail	The Great Bear
6	The Little Plough-Tail	The Little Bear
7	The Great Ship	Navis
8	The Bald Ship(?)	
9	Arthur's Yard (Wain)(?)	Orion
10	Theodosius' Group (Twr Tewdws)	The Pleiades HT
11	The Triangle	Triangulum(?)
12	The Palace of Don (Llys Don)	Cassiopeia
13	The Grove of Blodeuwedd	
14	The Chair of Teyrnon	BT
15	The Court of Eiddionwydd	
16	Caer Sidi	The Zodiac HT
17	The Conjunction of 100 circles	
18	The Camp of Elmur	TYP
19	The Soldier's Bow	

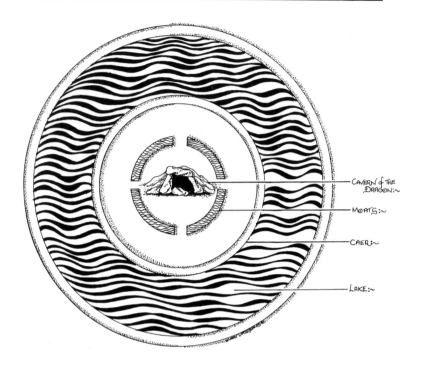

Figure 23   The Protection of the Honey Isle.

20	The Hill of Dinan	
21	The Eagle's Nest	
22	Bleiddyd's Lever (Bleidad?)	
23	The Wind's Wing	
24	The Trefoil	
25	The Cauldron of Ceridwen	HT
26	Teivi's Bend	
27	The Great Limb	
28	The Small Limb	
29	The Large-Horned Oxen	The Twins(?)
30	The Great Plain	[Milky Way]
31	The White Fork	
32	The Woodland Boar	
33	The Muscle(?)	
34	The Hawk	
35	The Horse of Llyr	

36   Elphin's Chair
37   Olwen's Hall

In the *Vita Merlini* (54) Merlin studied the heavens from his 'observatory' which had seventy-two windows. In the **Saltair ne Rann** (130) and the *Senchus Mor* this is echoed at the end of the description of the making of the universe, where the passage of the sun through the constellations is described, each of the twelve divisions through which it passes having six windows with close-fitting shutters and strong coverings, which open to shed light by day, also making a total of seventy-two.

The Three Levels

Taliesin's personal cosmology divides very neatly into three. A number of influences, both inner and outer, affect him in different ways throughout his life. We can devise the following schema to explicate them:

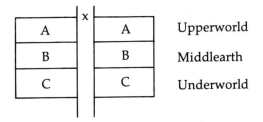

Figure 24: The Three Worlds.

A **Upperworld** Caer Arianrhod (Corona Borealis) and Caer Gwydion (the Milky Way) illuminate Taliesin's firmament. The Crown of the North, as it is called, has seven stars. Native Americans called it 'the Celestial Sisters' and believed it to be the cave wherein the Great Bear hibernated. The Milky Way has been known as a pilgrim route in many parts of Europe – both Compostella and Walsingham have legends about this. Its swirlings are like those of the druidic mist, the enchantments of Gwydion – a figure with whom Taliesin much identifies. Arianrhod seems, at times, to be an upperworld analogue of Ceridwen.

B **Middlearth** The constellations of Taliesin's middlearth are
Maelgwn, Gwyddno, Urien and Elffin; the men to whom he is
bound by bonds of relationship, patronage and homage.
C **Underworld** Taliesin associates with the underworld deities
of Ceridwen, Bran and Arawn, symbolised by the cauldron and
bag/coracle.

He thus maintains complex webs of relationship with the
three worlds, as well as with the Otherworld, which is not
understood to be an upper or other world.

x This is the central pole, described in **Hostile Confederacy**:

> I know who made the great pole/fork (**fforch**)
> which connects earth and heaven.

This is perhaps also referred to in his praise of the treetops
in **The Bright Trees**, which he sees as analogous to the
ancient poets of high tradition. The pole also penetrates the
underworld of Annwn, wherein he learns the wisdom of the
ancestral lore.

It is possible that this threefold division may account for
Iolo Morgannwg's division of the Celtic Otherworld into three
artificial levels: **Ceugant**, **Gwenfed** and **Annwn**. Only the last
named can claim any reality beyond Iolo's imagination though
once again, as stated elsewhere, the fact that he appears to
have invented the names does not invalidate the structure
which, despite his efforts to provide primitive analogies to
the Christian divisions of Heaven, Purgatory and Hell, does
have a valid place in that it meshes very neatly with the levels
recorded in the actual Celtic texts (335, 336).

We may certainly suppose that the Celtic shamans drew
upon such soul-maps to describe their own journeys and
that, since no two would ever have been quite the same, the
power which produced the similarities within the traditions
we do possess must have been very great indeed.

Knowledge of Wind and Wave

At the narrower end of the cosmological hierarchy is weather,
about which Merlin originally summoned Taliesin to discourse
in the *Vita Merlini*. The importance of weather-lore is shown
by a curious fragment which survived to be included in
the compendious collection of law tracts and other material

known as *Senchus Mor* (111) and also, in a slightly different version, in the Irish cosmological poem **Saltair Na Ran** (130). Here we find the winds not only named but also linked to specific colours. There were, we are told 'four chief winds and four subordinate winds, and four other subordinate winds, so that there are twelve winds.' The four chief winds blow from North, South, East and West, and between each two points of these there are two subordinate winds. Each of these also had a specific colour, as in the diagram printed below.

The importance of the winds to the ancient Irish is further demonstrated by the following poem, dated to the 10th Century, which deals with the particular blessings or calamities

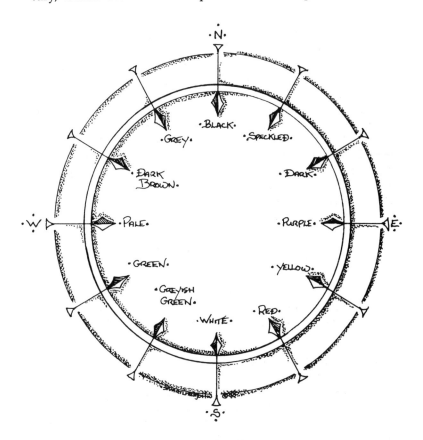

Figure 25   The Wheel of the Winds.

which follow upon the blowing of each wind. Invoking Christ,
the poet asks

> That I may tell what signifies the voice
> Of the wind on the kalends of January.
> Solanus of the hundred battles,
> It is fruitful though productive of plague,
> It rejects chiefs only,
> Many are its diseases.
>
> Africus from the south-east, not bad,
> It signifies specially good fruit,
> Fish and corn, while it lasts,
> It is unique in its excellences.
>
> As for Saronicus from the South,
> It signifies to you a rich harvest,
> A great quantity of full fruit,
> Marvellous huge fish.
>
> Goods will be destroyed, a track not narrow,
> If it is Favonius from the south-west:
> It signifies every corn-crop laid low,
> Battles and scant harvest.
> It denotes the death of a king if from the West.
>
> It is Puinina around the ocean,
> Great bloodshed, and slaying of men,
> And a plague on [wrongdoers].
>
> Pessima from the north-west only,
> Dearth, and slaughters,
> And fall of blossoms it says
> Without . . .
>
> If it is Faiccina from the north,
> There will be noise of red-sworded battle,
> Death of the [false], plague and heat,
> Drought and heavy distress.
>
> A fair multitude of fish, petty commemoration!
> If it is Altanus from the north-east,
> Sickness in it, battle with venom,
> Many fruits it brings to us.
>
> *Hibernica Minora*, trans. Kuno Meyer, 206

270

This is more than simple weather-lore, and less than magic. It relates to an almost symbiotic relationship with the elements, such as all shamans must possess. Though late, and Christian in tone, its Latinate names cannot disguise the primate beliefs beneath its outer layer.

Hu The Mighty

No discussion of Celtic cosmology would be complete without mention of Hu Gadarn. This figure dominates modern revival druidry as a principal deity. Hu the Mighty, as **gadarn** is generally translated, is pictured as a Ploughman God, leading the Cymry out of the Summer Country, otherwise known as Deffrobani or Constantinople. That no trace of him has ever been discovered earlier than the 14th Century has led many commentators to the conclusion that he was yet another 'invention' of the redoubtable Iolo Morgannwg who refers to Hu in several of the so-called **Third Series** of the **Welsh Triads**, originally published in *The Myvyrian Archaiology of Wales* (145), and more recently edited by the leading authority on the **Triads**, Rachel Bromwich (34).

The version quoted here is not Iolo's own, but that of W. Probert, published in 1823 as an appendix to his *Ancient Laws and Institutes of Wales*. There are altogether seven references to Hu, as follows:

There are three pillars of the nation of the Isle of Britain. The first was Hu the Mighty, who brought the nation of the Cambrians first to the Isle of Britain; and they came from the Summer Country, which is called Defrobani (that is, where Constantinople now stands); and they came over the Hazy Sea to the Isle of Britain, and to Armorica, where they settled. (*Triad 4*)

There were three social tribes of the Isle of Britain. The first was the Cambrians, who came to the Isle of Britain with Hu the Mighty, because he would not possess a country and lands by fighting and pursuit, but by justice and tranquillity. (*Triad 5*)

The three over-ruling counter energies of the Isle of Britain: Hu the Mighty, who brought the Cambrian nation from the Summer Country, called Defrobani, unto the Isle of Britain. (*Triad 54*)

The three benefactors of the Cambrian nation. First, Hu the Mighty, who first taught the Cambrians the way to plough, when they were in the Summer Country, before they came to the Isle of Britain (*Triad 56*)

271

The three primary inventors of the Cambrians. Hu the Mighty, who formed the first mote and retinue over the nation of Cambria . . . (*Triad 57*)

The three inventors of song and record of the Cambrian nation: . . . Hu the Mighty, who first applied vocal song to strengthen memory and record . . . (*Triad 92*)

The three primary and extraordinary works of the Isle of Britain . . . the large horned oxen of Hu the Mighty, that drew the [**Avanc**] from the lake to the land, so that the lake did not burst forth any more . . . (*Triad 97*)

These **Triads** are all generally ascribed to Iolo himself, and Hu Gadarn has been dismissed as a figment of either his own or, at best, some medieval author's imagination. However, the work of A. C. Rejhon (258), coupled with that of Rachel Bromwich (34), has recently indicated that there is more to Hu than was at first apparent.

The initial problem is the name itself. The prefix **hu** simply means 'the', though it is also used as an intensifier to indicate a more powerful stress to the word which follows it. Its nearest equivalents are the Gaulish **su**, 'good', Old Irish **so** or **su** which have the sense of 'ready, quick, mighty, bold, resolute' (258), while **Gadarn** (or **Cadarn** as it is sometimes written) is generally taken to mean 'warrior'. One could break down the name as **Hu Cadarn**, 'the mighty-battle-man' or 'warrior'. How this powerful figure came to be associated with the idea of a divine ploughman is less easy to explain, although Rejhon's argument (summarised below) seems, to me, to hold water.

Some scholars believe that we need look no further than the 14th Century poet Iolo Goch for an immediate source. A poem does indeed exist which describes Hu Gadarn as an archetypal ploughman, an emperor of land and sea, and a 'constable of golden corn'. However, it is possible to look elsewhere for a possible basis for the character.

Even Iolo Morgannwg (or rather his editor) recognised that a relationship existed between the figure of Hu Gadarn and the French hero Hugon Le Fort, who appears only in the Chanson de Geste called *Le Pélérinage de Charlemagne à Jerusalem et à Constantinople*, 'The Journey of Charlemagne to Jerusalem and Constantinople' (318). This text tells how the Emperor Charlemagne visited Hugon after hearing himself unfavourably compared to his host. Given lodging, the Emperor and his twelve peers were overheard making several boasts about their

272

prowess, and next day were required to prove their abilities which they did, though not without divine intervention. Hugon himself was said to plough his fields with a golden plough, seated on a golden chair. In the 13th Century Welsh version of this story Hugon is translated as Hu Gadarn – the question is whether this was the *origin* of the name in Welsh myth and Bardic lore, or whether there was an *already existing* figure who became, by association, identified with Hugon the Strong. Certainly the evidence of a later summary of a lost version of the **Pélérinage** found in the *Myreur des Histors* by Jean d'Outremeuse, which dates from the end of the 14th Century, suggests that this may be so. In this the character known as Hugon is called, instead, 'Gadars', a name which seems likely to have derived from the Welsh 'Gadarn'. We are thus left to assume either that the French author used a Welsh text as his source – which is unlikely – or that the name Gadarn referred to the *original* hero of the tale.

This same story, with certain variations, is told in the ballad of **King Arthur and King Cornwall**, with Arthur playing the role of Charlemagne, and King Cornwall that of Hugon. The latter has been identified (318) with the archetypal figure who appears throughout the Arthurian mythos as the abductor of Guinevere (others are Melwas, Meleagraunce, Cador and Mordred) and, through him, with the Irish hero Eochaid Airem, whose own wife, Etain, is abducted by the otherworldly king, Midir. Eochaid himself is described, in the 11th Century text **Tochmarc Etaine**, 'The Abduction of Etain' (25), as being 'the first of the men of Ireland to put a yoke upon the necks of oxen', and it was said that he was following the example of 'the folk of the elf-mounds', who yoked their oxen across the shoulders rather than the forehead (25).

Thus Eochaid is said to be the first ploughman in Ireland, and is involved in an episode similar to that found in **King Arthur and King Cornwall** and the **Pélérinage de Charlemagne** where both leaders are shown as either submitting or being submitted to by men of more than mortal stature, and where, in the case of the Charlemagne text, the place ruled over by Hugon is Constantinople – from which city Hu Gadarn is said to have led the Cymry.

The argument is circular, but to my mind it suggests that Hu was indeed an established figure in his own right, before the advent of the Charlemagne story. The later redaction alone seems to prove this. Whether he was really the divine figure that Iolo believed him to be is a matter for further discussion than we have room for here. That he does not, apparently, appear to be mentioned in any of the insular inscriptions which name the other Celtic deities is a serious stumbling block to belief in Hu as a god-figure. However, we must not forget that we may be dealing with folk-belief rather than established oral tradition, and in the light of this may perhaps tentatively suggest that 'hu Gadarn' was a title rather than a distinct figure, and that he could thus have been the supreme deity – assuming that such was recognised – of the Druids.

Thus we come to the end of this exploration of the traditions relating to Taliesin. The second part of the book consists of new translations of the major mythological poems attributed to him. Attached to each of these is a brief commentary intended to enable the reader to find a way through the crowded garden of symbolism and reference. The Myth of Taliesin is about the attaining – not always easily – of wisdom. As such there is much that it can tell us today about the perils and pitfalls of knowing too little or too much. It tells us something, also, about initiation, about the way it can come and the feelings it evokes. There is, perhaps, little of the personal in Taliesin's poems, but there is enough to acquaint us with his compassion, sense of justice, his unwillingness to suffer fools gladly, and his abiding interest in everything from the merest raindrop to the farthest star. His work is an embodiment of the innate curiosity of the human spirit, which hungers and thirsts for knowledge (sometimes against its best interests) and which has never really changed in this respect since the beginning of time.

The study of these materials leads us into every possible area of Celtic life and lore. It shows us the way into the realm of the Otherworld, which is also that of the Celtic shamans, and gives us valuable insights into the techniques which were once practised by them. We are fortunate indeed that, despite their corrupt state, lateness of manuscript, tradition, etc., we can still find our way around in the tangled forest, and that we have, at last, begun to perceive faint, but well trodden, paths through the undergrowth.

PART TWO

The Poems of Taliesin Pen Beirdd

(In a New Translation with Commentary)

by

John and Caitlín Matthews

THE POEMS OF TALIESIN
PEN BEIRDD

This section contains translations with notes, glosses and brief commentary of all the major poems attributed to Taliesin which are felt to be part of the authentic tradition. Most are by Caitlín and John Matthews, and appear here in this form for the first time. Others are taken from various sources, including D. W. Nash's *Taliesin* (8), W. F. Skene's *Four Ancient Books of Wales* (10) and the idiosyncratic translations of J. Gwenogryfan Evans (4). Some constitute reconstructions from longer works contained within all these sources, and are printed here in full, separately from the text, for the sake of clarity. A detailed description of the methods employed will be found in the Introduction and Chapter Three. Poems from Nash are indicated by an **N** after the title; those from Skene by an **S**; Evans by an **E**. The remainder are original translations by John or Caitlín Matthews. We have omitted all those poems addressed to or about Owein Gwynedd, partly because they are very readily available in excellent translations, and partly because they have been very specifically and accurately identified as the authentic compositions of the 6th Century bard Taliesin. The divergence between this figure and that of the Taliesin tradition is, as stated throughout, wide. Those who wish to know more of the historical figure are referred to the bibliography. For the purposes of the present work it was felt that these fell outside the compass of our study into the mythological and shamanic traditions relating to Taliesin.

List of Poems from the Book of Taliesin

This list is by no means complete. It follows roughly the order established by Skene (10), which is not necessarily that of the original manuscripts. It lists all those poems which appear, after investigation, to belong to the Taliesin tradition, including various poems of a theological nature which nonetheless show signs of deriving from an original (rather than a clerkly) source. The page on which each poem can be found is indicated in brackets after each title. The various categories into which the poems fall are indicated as follows.

1 **Bold** = the major poems of Taliesin translated here.
2 † = poems from the *Hanes Taliesin* which do not appear in the *Book of Taliesin*.
3 ( ) = our title.
4 * = poems from other sources containing references to Taliesin.
5 + = poems **not** translated here.

† **The Consolation of Elffin** (280)
† **Taliesin's Song of his Origins** (281)
+† The Nature of Water
† **Journey to Deganwy** (282)
† **Primary Chief Bard** (283)
† **The Chair of Deganwy** (286)
† **The Three Fountains** (287)
† **The Contention of the Bards** (289)
† **The Rebuke of the Bards** (290)
+† The Spite of the Bards
+† The Pillar of Song
+ The Reconciliation of Lludd and Lleflys
Death Song of Cu Roi Mac Daire (291)
+ Death Song of Erof
+ Madawg, ap Uthyr
+ Death of Cunedda ap Edern
Chair of the Sovereign (292)
Preiddeu Annwn (in main text on pages 251–2)
+ Daronwy
+ Praise of Lludd the Great
(Defence of the Chair) (294)
Cad Goddeu (296)
(Taliesin's Bardic Lore) (301)
+ Death Song of Dylan eil Ton
+ (Taliesin's Predictions)
The Chair of Ceridwen (304)

The Death Song of Uther Pendragon (306)
+ (The Archdeacon)
+ The Praises of Taliesin
* **(Seithenhin)** (308)
+ Praise of Tenby
+ (Praise of Gwallawg I)
+ (Praise of Gwallawg II)
+ (Kings of Rheged)
+ Satisfaction of Urien
+ Spoils of Taliesin
+ (Battles of Owain ap Urien)
+ The Affair of Argoed Llwyfain
* Death Song of Owain
Dialogue of Myrddin and Taliesin (in main text on pages 208–9)
(Protection of the Honey Isle) (309)
+ (Contention of Powys)
+ Armes Prydein
Lesser Prophecy of Prydein (in main text on page 196)
+ (Cadwaladr)
+ Satire of Cynan Garwyn son of Brochwael
* **(Cuhelyn's Song)** (310)
+* (Blessings)
+* (The Trinity)
Fold of the Bards (311)
Hostile Confederacy (312)
Chair of Taliesin (319)
Song to the Wind
+ Song to Mead (II)
(Song of the Macrocosm) (321)
(Song of the Microcosm) (in main text on pages 262–3)
+ Elegy of the 1000 Sons
+ The Pleasant Things of Taliesin
+ (Taliesin's Dies Irae:)
+ (Taliesin's Lorica)
+ Plagues of Egypt
+ Rod of Moses
+ (The Promised Land)
+ (The Twelve Tribes)
+ The Contrived World
(Bright Trees) (323)

Excerpts from the following Poems
Horses (326)
Song of Ale (I) (327)
(Taliesin's Youthful Lore) (328)

The Consolation of Elffin

Fair Elffin, cease your sorrow!
Swearing profits no one.
It is not evil to hope
Nor does any man see what supports him,
Not an empty treasure is the prayer of Cynllo,
Nor does God break his promise.
No catch in Gwyddno's weir
Was ever as good as tonight's.

Fair Elffin, dry your cheeks!
Such sorrow does not become you,   (10)
Although you thought yourself cheated
Excessive sorrow gains nothing,
Nor will doubting God's miracles.
Although I am small, I am skilful.
From the sea and the mountain,
From the river's depth
God gives his gifts to the blessed.

Elffin of the generous custom,
Cowardly is your purpose,
You must not grieve so heavily.   (20)
Better are good than evil omens.
Though I am weak and small,
Spumed with Dylan's wave,
I shall be better for you
Than three hundred shares (of salmon).

Elffin of noble generosity,
Do not sorrow at your catch.
Though I am weak on the floor of my basket,
There are wonders on my tongue.
While I am watching over you,   (30)
No great need will overcome you.
Be mindful of the name of the Trinity
And none shall overcome you.

Taliesin's first song, sung on the occasion of his discovery by Elffin, son of Gwyddno Garanhir. Taliesin speaks of his being found in the

280

weir, and of the great good that will come of it, for though small in
the bottom of his basket, his abilities, both magical and poetic, will
bring only benefit to his patron. The last two lines are probably a later
interpolation.

Taliesin's Song of his Origins

Firstly I was formed in the shape of a handsome man,
in the hall of Ceridwen in order to be refined.
Although small and modest in my behaviour,
I was great in her lofty sanctuary.

While I was held prisoner, sweet inspiration educated me
and laws were imparted me in a speech which had no
    words;
but I had to flee from the angry, terrible hag
whose outcry was terrifying.

Since then I have fled in the shape of a crow,
since then I have fled as a speedy frog, (10)
since then I have fled with rage in my chains,
– a roe-buck in a dense thicket.

I have fled in the shape of a raven of prophetic speech,
in the shape of satirising fox,
in the shape of a sure swift,
in the shape of a squirrel vainly hiding.

I have fled in the shape of a red deer,
in the shape of iron in a fierce fire,
in the shape of a sword sowing death and disaster,
in the shape of a bull, relentlessly struggling. (20)

I have fled in the shape of a bristly boar in a ravine,
in the shape of a grain of wheat.
I have been taken by the talons of a bird of prey
which increased until it took the size of a foal.

Floating like a boat in its waters,
I was thrown into a dark bag,
and on an endless sea, I was set adrift.

Just as I was suffocating, I had a happy omen,
and the master of the Heavens brought me to liberty.

1–7 relate the birth process of Taliesin. The hall of Ceridwen is her womb, and her outcry the cries of labour.
8–17 relate the number of possible shapes which life might take.
18 is a metaphor of sexual union.
19 is the seed of life itself.
20–21 describe the embedding of the seed and the increasing of the womb.
22–24 describe life in the womb.
25–26 describe birth again.

Journey to Deganwy

I will set out on foot,
to the gate I will come,
I will enter the hall,
my song I will sing,
my verse I will proclaim,
and the king's bards I will cast down.
In the presence of the Chief,
demands I will make,
and chains I will break –
Elffin will be set at liberty.   (10)

And when the contention arises
in the presence of chieftains,
and the bards are summoned
to sing in faithful harmony,
with the magician's chess-board (*gwyddbwyll*),
with the druid's wisdom,
in the court of the sons of God, (*Deiion*)
there shall be some in the semblance
of cunning tricks
and crafty devices,   (20)
in grief and pain
because of the wronging of innocents.

Silent as fools,
as at the battle of Badon
with Arthur, chief giver of feasts,
with his tall blades red
from the battle which all men remember.
The King's battle against his enemies,
woe to those fools!
When his vengeance comes,   (30)
I, Taliesin, chief poet,

by means of brilliant druids' wisdom,
will release fair Elffin
from the prison of the proud tyrant.

There shall be remembrance of blood,
because of the wondrous horse,
(the battle of the woodshore in . . .)
which arose from the old North.
This shall bring an end.
No word of grace or blessing   (40)
upon Maelgwn Gwynedd,
because of this fearful wrong
and ingenious cruelty.
Vengeance shall be the ending
upon Rhun his heir.
May his life be short,
may his lands be wasted,
may his exile be long
– this upon Maelgwn Gwynedd!

1–10 are a statement of intent, like a journey itself.
15–16 are precisely translated.
17 *meibion Deiion* is given as 'scions of nobles' by Ford (2).
23–34 Taliesin images the terror and might of Arthur at Badon, which causes all viewers to gape like fools.
39–49 contain a fairly extensive and comprehensive cursing of Maelgwn's lineage. The wondrous horse is probably Meirchion, Elffin's great-grandfather, from the Gogledd (Men of the North) whose lineage will supplant or overthrow Maelgwn's. It may also have relevance to the end of the story, where Elffin's horse wins the race.

Primary Chief Bard

(following the order of verses as they appear in the
Book of Taliesin)

Primary chief poet
Am I to Elffin.
And my native country
Is the place of the Summer Stars.

John the Divine
Called me Merlin,
But all future kings
Shall call me Taliesin.

I was nine full months
In the womb of the hag Ceridwen.   (10)
Before that I was Gwion,
But now I am Taliesin.

I was with my king
In the heavens
When Lucifer fell
Into the deepest hell.

I carried the banner
Before Alexander.
I know the names of the stars
From the North to the South.   (20)

I was in Caer Bedion
Tetragrammaton.
I accompanied Heon
To the vale of Hebron.

I was in the canon
When Absalom was slain.
I was in Llys Don
Before the birth of Gwydion.

I was patriarch
To Elijah and Enoch.   (30)
I was there at the crucifixion
Of the merciful Mabon.

I was the foreman
At the construction of Nimrod's Tower.
I was three times
In the prison of Arianrhod.

I was in the ark
With Noah and Alpha.
I witnessed the destruction
Of Sodom and Gommora.   (40)

I was in Africa
Before the building of Rome.
I came here
To the remnant of Troy.

I was with the Lord
In the manger of the ass.
I upheld Moses
Through the water of Jordan.

I was in the sky (or, possibly, at the Cross)
With Mary Magdalene.   (50)
I received the muse
From Ceridwen's cauldron.

I was a harping bard
To Deon of Lochlin.
I have gone hungry
For the Maiden's Mabon.

I was at the White Mount
in the court of Cynfelyn.
In stocks and fetters
For a year and a day.   (60)

I was in the larder
In the land of the Trinity.
And no one knows whether my body
Is flesh or fish.

I was instructor
To the whole universe.
I shall be until the judgement
On the face of the earth.

I have sat in the perilous seat
Above Caer Sidi.   (70)
I shall continue to revolve
Between the three elements.

There is not a marvel in the world
Which I cannot reveal.

1–12 establish Taliesin's identity. (On the translation of line 4 see main
text discussion p. 237).
14–62 presuppose his prior presence to all great happenings.
63–66 show him to be analogous to the primeval substance from which
creation was formed (cf. *Hanes Taliesin*).
67–70 sum up his omniscience and omnipresence.

71–74 place him in the axial seat of the Corona Borealis, as master of the mysteries.

The Chair of Deganwy

Narrow-minded bards, I am contending
to keep the virtue of his powers.
I proclaim a prophetic song
to all who will listen.
I seek what is lost,
I believe in its finding completely:
Elffin suffers punishment
in Caer Deganwy.

Let them not lay on him
too many fetters or chains.   (10)
For the chair of Deganwy
I will be tried again.
Mighty my rejoicing here,
strong is my seeking.
Three hundred and more
are the songs of my singing.
The bard who does not know them
merits neither stone nor ring,
nor reward for his shield.

Elffin ap Gwyddno   (20)
is fallen under the spoils. (*anraithdro*)
Under thirteen locks,
for praising his teacher.

I am Taliesin,
Chief-poet of the West,
I shall release Elffin
out of the golden fetter.

15–16 the exact number of stories which every poet should know.
20 does not translate – the lines around it are slightly rearranged to make sense.
22 *Anraithdro* is booty, spoils, treasure and destruction in Welsh. It suggests the thirteen treasures of Annwn for thirteen locks. If so, was Elffin once a sacrificial guardian of the Hallows? Since Maelgwn is Pendragon at this time, he may have need of a Mabon (181).
26 Taliesin is chief bard to Elffin, comes from the Region of the Summer Stars, and here is chief-poet of the West.

The Three Fountains

If you are chiefs poets
versed in the arts,
relate the high mysteries
to the people of the wide world.

There is an odious worm
from Caer Satanas,
it has conquered all
between depths and shallows.

Its jaws are as wide
as the Alps (*mynnydd Mynnau*).　　　　　　(10)
Death cannot conquer it,
nor hand nor blade.

It weighs nine hundred stone;
its two paws are hairy;
one eye in its head
green as the glacial ice.

There are three fountains
in its (neck?);
the sea is speckled with the wash (*lit.* plough)
of those who swim through it –　　　　　　(20)
gentle cows and oxen.

The River of Gifts, the River of Blessing,
is the name of the three fountains.

Out of the ocean is produced
a creature of grey brine
which is from the (*corini?*)
To restore the wave,
over the Sea of Ages it vanishes.

The second, in perfection,
strikes the hill-foot,　　　　　　(30)
whence do we have rain outside:
through the sea-mist (*awyr dylan*)
fiercely slashing.

The third (is) in the veins of the mountains,
like a flowing sword-edge (*fal callestig wledd*);
the work of the King of Kings. (*Rex Rexedd*)

287

Are you boastful bards?
In proud anxiety
you are unable to satirise
the kingdom of Britain.   (40)

I am Taliesin,
Chief poet of the West,
I shall release Elffin
from the golden fetter.

This poem is very difficult and some lines hopelessly obscure. The images do not follow at all clearly. It follows on directly from **The Chair of Deganwy** in the text, and may be linked to it in some way. The poem is certainly cosmological and has the same riddling drift of many others in the canon.

5–8 The worm from Caer Satanas was perhaps not originally so odious and this therefore may be an interpolation, since the rest of the description of the three fountains is beneficial to humanity and not the reverse. This seems to be really a cosmological serpent, despite its great paws and single eye.

17–18 It is impossible to tell where the three fountains arise from and we merely follow Skene and Nash here. Three fountains similarly play before Caer Arianrhod in **Defence of the Chair**.

19–23 The image is familiar from **Preiddeu Annwn**, 38–39. Bulls and cows swimming or grazing in the sea is familiar from various accounts of the Otherworld, including **Bran Mac Febal**, where the fish are called *Manannan's cattle*.

22 *Deifr Ddonwy, dyfr Ddawn* may be actual rivers. We have translated the names literally. The sense seems to be like that of Connla's Well in Irish tradition with its five streams of enlightenment. Both words used – gifts and blessings – have the association of talents and abilities, and so would fit the *aos dana*, the gifted people or poets.

24 Taliesin's discourse in the *Vita Merlini* speaks extensively of rivers, wells, springs etc. The first fountain seems to be the source of the tides, ebbing and flowing from *Corini* – Corinth? Corranyeid? Or Korrigans who, perhaps, churn the waters?

28 *Moroedd* we have translated literally as 'sea of ages' though it may be a real place.

29 The second fountain seems to be responsible for rainfall – another preoccupation of *Vita Merlini* (see Chapter Nine).

34 The third fountain seems to be the source of springs, however it is difficult to be happy about this verse. Neither Skene nor Nash had any idea and the surface reading of *fal callestig wledd* seems to be 'like a flinty banquet'. Nash proffers 'liquid flint' in wild surmise, but this is a hard image to get into.

37 The suggestion of this verse is that Elffin is representative of Britain's sovereignty or that, like Mabon, Elffin's youthful innocence protects him from satire.

41 The same verse concludes **The Chair of Deganwy**.

Generally, the serpent may be taken as a kenning of Britain itself, or its Otherworldly overlay. It reads like the description of a mountain. The three fountains are elementally different: first, water of water – the salt brine and the returning tides; second, water of air – the condensation of cloud falling as rain; third, water of earth/fire – the underearth springs and volcanic lava.

The Contention of the Bards

Who was the first man
created by the Lord God?
What was the flattering speech
prepared by Eve (*Jeuaf*)?

What meat, what drink,
what was his first shelter?
What was his chief reproach?
His first roofing?

Who taught him to clothe himself?
Who brought renunciation   (10)
out of the crafty land
in the beginning?

Why is stone hard?
Why is a thorn sharp?
What is as hard as a stone
and salty as salt?

What is as sweet as honey?
What rides on the gale?
Why is the nose ridged?
Why is a wheel round?   (20)

Why does the tongue articulate
differently from other organs?
If your bards are skilful, Heinin,
let them make answer to Taliesin.

This riddle song is about the first man and woman, and is related to one of the **Four Pillars of Song**.
4 *Jeuaf* makes no sense whatever – it is hardly Jehovah, or indeed Adam himself. However, Eve flatters Adam into eating the apple.
10–12 is translated literally. The sense seems to be that a) Adam and Eve brought with them the seeds of renunciation from paradise because of

their actions, b) Adam reaped what he sowed outside paradise, or c) it refers to Lucifer's attempt to become master of creation before Adam and Eve were created.

The remaining riddles are fairly stock.

The Rebuke of the Bards

If you are skilled bards
of ardent **awen**,
don't be contentious
in the court of your king.
Unless you know the names of verse-forms
be silent, Heinin – unless you know
the name of **rimiad**,
the name of **ramiad**,
the name of your forefather
before his baptism.   (10)

And the name of the firmament,
and the name of the element,
and the name of your language,
and the name of your region.

Be gone, you bards above,
be gone, you bards below.
my dear one is below
in the fetter of Arianrhod.

It is certain you know not
the song on my lips,   (20)
nor the distinction
between truth and falsehood.

Why don't you flee?
The bard who cannot silence me
will never be silent,
until he comes to his grave,
beneath a gravelly floor.
Whoever shall listen to me,
let God listen to him.

Taliesin puts the challenge on a professional footing here, attacking Heinin's teaching of basic verse-forms and procedures.
9–14 gets personal for Heinin, who should know these basic constants as a basis for his practice.

290

18 is an odd line, in the context of the story, for it was Taliesin, not Elffin who was imprisoned thus, previously. Odd, that is, unless, Elffin is undergoing another kind of captivity: of mythic or poetic nature.
23–29 imply that only those who know more than Taliesin should even dare to speak after they have tried him, and that his wisdom is so great that even God will listen to those who have learned from him!

The Death Song of Cu Roi Mac Daire

Into the mighty fountain flows the tide
Flows in, flows out, grinding, rushing.
Cu Roi's death-song moves me –
Sorrow for the death of one so fierce!
Who has had more terrible fortune
Since he crossed the Southern sea?
Renowned was he before being imprisoned.

Into the mighty fountain flow the waves,
Flow in, flow out, rushing, crushing,
Cu Roi's death song moves me –   (10)
Sorrow for the death of one so brave!

Into the mighty fountain gushes the deep,
Grinding, smashing at the grim shore,
A conqueror, mighty its onslaught.
After Manaw, many turned for home,
Departing from the heaped-up slaughter.

I know all the tales of Cu Roi and Cuchulainn,
Of their hundred battles on border lands.
At the last, as Cu Roi fell, his people lamented.
The Fair Ones received him in Caer Golydd.   (20)

This is a very difficult poem, many lines of which are corrupt and virtually meaningless. Skene's translation has so many bad lines I was forced to abandon it and turn to Patrick Simms-Williams' version (280). Professor Williams had solved many of the problems, but does not seem to completely understand the poem.

The repeated references to the sea, pouring into the 'mighty fountain' (perhaps a river) give the work a melancholy feel. Cu Roi himself had strong associations with the sea, so perhaps the metaphor is intended to make the parallel between the hero's furious assaults and those of the waves.

The translation of the last two verses is extremely tentative, and may be said to derive from reading 'between the lines'. If we are correct in our reading the poet seems to be referring to the warriors departing from a great battle in which Cu Roi was a victor and caused great slaughter, but in which he was wounded. At least, the final lines seem to refer to his soul being received into the Otherworld. (The text reads **Caer yssy Gulwyd**, literally 'Castle of the Lord' – I take this to be a Christian gloss and have substituted **Golydd** as in the **Preiddeu Annwn**.)

We may be surprised that Taliesin should write about the Irish Hero, but this is in keeping with the nature of the other material which derives from as wide a range of sources as possible. Perhaps the author was aware of the story in which Cu Roi helped Cuchulainn steal a great Cauldron, and therefore thought to relate it to the Taliesin tradition.

The Chair of the Sovereign
(Kadeir Teyrnon)
(N)

Sing a brilliant song
of boundless inspiration,
Concerning the Man who is to come
To destroy the nations. [Arthur?]
His staff and his entrenchment,
And his swift devastations,
And his ruling leadership,
And his written number,
And his red purple robes,
And his assault against the rampart,   (10)
And his appropriate seat
Amid the great assembly.

Has he not brought from Annwn
The horses of the pale burden-bearer, [Rhiannon]
The princely old man,
The cupbearing feeder? [Gwyddno? Bran? Grail?]
The third deeply wise one,
Is the blessed Arthur.
Arthur the blessed
Renowned in song,   (20)
In the front of the battle
He was full of activity.

Who were the three chief ministers
Who guarded the land?
Who were the three skilful ones
Who preserved the token,
And came with eagerness
To receive their Lord?

Great is the mystery of the circular course.
Conspicuous is the gaiety of the old.   (30)
Loud is the horn of the traveller.
Loud the cattle towards evening.
Conspicuous is truth when it appears,
More so when spoken.

Conspicuous when came from the cauldron
The three inspirations of Ogyrwen. [Ceridwen?]
I have been Mynawg wearing the collar, [Mynweir/Rhiannon]
With a horn in my hand.

He does not merit the Chair,
Who does not preserve my word.   (40)
Mine is the splendid chair,
The inspiration of my ardent song.

What are the names of the three cities
Between the sea and the land?
No one knows who is not earnest,
The offspring of their lord.

There are four cities
In peaceful Britain.
Tumultuous chiefs
Have not been nor shall be,   (50)
Shall not be nor have been.

There shall be a conductor of fleets.
The billows shall cover the strand,
Overwhelming the land;
Nor rock nor roof,
Nor hill nor dale,
Not the least shelter
From the wind when it shall rage.

The Cadeir Terynon,
Skilful is he who keeps it.   (60)

Is there here one who is enquiring,
A bottomless enquirer,
For the lost warriors?
I think with wrathful gesture
Of the destroyed Chieftain,
Of the lacerated form
Of the corslet-wearing Leon.

Exalted be the Lord,
To the end be his name celebrated.

Brittle are the young shoots of the tree, (70)
Frail like them,
A little while and we melt away;
At the end of our toil,
Languages shall pass away.

The ardent soul
Shall be voyaging through the clouds
With the children of the Seraphim,
Gliding on shall be thy people,
To the liberation of Elffin.

12 Skene 'company of the Wall' – the legions.
13 Skene 'Cawrnur' = the Great Wall.
23 According to the Welsh *Triads*: Caradoc ap Bran, Caurdof ap Caradawg, Owain ap Macsen Gwledig
43 Skene 'What are the names of the three Caers?'
70 Skene 'Loricated Legion.'

Defence of the Chair

There was a battle after a feast of joyless drinking,
a battle between the sons of Llyr in Ebyr Henfelen.
I have seen in the terrible, tumultuous battle
the brilliant shining lances over the men.

There was a battle against the glorious lord in the vale of
  Severn,
against Brochmael of Powys who enjoyed my **awen**,
a battle in which the first assaults were made against Urien.
It ran to our feet, the blood of that destruction.

The chair and cauldron of Ceridwen, have they no defence?
My tongue is it not free in the Goddess's sanctuary
  (enclosure)? (10)
For the glory of the Goddess are offered,
the milk, the dew, the acorns.

I have meditated upon what I shall say.
I know that death's approach is certain
and that it overflows (menaces) the lands of *Enlli* and Dyfed
raising ships upon the surface of the plain.

I have been to Deganwy to contend
With Maelgwn, the greatest of criminals;
I have liberated my master with the aid of the Great Giver,
I have liberated Elffin, the sovereign of our endeavours. (20)

I possess three chairs of harmonious accordance
and I will chant until the judgement.
I was at the combat of Goddeu with Lleu and Gwydion
who changed the elementary forms of trees and grasses.

I was with Bran in Ireland,
I saw the death of Morddwyd Tyllon, [i.e. 'The Pierced
    Thigh']
I assisted in the bardic contest
between the Irish, those deathly distillers of men!

From Glasgow to Loch Ryan,
the Cymry are courageous heroes – (30)
Deliver the Cymry from oppression!

There are three truly pitiless races:
the Irish, the Picts and the Romans.
They create disorder and confusion.

Beautiful are the cities about Britain's borders.
(The worst battles) are those between chieftains over their
    mead-cups.
At the festivals of the Great Giver who gives me gifts,
the two chief druids received their guerdon.

My chair is in Caer Sidi,
where no one is afflicted with age or illness. (40)
Manawyd and Pryderi have known it well.
It is surrounded by three circles of fire.
[or Three organs/fountains play before it]

To the borders of the city come the ocean's flood,
A fruitful fountain flows before it,
whose liquor is sweeter than the finest wine.

22, 40–46 are a direct pastiche of the **Preiddeu Annwn**.
25–28 related the Wasting of Britain, as told in the story of Bran, alias
Morddydd Tyllon, he of the 'Pierced Thigh'.
19 and 38 we have translated Distributor as Great Giver, since the
Christian dedications at beginning and end seem to be stuck on to

all poems regardless of their origin, and Taliesin's inspiration was most definitely in the gift of Ceridwen.

17–20 are straight autobiography.

23–24 may possibly refer to Cad Goddeu, at which Lleu was not a named combatant!

The poem is, then, despite its historical furniture, about the defence of Britain on a surface meaning, but about the deeper defence of the Otherworld *within* the world of Britain. Taliesin is cosmologically at the centre of the whole image, in the chair, in the tower of Caer Sidi, surrounded by three fires, a fountain and the waves of the sea (see Fig. 20 in Chapter Nine). He refers to the encroaching death by sea (invasion, bringing new customs and disordering the traditional lore) in lines 13–16, where Ynys Enlli (Bardsey) is mentioned – the Isle of Saints. For him, his chair is established for all time in Caer Sidi ('Perfect is my Chair . . .' – **Preiddeu Annwn**), but his three chairs in the three worlds, which are 'harmoniously accordant' (line 21) are threatened.

12 The milk, dew and acorns are the natural gifts of Ceridwen – milk for men, dew for the land, acorns for swine and other magical beasts.

1–5 refer to an unknown battle of the sons of Llyr, God of the Sea. The encroaching waters, in lines 13–16, may also be referred to in line 5 as the Severn Bore, which traditionally is said to be caused by the warring kings of the river. The Hafren (Severn) may well be the setting of many another mythical combats, including that of Pwyll and Hafgan in the first branch of the *Mabinogion*.

Cad Goddeu

I have been in many shapes
Before I assumed a constant form:
I have been a narrow sword,
A drop in the air,
A shining bright star,
A letter among words
In the book of origins.
I have been lanternlight
For a year and a day,
I have been a bridge   (10)
Spanning three score rivers.
I have flown as an eagle,
Been a coracle on the sea,
I have been a drop in a shower,
A sword in a hand,
A shield in battle,
A string in a harp.
Nine years in enchantment,
In water, in foam,
I have absorbed fire,   (20)
I have been a tree in a covert,

296

There is nothing of which
I have not been part.

I fought, though small,
At the battle of Goddeu Brig.
With Prydain's ruler,
With his rich-laden fleet.
Unwise bards pretend
A terrible beast
With a hundred heads –   (30)
The battle was contested
At the root of its tongue,
At the back of its skull.
The hundred-clawed black toad,
The crested, speckled snake
Are the soul's punishment,
A torment to the flesh.

I was at Caer Nefenhir,
Where grass and trees came swiftly –
Wayfarers perceived them,   (40)
Warriors stood astonished,
At the might of the Britons,
Shown forth by Gwydion.
Men called upon the Christ,
On the Saints as well,
To deliver them swiftly
From terrible rage.
Answer they got
In elemental language:
Rush, ye chiefs of the Wood   (50)
With the princes in your thousands,
To hinder the hosts of the enemy.
The trees were enchanted
For work of destruction,
The battle was joined
with the music of harps.
In the tumult many fell,
But brought forth new heroes . . . [four lines omitted].

The Alders, first in line,
Thrust forward in time.   (60)
The Willows and Mountain Ash
Were late to the array.
The Blackthorns, full of spines,

And their mate, the Medlar
Cut down all opposition.
The Rose marched along
Against a hero throng.
The Raspberry was decreed
To serve as useful food,
For the sustenance of life –   (70)
Not to carry on the strife.
The Wild Rose and the Woodbine
With the Ivy intertwined
How the Poplar trembled,
And the Cherry dared.
The Birch, all ambition,
Was tardily arrayed;
Not from any diffidence, but
Because of its magnificence
The Laburnum set its heart   (80)
On beauty not bravery.
The Yew was to the fore,
At the seat of war.
The Ash was most exalted
Before the sovereign powers.
The Elm, despite vast numbers,
Swerved not half a foot,
But fell upon the centre,
On the wings, and on the rear.
The Hazel was esteemed,   (90)
By its number in the quiver.
Hail, blessed Cornell,
Bull of battle, King of all.
By the channels of the sea,
The Beech did prosperously.
The Holly livid grew,
And manly acts it knew.
The White Thorn checked all –
Its venom scored the palm.
The Vines, which roofed us,   (100)
Were cut down in battle
And their clusters plundered.
The Broom, before the rage of war
In the ditch lay broken.
The Gorse was never prized;
Thus it was vulgarised.
Before the swift oak-darts
Heaven and earth did quake.
The Chestnut suffered shame

At the power of the Yew. (110)
Forest, that caused obstruction,
Thy multitude was enchanted,
At the Battle of Goddeu Brig. [12 lines omitted]

Not of mother nor of father was my creation.
I was made from the ninefold elements –
From fruit trees, from paradisiacal fruit,
From primroses and hill-flowers,
From the blossom of trees and bushes.
From the roots of the earth was I made,
From the broom and the nettle, (120)
From the water of the ninth wave.
Math enchanted me before I was made immortal,
Gwydion created me with his magic wand.
From Emrys and Euryon, from Mabon and Modron,
From five fifties of magicians like Math was I made –
Made by the master in his highest ecstasy –
By the wisest of druids was I made before the world began,
And I know the star-knowledge from the beginning of Time.

Bards are accustomed to praises.
I can frame what no tongue utters. (130)
I slept in purple,
I was in the enclosure
With Dylan Eil Mor,
I was a cloak between lords,
Two spears in the hand of the mighty,
When the torrent fell
From the height of heaven.
I know four hundred songs
Which bards both older and younger cannot sing –
Nine hundred more, unknown to any other. (140)
I will sing concerning the sword
Which was red with blood.
I will sing the boar-slaying,
Its appearance, and its vanishing –
Of the knowledge it carried.
I have knowledge of splendid starlight,
The number of ruling stars
Scattering rays of fire
Above the world.

I have been a snake enchanted on a hill, (150)
I have been a viper in a lake;
I have been a star, crooked at first,

The haft of a knife, or a spear in battle.
Clearly shall I prophesy
Of battle where smoke comes drifting.
Five battalions of lads will dance on my knife.
Six yellow horses – the best of the breed –
Better than any is my cream-coloured steed,
Swift as a sea-mew along the shore.
I myself am a power in battle,   (160)
A cause of blood from a hundred chieftains.
Crimson is my shield, gold my shield-rim.
Only Geronwy, from the dales of Edrywy,
Is better than I.

Long and white are my fingers.
Since I was a shepherd,
Since I was learned,
I have travelled the world;
I have made my circuit,
I have dwelled in a hundred islands,   (170)
In a hundred caers.
O wise and proficient druids
Do you prophesy of Arthur –
Or is it I you celebrate?
I know what is to be –
You what has been;
I know the saga of the flood,
Christ's crucifixion,
The day of doom.
Golden, jewelled,   (180)
I shall be richly bedecked
Luxury shall attend me
Because of Virgil's (or 'the Ffyrllt's') prophecy.

This is another miscellany of poems, of which only the central section,
lines 38–113, actually concerns the famous battle of Goddeu Brig, the
Battle of the Trees which may indeed refer to either an actual battle or
a kenning account of the Ogam alphabet (see Chapter Eight).
1–23 add further to the catalogue of objects whose nature the poet has
assumed.
24–37 apparently refer to the battle as a real struggle between flesh
and blood adversaries. However, the references to the beast and to the
battle fought at the root of the tongue and the back of the head led
Robert Graves to the belief that the whole poem concerns the struggle
to discover the secret names and mysteries of the opposing armies (101).
This is not at all inconsistent with the sense of the poem. Twelve lines
are omitted at the end of this section as having nothing to do with the
rest of the poem.

38–113 constitutes the main poem on the battle. Our version owes considerably to that of J. Gwenogryvan Evans (4), though we have diverged at certain points where his text made less sense. The various attributes of the trees could well be a way of describing the letters of the Ogam alphabet in riddling form.

114–128 has been consistently described as referring to the creation of Blodeuwedd, whose story is found in the *Mabinogion* (144). However, it may just as well be seen as a description of Taliesin's own interior growth and to his eventual rebirth.

129–154 continues the pattern of inner identification begun in line 23. There are references to the lost story of Dylan, which is begun in the *Mabinogion*.

155–164 appears to be a separate poem concerning a warrior who is perhaps taking part in Cad Goddeu, or in some historical struggle in which Arthur is also present.

From here until the end the speaker is again Taliesin. The poem ends with the mysterious reference to Virgil or possibly to the Ffyrllt, whose books Ceridwen was supposed to have consulted. (See Chapter One.) The word Ffyrllt may well be a corruption of Virgil.

Taliesin's Bardic Lore

Here is a chant of a primordial kind.
Who existed before darkness or light?
Where are the roots of the world?
On what day was Adam created?

Common men do not receive knowledge.
Sorrowful is he who by evil deeds
has lost the friendship of heaven's country.

Whence comes night and day?
Why is the eagle grey?
Why is night dark? (10)
Why is the linnet green?
Why does the sea swell?
Why is this not known?

There are three fountains
on the mountain of skill,
there is a citadel
over the ocean's wave.
Fawning praiser,
tell me the name of its porter?

Who was the confessor (20)
Of the Mary's Mabon?

What was the best deed
Adam ever performed?

Who will measure Annwn?
Who can tell the thickness of its veil?
Who can tell the size of its maw?
Who can tell the value of its stones?

Why do the treetops bend and bow?
What is this smoke amid the trees?
Perhaps Llew and Gwydion   (30)
perform their magic there?
Do they know the ancient books
when they perform their art?

Whence comes darkness
When the day ends?
Where does it go
When the day dawns?

I wander through native lands
To help the clans:
Loudly, I induce portent,   (40)
Seeking answer at the Strong Door.
While we wander
men seek the two wizards; [Math and Gwydion]
the dawn brings ships in close
seeking the shoe-makers.

                    *   *   *

Everywhere the company finds
distress among the Cymry.
Wandering hordes of Saeson
Have tried the very soul.
The Cymry have lost   (50)
the blessing of the Mass.
Ships will come to shore,
councillors to the Angles.
Signs of deliverance
are seen from the Saeson,
long enclosed in Seon.
Our leaders must act
against the bold Picts
and the sea-roving Scotti.
Blessed good fortune   (60)
will alleviate calamity,

ease our disunity –
assaults will end.

He was in conflict constantly
while he lived –
worshipping the Creator,
defending the realm,
civilising, chiding,
conquering with sharp steel.

* * *

I have been with the initiates,   (70)
with old Math and the smiths,
with Hefydd and Elestron in the trials,
a whole year in the City of Smiths. (Caer Gofannon)

I am old, I am young, I am Gwion,
I am universal,
I am gifted with a perceptive spirit.
I remember the ancient wisdom
of the Gwyddylffitchi,
defenders of the Cauldron's fire.

I am a bard,   (80)
I do not vouchsafe my secrets to slaves.
I am a guide, I am a judge.
If you sow, you labour;
yet, though you labour,
still you do not reap.

A party of swollen-breasted bards came here,
admitting, drunkenly,
to seeking the muse only rarely.
Though they seek rewards
they shall not get them –   (90)
and so they seek
to create mischief
for anarchy's sake.

Have you seen the strong lord?
Do you know the master's prophecy
concerning Uffern?

Before I long for my life's ending,
before I foam at the mouth,

303

before I am planked,
let there be celebration in my soul.   (100)
Books of learning hardly tell us
of the sufferings after the death-bed.
Whoever shall hear **my** bardic books,
shall find sanctuary in the Otherworld.

6 gives the keynote of this poem – loss of the Otherworld. This is
answered in 54–55, whereby Taliesin proclaims that his own redemptive
story is also a way to the Otherworld.
3–18 seem to be a brief portrait of the inner realms.
18–22 reveal the key figures in the redemption. The porter in hell (Judas),
Christ's confessor (Peter), and Adam's *felix culpa* – performed by Eve.
23–30 speak of the mystery of the Underworld.
31–39 speak of past initiates of wisdom.
38–45 refer to the story of Math and Gwydion who, in the second branch
of the *Mabinogion* spent some time disguised as shoemakers. This theme
is partly taken up again at line 70.
45–69 seems to constitute a separate poem. It may well be that the
dominus fortis, the Strong Lord, mentioned in line 92, is Arthur himself
and that his deeds are referred to here.
73 Caer Gofannon does not appear anywhere else in Celtic literature,
but is alluded to in numerous folk-tales about the Goban Saer. The
apprenticeship to the smith gives wisdom, as in the case of Niall of
the Nine Hostages in Irish tradition.
77–78 seems to suggest that Taliesin learned some of his wisdom from
the Gwyddylffitchi, the Irish and the Picts.
86–93 is yet another attack on the false bards.
97–104 'sufficient unto the day is the evil thereof' – the deathbed has
its own sufferings, but afterwards the books are silent on what the soul
experiences.

The Chair of Ceridwen

Sovereign of the power of air,
fulfil my heartfelt vows . . .
From midnight till daybreak
have my lights shone forth.

                    *   *   *

Noble was the life
of Minawg ap Lleu
whom I saw awhile since.
He met his end on the mound of Lleu.
Eager was his rash assault.

Afagddu, my own son,   (10)
he was blessed by the Lord

in the bardic trials.
His wisdom was deeper than mine.

The most skilful man I have ever heard of
was Gwydion ap Don, endless his resources,
who made a woman out of flowers,
and drove pigs from the South,
for he has the finest art.

From the soil of the courtyard
with bent and plaited chains   (20)
he made horses
and wonderful saddles.

When all the chairs are compared,
mine is pre-eminent.
My chair, my cauldron, my laws
my searching speech give them consistency.

I am an initiate of the court of Don.
I and Euronwy and Pryderi. (Euron)

I saw a terrible conflict in Nant Ffrancon,
– it was dawn on a Sunday –   (30)
between *Gwythaint* and Gwydion. [The Angry One]

One Thursday he came against the men of Mon,
seeking shadows and enchantments.
Beautiful Arianrhod, fair as the dawn –
a great disgrace to the wonder of the land of Britain –
throws her encircling rainbow around the court,
a river which drives back the attack against her land.
Its poison surrounds the earth.

                          *   *   *

The books of Bede do not lie,
the chair of the guardian is here,   (40)
and shall so continue in Europe till the judgement.
May the Trinity grant us
mercy on that day
and generous patronage.

This poem mentions a series of clever initiates, primary among whom
is Ceridwen, for she is the narrator.

305

1–4 and 39–44 are clerical interpolations.

5–8 There is no known Minawg ap Lleu (Generous son of Light) although Taliesin describes himself as Mynawg Mwynfawr (the Generous Rich One) in another poem. Is this supposed to be an epithet for Taliesin also? For he 'met his end' as Gwion, an act certainly witnessed by Ceridwen.

10–13 praise Afagddu as though he had indeed received the gifts of the cauldron.

14–22 speak of Gwydion's skill.

23–28 Ceridwen declares herself to be the keeper of the pre-eminent chair and speaks of herself as 'skilled in the courts of Don' – Llys Don is Cassiopeia, itself a mythic chair which, as a constellation, turns about the North Star.

29–38 seem to relate to the two assaults on Arianrhod by Gwydion and Llew, in order to gain a name for the former and arms for the latter. However, another interpretation suggests itself. *Gwythaint*, or the Angry One, refers perhaps to Arianrhod herself, in disgrace from the court of Math. This is reinforced in line 35. Arianrhod is presented as defending herself with the rainbow of her Corona Borealis, the poison of which (a most specific reference) infects the whole world. Paralleled is the breaking out of poison from the shattered cauldron.

Is Ceridwen using this incident as a metaphor of her own overcoming by Taliesin? Taliesin frequently likens himself to Gwydion favourably. Like Arianrhod, Ceridwen is wronged and tricked into giving up what she would rather keep. Perhaps a more ancient story related to Llys Don also exists? (See Chapter Nine for fuller discussion of this.)

Death Song of Uther Pendragon

Am I not powerful in the assault?
Am I not restless to avert the bloodshed of hosts?

Am I not called Gorlassar? (Blue Enamel)
My belt was a rainbow's circuit round the foe.
Am I not a prince of shadows
to him who sieves the two chief baskets?

Am I not the shelter of the basket, ploughing?
Am I not restless to avert the bloodshed of hosts?
Am I not he who extends his protection
Suppressing the kinsman of anger? (Casnur)   (10)
Am I not habitually harming Gwythyr –
a daring sword-stroke against the sons of Casnur?

Do I not share my protection,
a ninth part to the battling Arthur?

Am I not the destroyer of a hundred Caers?
Am I not the killer of a hundred stewards?
Am I not winner of a hundred sails? (**Ilen** – tents?)
Am I not the cutter of a hundred heads?

Did I not cut off the Old Head (*Henpen*)?
The best sword-stroke of the enchanter.   (20)
Am I not the best enchanter
of the Strong Door (*Hayarndor*) to ascend the mountain?

Widowed with grief, age wasted my frame,
Yet no time, no world shall be without my seed.

I am a praiseworthy poet of skill.
Fervent the song of ravens and eagles in their anger.
Afagddu had a pair (of them)
When four battle-hosts fed between two plains.
To climb to heaven has long been my desire,
From the eagle, from fear of injury.   (30)

I am a bard and harper,
I am a piper and crwth-player,
of sevenscore singers,
the very best enchanter.
From the lime of competition
I take my winged ascent.

Thy son, thy poetic one,
thy prophetic bard.
My tongue will sing of death.
May these stones of song   (40)
Ever brighten the treasury of Britain.
May the Lord of Heaven not deny me wisdom.

Uther here describes himself as a protector of Britain.
3 Uther is Gorlassar – Blue Enamel. Does he equate with Llassar Llaes
Gefnewid – the gigantic bearer of the Cauldron in the Mabinog of
Branwen?
4 Like the cloak of Caswallawn, or the druidic magical mist, Uther's
belt confuses the enemy.
5–7 The basket references are literal but obscure. Gwyddno's **mwys** or
weir catches Taliesin/salmon.
19–22 suggests a further stage of the Pen Annwn cycle. The word **goreu**,
'best', appears here twice, in connection with Goreu's sword-blow to
behead Yspaddaden (183).
23–24 is Uther's bequest – no age shall be without its cycle of Mabon,
Pendragon, Pen Annwn (181).

25–36 seem to be interpolation referring to Taliesin himself, since Uther is a battle-leader and defender of the realm, not a poet.

35–36 The image of a bird in lime is hidden in these lines, escaping from the grounding influences of patronage into spiritual freedom.

37–41 may also be Taliesin himself. Does this suggest that he is the lineal bard of the Pendragons?

39–40 are very difficult, and this is an inspired guess.

Seithennin

Seithennin, stand thou forth
And behold the billowy waves:
The sea has covered the plain of Gwyddno.

Accursed be the damsel,
Who, after the wailing,
Let loose the Fountain of Venus, the raging deep.

Accursed be the maiden,
Who, after the conflict,
Let loose the fountain of Venus, the desolating sea.

The cry of *Mererid* rises to Fand's Tower,   (10)
Today not even to God does supplication come:
Common after excess there ensues restraint.

A cry from the roaring sea overpowers me this night,
And it is not easy to relieve me;
Common after excess succeeds adversity.

A cry from the roaring sea comes upon the winds;
The mighty and beneficent one has caused it;
Common after excess is want.

A cry from the roaring sea   (20)
Impels me from my resting place this night;
Common after excess is far-extending destruction.

The grave of Seithennin, the weak-minded,
Between Caer Cenedir, Cinran,
And the shore of the great sea.

This clearly refers to the famous story of the inundation of Cant're Gwaelod, the home of Elffin's father Gwyddno Garanhir. Seithennin was the drunken warden of the sea-wall. One night he became so intoxicated that he opened the sluice gates and the entire area (believed to be the present Cardigan Bay), was overwhelmed. In other versions Seithennin rapes the maiden who holds the key to the sluice-gates, and who afterwards opens them. She is referred to here as the cursed maiden. Gwyddno's epithet 'Garanhir', 'Crane's legs', seems wholly in keeping with the story.

The three names of the sea are given as **The Field of Gwenhidwy**, **The Court of Neifion**, and **The Fountain of Venus**, though we have not chosen to translate them here. Perhaps this is an oblique reference to the three fountains mentioned in **The Defence of the Chair**.

Mererid may be a corruption of the Irish **muruach**, mermaid.

Protection of the Honey Isle

A great festival
About two lakes.
A lake surrounds me,
encompasses the Caer
which surrounds another circle
with deep moats.

A deep cavern
opens before me,
shadowed by great rocks.
The dragon comes out   (10)
and crawls towards
the cups of song,

of the song
of the cups of gold.
The golden cups
are in his hand,
his hand is on the knife
and the knife is
above my head.

Glory to you,   (20)
victorious Beli,
son of King Manogan,
who defends the Honey Isle.

9 It is implied that Beli, one of the primal gods of Britain, is the dragon. He has become the guardian spirit of Britain – a real Pen Annwn. He is drawn to the offerings of song in a shamanic manner.
18 Taliesin's song impels the defence of Britain because he is always aware of Beli's sword.

The **Stanzas of the Graves** (No. xxiii) has:
Who owns the grave in the great plain? (Salisbury)
Proud his hand upon his lance –
The grave of Beli, the son of Benlli Gawr

Cuhelyn's Song

According to the sacred song of Ceridwen,
The **Ogyrven** of many seeds –
The seeds of poetic harmony,
The exalted speech of the initiated poet,
Cuhelyn the wise, a true Cymraig,
Will skilfully sing the rights of Aedan the Lion.
A full song, a powerful composition,
Worthy of a Chair.
May he receive eulogy from suitors,
And they gifts from him,   (10)
A sovereign's bond,
The subject of harmonious contest.
Splendid his horses, great his respect,
Skilful men seek this chieftain:
The circle of deliverance,
The people's refuge.
A treasure beyond reproach.
To jest with him, the venerable one,
I greatly desire –
Who is both broad defence,   (20)
A ship to a drowning man,
A haven for the singer.
Swift as lightning, a powerful chief,
A luminous mind, knowing much,
Accomplished –
May the hero of the feast,
By peaceful means,
Establish tranquillity from this moment on.

This poem is from the *Black Book of Carmarthen* and is almost certainly
not by Taliesin. It is interesting, however, for a number of reasons,
not the least of which are the opening lines. We have retained the
ambiguity of the reference to Ceridwen, which could be read either
to mean that she herself is the 'Ogyrven of many seeds' or that the
poet is drawing upon the power of the seeds of poetic harmony for
his **awen**. The subject of the poem may be the Irish hero Cuchulainn,
though this is not certain. If so, lines 26–28 may well refer to the story
of **Bricriu's Feast** (59).

The Fold of the Bards

With discretion I try
the vain poems of Britain's bards,
in contentious competitions,
careful as the smith's skilled hammer.

The fold of the bards (bards' enclosure), who knows it not?
Fifteen thousand the doors (*drostau*)
of its qualifications (*gymhwyssau*)

I am a musician, I am a bright chanter.
I am a magician (*dur*), I am a seer.
I am a maker, I am a wiseman. (10)
I am a serpent, I am the fellowship of the feast.

I am not a bard, dumbstruck or hesitant.
When the chanter sings from memory,
I am not he who cries out in amazement.
It falls to me to compete with them:
like donning clothes without lice,
like sinking in a lake without being able to swim.

The gathering sea holds its bold course,
loudly it rushes to the sea-board towns.
The sea-girt rock, by a great design, (20)
will be our protection from the enemy.
The crag of the chief (*pen perchen*), the peaceful chief,
will enjoy intoxicating mead.

I am a cell/secret, I am a bower, I am a faithful one,
I am a satchel of song, I am a place of increase (*lle ynnet*).
(But as) I love the woods, the best shelter,
And a constructive bard who does not buy gifts,
so I do not like bribetakers.
Who curses the singer, shall not have mead.

It is high time to go to the drinking, (30)
and share with the skilful,
and sing dense verse (*a cham clwn*),
according to the country's custom,
(to) the shepherd of the region, the keeper of the pen,
like a company without stumbling at the gate.
He could not progress without a foot,
he could not go nutting without (his) trees.

311

Like seeking bees in heather,
like *mal peireint aureith ynuut*
like a battle-host without a head,   (40)
like feeding the homeless with husks,
like ridging the wasteland of the country,
like reaching for the skies with a hook,
like avoiding blood when in thistles,
like fashioning light for the blind,
like sufficient clothes for the naked,
like scattering foam on the shore,
like feeding fish on milk,
like roofing a hall with leaves,
like *mal lladu llyry a gwyeil.*   (50)

I am a bard of the hall. I am a chick of the chair.
I frustrate the loud bards.
Before I'm ferried to my hard-won reward,
may I win a place in your fold, O Son of Mary.

This poem has some of the most sustained images we have encountered
– the fold or enclosure of the bards is the poetic assembly, held under
the aegis of Britain's Pendragon or a great chief.
16–17 These odd images suggest no competition, no scratching, no
effort to swim against the waters.
18–23 is very like the **Protection of the Honey Isle**.
24 shows Taliesin's true power. He is the repository of his craft. Whoever
doesn't uphold it is satirised and excluded from the feast.
34 The pastor or shepherd is the keeper of the fold itself, the king
or chief.
36–37 The king could not proceed without the basis of tradition, i.e. his
bards, nor could he gather the fruits of wisdom – poetry.
38–50 seems to qualify lines 35–37. It would be an utter waste of time
to attempt any of these things, so essential is the poetic art.
39 is virtually untranslatable. A pure guess might be 'like pissing in a
golden cauldron'(!)
50 Another impossible line. At a guess it might mean: 'Like standing
on one's head in the dust'.
51 Taliesin describes himself appositely as a 'chick of the chair' –
reference to Ceridwen as the hen and keeper of the chair.
53–54 The image is sustained to the end of the fold in heaven.

The Hostile Confederacy

Behold a bard who has not chanted yet.
But he will sing soon
and by the end of his song
he will know the starry wisdom.

No recompense for my song –   (5)
No one heeds the words of Taliesin.

The day dawns when
Kian will recite
a host of praises.
My reward will be the speech intended for Afagddu. (10)

It was an ingenious exchange –
The Lord's song
Became Gwion's utterance –
His speech, a chance occurrence.

Gwion could make the dead alive –   (15)
A difficult endeavour.

Gwion kept the cauldron
Steadily boiling.
Gwion of small merit
Shall be until the ages of ages.   (20)

The peace that you bring to me
In the depth of your praises
Does it not rather resemble a hostile conspiracy?

What then is this custom?
your tongue recites   (25)
so many native songs
that you are no longer able to say
words of blessing over the clear liquid
which is the theme of your eulogy.

I alone am your custom   (30)
the third among equal judges.

Three score years
I have suffered earthly existence,
in the water of the law and the crowd,
in the elements of the earth.   (35)

Surrounded by a hundred servants
a hundred kings making oaths
a hundred leaving them
a hundred returning to them,
a hundred bards chanting   (40)
and predicting this.

Small was her desire
for gold and silver –
Lladdon, daughter of the Wave. (Latona?)

Who is the mortal who left her   (45)
With a bloody breast?
He will be spoken of later
and he will be greatly praised.

I am Taliesin
and I defend the true lineage   (50)
until the end of time
to Elffin's profit.

Is it not a tribute
of gold that is given
when one is loathed and unloved?   (55)

Perjury and treason,
I no longer desire them.
In the stream of our song,
no one recognises
the brother who greets me.   (60)

I am a wiseman of the primal knowledge,
I am an experienced astrologer,
I pronounce anger, I pronounce solutions,
I speak to habitual fawners.
Continue, behold God.   (65)

In the language of Talhearn,
baptism was the judgement,
whoever expounded to him the nature
and the power of poetry
To him is wisdom bestowed,   (70)
and inspiration without fail.

Seven score goddesses
have shares in inspiration,
but of these scores, only one truly.

Anger will cease in the depths,   (75)
in the depths anger will swell,
in the depths, under the earth,
in the sky over the earth,

314

only one truly knows
what is the sadness   (80)
that is better than joy.

I know the law
of fertile inspiration
when it is skilful,
to those happy days,   (85)
to a quiet life,
to the defence of the times,
to kings of whom long is the consolation
to the things who are on the face of the earth.

It is difficult to perform   (90)
a task on a new garment.
Why is the harp-string lamenting?
Why does the cuckoo lament, why does it sing?
I know it as I know many pleasant things.
I know why Geraint and Arman   (95)
abandoned their camp,
I know when the spark
of hardness works from the stones,
I know why the honeysuckle smells good,
why crows are the colour of wax.   (100)

Talhearn is
the great master of stars,
he knows the mind of trees,
he knows that meditation is the day's pleasure,
he knows good and evil.   (105)
I know the cup where the wave has flowed,
I know the end of the dawn,
I know who has preached
to Eli and Eneas.

I know the cuckoos of summer,   (110)
I know where they go in winter.

The inspiration that I sing
I have brought it up from the depths.

A river of it flows,
I know its length,   (115)
I know when it disappears,
I know when it refills,

315

I know when it overflows,
I know when it disappears,
I know which foundation   (120)
there is under the sea.
I know its measure,
I know each (one) and what surrounds it.

I know how numerous are the hours of the day,
I know how numerous are the days in the year,   (125)
how numerous are the spears in battle,
how numerous are the drops of a shower
gently dispersing . . .

I know all the craft of Gwydion
who made great mockery and nearly a disgrace.   (130)

I know who it is
who fills the river
and its release on the people of Pharaoh,
I know who averts
the present questions.   (135)

I know what made enduring patience
when the sky was raised.

When the great knowledge of the stars is imparted
then will be understood every high thing.
I know when the spirit is working,   (140)
when the sea is pleasant,
when the race is valiant,
when the Most High is implored,
I know the extent over the earth
of the sun which shines upon us,   (145)
I know when the bird of anger goes to its rest,
the bird of anger goes to its nest
when the earth becomes green.
I know who sings the psalms,
and by whom the songs are psalmed,   (150)
if one truly considers them
and collects them together in a book.

I know the number of the winds and streams,
I know the number of the streams and winds,
how many are the rivers,   (155)
I know size of the earth

and its thickness.
I know the sound of blades
reddened on all sides under the sun,
I know the Regulator　　　　　　　　　　　　　　　(160)
of the Heavens and of the Earth.

I know why a hill resounds,

I know why devastators win land,
I know why the silver vault is reknitted,
why breath is black,　　　　　　　　　　　　　　　(165)
why it is better,
why the valley is radiant.

I know why the cow is horned, (*The Essences*)
why a wife is loving,
why milk is white,　　　　　　　　　　　　　　　　(170)
why holly is green,
why the goat is bearded,
in the many fields,
why it is bearded,
why the parsnip is crested,　　　　　　　　　　　　(175)
why the wheel is round,
why the mallet is flat,
why the kid is speckled,
why salt is in brine,
why beer is a lively medium . . .　　　　　　　　　(180)

I know why the alder is purple coloured,
why the linnet is green,
why hips are red,
why a woman is never still,
why night comes,　　　　　　　　　　　　　　　　(185)
I know the nature of the flood
but no one knows why the interior of the sun is red.

I know who made the great pole
which connects earth and heaven,
I know the number of fingers in the cauldron.　　(190)
on the one and only, on the hand,
I know what name of two words
will never be taken from the cauldron.

I know why the ocean rolls about us,
why fish are black,　　　　　　　　　　　　　　　(195)
of sea food will their flesh be,

until the time when it will be transformed
when the fish will lock it up. (the sea?)

I know that the white swan's foot is black,
I know that the sharp spear is four-sided, (200)
I know that the heavenly race are unfallen,
I know that there are four elements
but their end is not known to me.
I know the wanderings of the boar and the deer.

I salute you, bard of the border, (205)
how do you stand beside he whose bones are of the fog
in a place where the two cataracts of the wind combat?

My knowledge declares itself
in Hebrew, in Greek,
In Greek and Hebrew, (210)
laudate, laudate Iesu.

A second time was I created, [*The Enduring Things*]
I have been a blue salmon,
I have been a dog, I have been a deer,
I have been a goat on the mountain, (215)
I have been trunk, I have been a beech,
I have been an axe in the hand,
I have been a pin in the tongs.

For a year and half,
I have been a white speckled cock, (220)
among the hens of Eiddyn. [Edinburgh]
I have been a stallion at stud,
I have been a battling bull,
I have been a yellow goat.

Fecund and nourishing, (225)
I have been a grain discovered
and I have grown on the hill.
The harvester took me
in a corner full of smoke
in order to free my essence. (230)

I have been in great suffering;
a red hen took me,
she had red wings and double comb;
I rested nine months

in her belly, as a child.   (235)
I have been matured,
I have been offered to the king,
I have been dead, I have been alive,
I have possessed the ivy branch,
I have had an escort;   (240)
before God I have been poor.

The Protector has also instructed me
between his red hands. He who has spoken of me
will find it hard to be happy;
that he may find great glory in it.   (245)

I am Taliesin
and I defend the true lineage
until the end of time
to the profit of Elffin.

For commentary see main text pages 94–108.

Chair of Taliesin

Mine is the eloquence of the wave
in the praise of the Lord God,
the course of all metre,
the song of prophecy.

A bard with the breast of a magician:
when he recites,
his store of **awen** flows
in midnight's stony-dark. (*ar feinoeth feinydd*)

Bards of brilliant speech,
their satires are unsubtle.   (10)
From valley to border,
great deception is their portion.

But I am no silent bard:
pre-eminent among the country's bards,
I enthuse the reckless,
I quicken the credulous,
I waken the onlooker,
I praise ardent lords.

I am no shallow bard:
pre-eminent among the bards of the kindred, (20)
bath vadawl idas?
The deep ocean is fitting.
Who is filled with hate?

In the contest, everything is revealed:
when dew is distilled,
and wheat is reaped,
and bees yield up their store,
and incense is offered,
and the golden pipes of Lleu, (*ac aur bib lleu*)
and the silver boat is fitted, (30)
and the ruby gems of berries,
and the foam of the ocean;
why the swift fountain
produces cresses,
what is the connection of the people
to the foaming noble drink,
and why the burden of the moon is wasted,
its joyful form pared,
and the beholding of wonders:
with the stars about the moon, (40)
and the bright appearances of men (*a gofrwy gwedd gwyr*)
against the winds of the airs,
and the bright sea,
the sanguine sea,
and the glass vessel
in the hand of the pilgrim,
and the strong and dark,
and the exalted sacrifice.
And medicinal herbs,
the place of summoning, (50)
and the bards and (with) flowers,
and the hidden thorns,
and the primroses in their frailty,
and the tops of forest trees,
a mall ameuadd (and bright doubt)
and frequent refilling,
and the overflowing wine cup,
from Rome to Rossed,
and the flowing flood
is God's own gift. (60)

Is not the tree the musician's treasure?
The fruit of its increase,

its inspiring brew,
ages over five cauldrons, (brewing)
and Gwion's river,
and good weather,
and honey and clover,
and intoxicating mead
pleasing to the Pendragon,
a gift of the druids.   (70)

This is most obscure. Its listings occur without let or explanation, in the manner of *The Chair of Ceridwen*, where a slow synthesis of one poem into another is the norm. Images of water are particularly marked. Many of the ingredients of the initiatory drink are hidden within this text.
1 sets the tone of the poem – Taliesin has the eloquence of the wave – presumably, that upon which he sets out in his coracle/bag, the birth-waters, as well as the waters of *awen*.
5 This is a revealing phrase, literally translated; better would be 'with a magician's heart', perhaps?
15–18 These are the qualities of the sea, as well as of poetic inspiration.
22 The **awen** is taking hold and he is about to give forth in a prophetic/shamanic manner.
24 *Camp ymhob noethas* suggests that poetry reveals the forms of everything, uncovering mysteries – *camp* means feat or game. When poetry is let loose it unveils everything.
29 The images become very Otherworldly suddenly, but this seems like the Otherworldly overlap which transforms the poet: he hears the golden pipes of Lleu, sees the silver boat readied, tastes the Otherworldly fruit, etc.
45 This image is straight from the *Voyage of Bran* (209).
48 'Exalted sacrifice' has the meaning of the mass or offering.
49–60 brings the poet to his appointed place within, in the company of poets, both high and low – the tops of trees and hidden thorns.
61–64 Our reading differs from others – the musician's tree is either the Otherworldly tree or else the wood of the poet's instrument. Its fruit are its notes, the words sung to the notes, all boiled up in Ceridwen's cauldron (the text clearly says five cauldrons, not 'a sweet cauldron of five trees' as suggested elsewhere).
68–70 The resulting brew pleases the king through the craft of druids.

Song of the Macrocosm

I praise my Father,
my God, my strength,
who infused in my head
both soul and reason,
who, to keep guard over me,

did bestow my seven senses,
from fire and earth, water and air:
the mist and flowers,
the wind and trees,
and much skilful wisdom   (10)
has my father bestowed on me.

One is for instinct,
two is for feeling,
three is for speaking,
four is for tasting,
five is for seeing,
six is for hearing,
seven is for smelling.

As I have said,
seven heavens there are   (20)
above the astrologer's head,
and three companies (parts) of the sea;
the sea beats on the strand,
the sea is great and wonderful,
the world itself likewise.

On high, God made
the planets:
He made the Sun,
He made the Moon,
He made Mars,   (30)
He made Mercury,
He made Venus,
(He made Veneris,)
He made Jupiter,
Seventhly, He made Saturn.

The good God made
five zones of the earth,
for as long as it lasts:
the first is formed cold,
the second is formed cold,   (40)
the third is formed hot,
injurious to flowers,
unpleasant and hurtful.
The fourth is paradise,
which people shall enter.
The fifth is temperate,
the habitable part of the universe.

Into three it is divided,
Into determined regions:
the first is Asia,   (50)
the second is Africa,
the third is Europe,
blessed by baptism,
lasting until doomsday
when everything will be judged.

He made my **awen**
with which I praise the king.
I am Taliesin,
I have a prophet's voice.
Continuing until the end   (60)
for Elffin's deliverance.

1–11 Taliesin speaks of his senses having been formed from the elements
and sub-elements.
12–18 The seven senses: instinct and speech are added to the usual
five.
19–25 The seven heavens are not enumerated. It is not clear whether
the three parts of the sea are also celestial in kind.
26–35 The planets have another added: Veneris – another name for
Venus – but possible implication of love/hunting in Artemis, the goddess
of venery.
36–47 He distinguishes five zones, three of which are unendurable, one
of which is habitable, and the last is paradise – a future habitation (see
Chapter Nine).
48–55 The three continents are named (excluding the Americas and the
Antipodes). Europe is the most blessed because it is Christian.
56–61 The standard ending.

Bright Trees
(S)

Bright are the ash-tops; tall and white will they be
When they grow in the upper part of the dingle;
The languid heart, longing is her complaint . . .

Bright are the willow-tops; playful the fish
In the lake; the wind whistles over the tops of the branches;
Nature is superior to learning.

Bright the tops of the furze; have confidence
In the wise; and to the universe be repulsive;
Except God, there is none that divines.

323

Bright are the tops of the clover; the timid have no heart;
Jealous ones weary themselves out;
Usual is care upon the weak.

Bright the tops of the reed-grass; furious is the jealous,
And he can hardly be satisfied;
It is the act of the wise to love with sincerity.

Bright the tops of the oat; bitter the ash branches;
Sweet the cow-parsnip, the wave keeps laughing;
The cheek will not conceal the anguish of the heart.

Bright the tops of the dogrose; hardship has no formality;
Let everyone preserve his purity of life.
The greatest blemish is ill manners.

Bright the tops of the broom; let the lover make assignations;
Very yellow are the clustered branches;
Shallow ford; the contented enjoy sleep.

Bright the tops of the apple tree; circumspect is
Every prudent one, a chider of another;
And after loving, indiscretion leaving it.

Bright the hazel-tops by the hill of Digoll;
Unafflicted will be every neglected one;
It is an act of the mighty to keep a treaty.

Bright the tops of reeds; it is usual for the sluggish
To be heavy, the youth to be learners;
None but the foolish will break the faith.

Bright the tops of the lily; let every bold one be a servitor;
The word of a family will prevail;
Usual with the faithless, a broken word.

Bright the tops of the heath; usual is miscarriage
To the timid; water will be intrusive along the shore;
Usual with the faithful, an unbroken word.

Bright the tops of rushes; cows are profitable,
Running are my tears this day;
No comfort is there for the miserable.

Bright the tops of fern, yellow
The charlock; how reproachless are the blind;
How apt to run about are youngsters!

Bright the tops of the service-tree; accustomed to care
Is the aged one, and bees to the wilds;
Except God, there is no avenger.

Bright the tops of the oak; incessant is the tempest;
The bees are high; brittle the dry brushwood;
Usual for the wanton is excessive laughter.

Bright the tops of the grove; constantly the trees
And the oak leaves are falling;
Happy is he who sees the one he loves.

Bright the tops of the oaks; coldly purls the stream;
Let the cattle be fetched to the birch-enclosed area;
Abruptly goes the arrow of the haughty to give pain.

Bright the tops of the hard holly; let gold be distributed;
When all fall asleep on the rampart,
God will not sleep when he gives deliverance.

Bright the tops of the willows; inherently bold
Will the war-horse be in the long day, when leaves abound;
Those with mutual friends will not despise each other.

Bright the tops of the rushes; prickly will they be
When spread under the pillow;
The wanton mind will be ever haughty.

Bright the tops of the hawthorn; confident the steed;
It is usual for a lover to pursue;
May the diligent messenger do good.

Bright the tops of the cresses; warlike the steed;
Trees are fair ornaments for the ground;
Joyful the soul with what it loves.

Bright is the top of the bush; valuable the steed;
It is good to have discretion with strength;
Let the unskilful be made powerless.

325

Bright are the tops of the brakes; gay the plumage
Of birds; the long day is the gift of the light;
Mercifully has the beneficent God made them.

Bright the tops of the meadow-sweet; and music
In the grove; bold the wind, the trees shake;
Interceding with the obdurate will not avail.

Bright the tops of the elder-trees; bold is the solitary singer;
Accustomed is the violent to oppress;
Woe to him who takes a reward from the hand.

Skene's translation, slightly amended. A curious poem which contains
most of the trees from the Ogam sequence. Each tree reference is
combined with a statement of gnomic wisdom – much of it trite and
obvious. The poem is from *The Red Book of Hergest* and may not be
by Taliesin at all. It is included here for the evidence it offers to the
continuing use of tree lore and Ogam in the Middle Ages. Four verses
which appear to be interpolations are omitted.

Fragments Containing References to the History of Taliesin

Many poems in the *Book of Taliesin* and elsewhere contain references
to the life or deeds of the bard. Lack of space does not allow complete
translations of these works, but the following extracts include most of
the longer passages of this kind.

from Horses

I have been a sow, I have been a buck,
I have been a sage, I have been a snout,
I have been a horn, I have been a wild sow,
I have been a shout in battle.
I have been a gushing torrent,
I have been a wave on the long shore.
I have been a gentle rain.
I have been a speckled cat in a forked tree.
I have been a circle, I have been a head,
I have been a goat in an elder tree.
I have been a crane bag well filled,
– A sight to behold.

Skene's translation, slightly modified.
   One of the most interesting lists of Taliesin's transformations, which
seems to have nothing to do with the rest of the poem. Of particular
interest is the reference to the crane bag. The line actually reads 'a

crane well filled', but the meaning is obvious in the context of the poet's statements. (See Chapter Five for a full discussion.)

from **The Song of Ale I**

He was a swift traveller,
The one who harnessed the wind;
Far he flew
Above the noisy world . . .

I myself am the guardian . . .
Who knows the secrets of song?
What is the retreat of Callofydd,
Wrapped in his robe,
When he opens the gate?
Who took a false oath?   (10)
Who began the tumult
In the loud dispute?
Fortunate his hasty flight.
He will awake the sleeper.
He will redeem the wild boar
Of Wales spread over with stones . . .

Who will pay the ransom
For Caer Wyrangon? [Worcester]
Is it Maelgwn of Mona?
Is it Aeron of Dyfydd?   (20)
Is it Coel, is it Cenau,
Is it Gwrweddw and his sons?
Not without honour his foes –
The hostages from Ynyr.
He is the resort of minstrels,
The star of Caer Seiont. [Segontium, near Carnarfon]
Have I not proclaimed the secrets
To Elffin on the seashore,
By the waters of Gododdin?
He is a true diviner,   (30)
A raven who prophesies at dawn.
I am an old wanderer,
A promoter of joy –
But I am silenced by anger
That no one praises Urien . . .

An intriguing glimpse into Taliesin's relationship with the great men of his day. The references are not always clear, but there is little doubt that this is a fragmentary account of the struggles of Briton against Saxon. The reference to Gododdin in line 29 suggests that Taliesin may have had a connection with this famous battle. The opening lines of the great cycle of poems, generally attributed to Aneurin, which deal with a struggle between the Men of the North (**Y Gogledd**) and the Angles of Bernicia, translate as follows:

I, Aneurin, will sing
What skilful-minded Taliesin knows.
There shall be a song of the Gododdin
Before the bright day dawns.

1–4 possibly refer to Bladud, the eponymous king of Bath (Caer Bladdon) who made winds and crash-landed at the site of what was to become a temple to the sacred waters (292).

24 Nash notes the reference in **Culhwch and Olwen** in which Glewlwyd Gavaelwawr says: 'I was in that battle of Dau Ynyr when the twelve hostages were brought from Llychlyn.'

from **Taliesin's Youthful Lore**

I will ask my lord
To listen to the **awen**.
Before the days of Ceridwen
He sustained her . . .

What are you when sleeping?
A body or a spirit,
Or a being of light?
O skilful minstrel,
Will you not answer?
Know you where night   (10)
Awaits the day?
Know you how many
Leaves are on the bush?
How the mountain was raised
Before the elements settled?
What supports the world,
what makes it habitable . . . ?

Oldest at its birth,
Time (or man) grows younger.

1–4 imply that Elffin sustained Taliesin *before* his rebirth from the womb of Ceridwen (the 'her' refers to the muse or **awen**).

5–7 suggest a glimpse of metaphysical speculations regarding the soul, but this may be a Christian gloss.

8–17 is yet another catalogue of lore *un*known to the boastful bards.

18–19 can be translated either to refer to man's, or time's gradual youthening.

A cassette of readings of the poems translated in this book will be available shortly. John and Caitlín Matthews give courses and workshops on this and other aspects of the Western Tradition, including Celtic shamanism. For further details write to the address below, enclosing four first-class stamps or two International Reply-Paid Coupons.

BCM Hallowquest,
London WC1N 3XX.

SELECT BIBLIOGRAPHY

1   Texts and Translations relating to Taliesin

1.   Ford, P. K., ed. and trans., 'A Fragment of the Hanes Taliesin by Llewelyn Sion', *Etudes Celtiques*, vol XIV pp. 451–460, 1975
2.   Ford, P. K., ed. and trans, *The Mabinogion and Other Medieval Welsh Tales*, Berkley, University of California Press, 1977
3.   Gwenogvryn Evans, J., ed., *Facsimile and Text of the Book of Taliesin*, Llanbedrog, privately printed, 1910
4.   Gwenogvryn Evans, J., ed., amended and trans., *Poems from the Book of Taliesin*, Llanbedrog, privately printed, 1915
5.   Guest, Lady C., ed., *The Mabinogion*, J. M. Dent, 1906
6.   'Idrisson', 'The Mabinogi of Taliesin', *Cambrian and Caledonian Quarterly*, pp. 198–382, 1833
7.   Morris-Jones, J., 'Taliesin' *Honourable Society of the Cymmrodorion* vol 26, 1918
8.   Nash, D. W., *Taliesin, or the Bards and Druids of Britain*, J. Russell Smith, 1858
9.   Pennar, M., trans., *Taliesin Poems*, Llanerch, Llanerch Enterprises, 1989
10.   Skene, W. F., ed. and trans., *The Four Ancient Books of Wales* (2 vols), New York, AMS Press, 1984–5
11.   Stephens, T., 'The Poems of Taliesin', *Archaeologica Cambrensis* (n.s.), No. 2, pp. 149–155, 204–219; No. 8, pp. 261–274, 1851
12.   Turner, S., *A Vindication of the Genuineness of the Ancient British Poems of Aneurin, Taliesin, Llywarch Hen and Merdhin, with Specimens of the Poems*, E. Williams, 1803
13.   Williams, I., *The Poems of Taliesin* (English version by J. E. Caerwyn Williams), Dublin Institute for Advanced Studies, 1975

2   Secondary Sources and Studies

14.   Adamnan, *Life of St. Columba*, ed. W. Reeves, Llanerch, Llanerch Enterprises, 1988
15.   Aebischer, P., *Le Pélérinage de Charlemagne à Jerusalem et à Constantinople*, Geneva, Librairie Droz, 1965
16.   An Chraoibhin, 'Cailleach an Teampuill', *Bealoideas* III, 1932
17.   Aneirin, *Y Gododdin: Britain's Oldest Heroic Poem*, ed. and trans. A. O. H. Jarman, Dyfed, The Welsh Classics, 1988
18.   Anwyl, E., 'Prologomena to the Study of old Welsh Poetry', *Transactions of the Honourable Society of the Cymmrodorion*, pp. 59–84, 1903–4

19. Apuleius, *The Golden Ass*, trans. Robert Graves, Harmondsworth, Penguin Books, 1950

20. Atkinson, G. M., 'Some Account of Ancient Irish Treatises on Ogham Writing, Illustrated by Tracings from the Original MSS', *The Journal of the Royal Historical and Archaeological Association of Ireland* (4th series), Vol 3 (1874/5), Dublin, 1876

21. Bartrum, P. C., *Early Welsh Genealogical Tracts*, Cardiff, University of Wales Press, 1966

22. Bartrum, P. C., 'The Thirteen Treasures of the Island of Britain', *Etudes Celtiques* vol 10 pp. 435–477, 1963

23. Bergin, O., *Irish Bardic Poetry*, Dublin Institute for Advanced Studies, 1970

24. Bergin, O. and Best, R. I., *Leabhar na hUidre* (Book of the Dun Cow), Dublin, Early Irish Text Society, 1929

25. Bergin, O. and Best, R. I., 'Tochmarc Etaine', *Eriu* 12, pp. 137–165, 1938

26. Bergin O. J., Best, R. I., Byrne, M. E., Meyer, K. and O'Keefe, J. G., eds., *Anecdota from Irish MSS* (5 vols), Dublin, Halle, 1907–13

27. Best, R. I., 'The Settling of the Manor of Tara', *Eriu* 4, pt. 2, pp. 121–172, 1910

28. Best, R. I. and O'Brien, M. A., *The Book of Leinster*, Dublin, Early Irish Text Society, 1954–67

29. Bloomfield, M. W. and Dunn, C. W., *The Role of the Poet in Early Societies*, Cambridge, D. S. Brewer, 1989

30. Bonwick, J., *Irish Druids and Irish Religions*, Marlboro, Dorset Press, 1986

31. Breeze, A., 'Sion Cent, the Oldest Animals and the Day of Man's Life', *Bulletin of the Board of Celtic Studies* vol XXXIV, pp. 70–77, 1987

32. Brennan, M., *The Boyne Valley Vision*, Portlaoise, The Dolmen Press, 1980

33. Bromwich, R., 'The Character of Early Welsh Tradition', *Studies in Early British History*, H. M. Chadwick et al., Cambridge University Press, 1954

34. Bromwich, R. (ed.), 'Trioedd Ynys Prydain: The Myvyrian Third Series', *Transactions of the Honourable Society of Cymmrodorion* pt 1, pp. 299–301, 1968; pt. 2 pp. 127–56, 1969

35. Bromwich, R., *The Trioedd Ynys Prydein in Welsh Literature and Scholarship*, Cardiff, University of Wales Press, 1969

36. Brown, A. C. L., 'Notes on Cauldrons of Plenty and the Land-Beneath-the-Waves', *Anniversary Papers by Colleagues and Pupils of George Lyman Kittredge*, ed. F. N. Robinson et al., pp. 235–49, Boston, Little, Brown and Co, 1913

37. Brehaut, E., *An Encyclopedist of the Dark Ages: Isidore of Seville*, New York, Columbia University, 1912

38. Brunaux, J. L., *The Celtic Gauls: Gods, Rites and Sanctuaries*, Seaby, 1978

39. Burland, C. A., *Echoes of Magic*, New Jersey, Rowman and Littlefield, 1972

40. Burns, R., *Keys to Transformation*, Enitharmon Press, 1981

41. Caesar, *De Bello Gallico* (trans. S. A. Handford), Harmondsworth, Penguin Books, 1951

42. Calder, G., *Auraicept Na N-Eces* (The Scholar's Primer), Edinburgh, John Grant, 1917

43. Campbell, J. F. and Henderson, G., *The Celtic Dragon Myth*, North Hollywood, Ca, Newcastle Publishing Co, 1981

44. Canfora, L., *The Vanished Library*, Hutchinson, 1989

45. Carey, J., 'Suibne Beilt and Tual mac Cairill', *Eigse* vol 20, pp. 93–105, 1984

46. Carmichael, A., *Carmina Gadelica* (5 vols), Edinburgh, Scottish Academic Press, 1928–1972

47. Carney, J., *Medieval Irish Lyrics with The Irish Bardic Poet*, Portlaoise, The Dolman Press, 1985

48. Chadwick, H. M., *The Heroic Age*, Cambridge University Press, 1967

49. Chadwick, H. M., and Chadwick, N. K., *The Growth of Literature* (3 vols), Cambridge University Press, 1932–40

50. Chadwick, N. K., 'The Borderland of the Spirit World in Early European Literature', *Trivium* 11/15, pp. 17–37, 1966/67

51. Chadwick, N. K., 'Dreams in Early European Literature', *Celtic Studies: Essays in Memory of Angus Matheson*, ed Carney, J. and Green, D., Routledge & Kegan Paul, 1968

52. Chadwick, N. K., 'Imbas Forosnai', *Scottish Gaelic Studies* 4, pp. 97–135, 1934/5

53. Chadwick, N. K., *Poetry and Prophecy*, Cambridge University Press, 1942

54. Clarke, B., ed. and trans., *Life of Merlin*, Geoffrey of Monmouth, Cardiff, University of Wales Press, 1973

55. Cockayne, O., *Leechdoms, Wortcunning and Starcraft of Early England* (3 vols), Rolls Series, 1866

56. Connellan, O., ed., *The Proceedings of the Great Bardic Institution*, Dublin, J. O'Daly, 1860

57. Corkery, D., *The Hidden Ireland*, Dublin, Gill & Macmillan, 1967

58. Cornford, F. M., *Principium Sapientiae*, Cambridge University Press, 1952

59. Cross, T. P., and Slover, C. H., *Ancient Irish Tales*, Dublin, Figgis, 1936

60. Curtin, J., *Irish Folk-Tales*, Dublin, The Talbot Press, 1944

61. Curtin, J., *Myths and Folk Tales of Ireland*, New York, Dover Publications, 1975

62. Davidson, H. E., ed., *The Seer in Celtic and Other Traditions*, Edinburgh, John Donald, 1989

63. Dexter, W. W., *Ogam, Consaine and Tifinag Alphabets*, Vermont, Academy Books, 1984

64. Diack, F. C., 'The Origin of the Ogham Alphabet', *Scottish Gaelic Studies* 3, pp. 85–95, 1934

65. Dillon, M., *Celts and Aryans*, Simla, Indian Institute of Advanced Studies, 1975

66. Dillon, M., *The Cycles of the Kings*, Oxford University Press, 1946

67. Dillon, M., 'Stories from the Law Tracts', *Eriu* XI, pp. 42–65

68. Diringer, D., *The Alphabet: A Key to the History of Mankind* (2 vols), Hutchinson, 1968

69. Dore, G., *Shaman's Path*, Boston and London, Shambhala, 1988

70. Drury, N., *The Shaman and the Magician*, Routledge & Kegan Paul, 1982

71. Dumézil, G., *The Destiny of a King*, University of Chicago Press, 1973

72. Dumézil, G., *The Destiny of the Warrior*, University of Chicago Press, 1969

73. Dumville, D., 'Some Paleographical Considerations on the Dating of Early Welsh Verse', *Bulletin of the Board of Celtic Studies* 27, pp. 249–251, 1976/8

74. Eliade, M., *Birth and Rebirth: the Religious Meanings of Initiation*, Harvill Press, 1961

75. Eliade, M., *A History of Religious Ideas* (vol 2), University of Chicago Press, 1982

76. Eliade, M., *Shamanism*, Princeton University Press, 1964

77. Ellis, P. B., *A Dictionary of Irish Mythology*, Constable, 1987

78. Esperandieu, E., *Bas-Reliefs de la Gaule Romaine*, Paris, Première Nationale, 1907–1914

79. Ettlinger, E., 'Omens and Celtic Warfare', Man XVIII, pp. 11–17, 1943

80. Ettlinger, E., 'Precognitive Dreams in Celtic Legend', *Folk-Lore* vol LIX, pp. 97–117, 1948

81. Evans, H. M. and Thomas, W. O., *Y Geiriadur Mawr*, Llandysul, Gwasg Gomer, 1971

82. Flower, R., *The Irish Tradition*, Oxford, Clarendon Press, 1953

83. Ford, P. K., 'The Death of Aneurin', *Bulletin of the Board of Celtic Studies* vol 34, pp. 41–50, 1987

84. Ford, P. K., 'Meredith Lloyd, Dr. Davies and the Hanes Taliesin', *National Library of Wales Journal* XXI, No 1, pp. 27–39, 1979

85. Ford, P. K., 'The Poet as Cyfarwydd in Early Welsh Tradition', *Studia Celtica* X/XI, pp. 152–62, 1975/6

86. Ford, P. K., ed. and trans., *The Poetry of Llywarch Hen*, Berkley, University of California Press, 1974

87. Ford, P. K., 'The Well of Nechtan' and 'La Gloire Luminesse', *Myth in Indo-European Antiquity*, ed. G. J. Larson, Berkley, University of California Press, pp. 67–74, 1974

88. Fraser, J., 'The First Battle of Moytura', *Eriu* Vol VIII, 1915

89. Gantz, J., *Early Irish Myths and Sagas*, Harmondsworth, Penguin Books, 1981

90. Gantz, J., 'Translating the Mabinogion and Early Irish Tales', *The Translator's Art*, ed. Radice, W. and Reynolds, B., Harmondsworth, Penguin Books, 1989

91. Garner, A., *The Guiser*, Hamish Hamilton, 1975

92. Giraldus Cambrensis, *The Historical Works*, ed. and trans. Wright, T., Bohn, G., 1863

93. Giraldus Cambrensis, *The Journey Through Wales/The Description of Wales*, trans. Thorpe L., Harmondsworth, Penguin, 1978

94. Glosecki, S. O., *Shamanism and Old English Poetry*, New York, Garland Publishing, 1989

95. Goetinck, G., 'The Wandlebury Legend and Welsh Romance', *Proceedings of the Cambridge Antiquarian Society* vol LXXVII, pp. 105–108, 1988

96. Gomme, G. L., 'Totemism in Britain', *The Archaeological Review* vol III, pp. 217–375, 1889

97. Goosse, A. *Jean d'Outremeuse, Ly Myreur des Histors*, Brussels, Palais des Academies, 1965

98. Gose, E. G., Jr., *The World of the Irish Wonder Tale*, University of Toronto Press, 1985

99. Graves, C., 'On the Ogam Beithluisnin', *Hermathena* vol 3, pp. 208–252

100. Graves, R., *The Crane Bag*, Cassell, 1969

101. Graves, R., *The White Goddess*, Faber & Faber, 1952

102. Green, M., *The Gods of the Celts*, Gloucester, Alan Sutton, 1986

103. Green, M., *Symbol and Image in Celtic Religious Art*, Routledge, 1989

104. Green, M., *The Wheel as A Cult Symbol in the Romano-Celtic World*, Brussels, Latomus, 1984

105. Greene, D., 'The Bardic Myth', *The Pleasures of Gaelic Poetry*, ed. S. Mac Reamoinn, Allan Lane, 1982

106. Greene, D. and O'Connor, F., ed. and trans., *A Golden Treasure of Irish Poetry*, Macmillan, 1967

107. Gwynn, E. ed. and trans., *The Metrical Dindsenchas*, Parts 1–5, Dublin, Hodges, Figgis, 1903–1935

108. Halifax, J., *Shamanic Voices*, Harmondsworth, Penguin Books, 1979

109. Hamp, E., 'Gwion and Fe Fi', *Eriu* 29, pp. 152–3, 1978

110. Hamp, E., 'Imbol Oimelc', *Studia Celtica* 14: 1, pp. 106–113, 1979

111. Hancock, W. N., ed., *Senchus Mor: The Ancient Laws of Ireland*, Dublin, Alexander Thom; London, Longman Green & Co, 1865

112. Harrison, A., *The Irish Trickster*, Sheffield Academic Press, 1989

113. Harvey, A., 'Early Literacy in Ireland: the Evidence from Ogam', *Cambridge Medieval Celtic Studies* No. 14, pp. 1–15, Winter, 1987

114. Hatt, J.-J., *Celts and Gallo-Romans*, Barrie & Jenkins, 1970

115. Hatto, A. T., *Shamanism and Epic Poetry in Northern Asia*, Luzac, 1970

116. Haycock, M., 'Metrical Modes in the Book of Taliesin', *Early Welsh Poetry*, ed. Roberts, B. F., (see Ref. 220)

117. Haycock, M., 'Preiddeu Annwn and the Figure of Taliesin', *Studia Celtica* 18/19, pp. 52–78, 1983

118. Haycock, M., 'Some Talk of Alexander and Some of Hercules: Three Early Medieval Poems from the Book of Taliesin', *Cambridge Medieval Celtic Studies* No 13, pp. 7–25, Summer, 1987

119. Heaney, S., 'The God in the Tree', *The Pleasures of Gaelic Poetry*, ed. S. Mac Reamoinn, Allan Lane, 1982

120. Heinberg, R., *Memories and Visions of Paradise*, Wellingborough, Aquarian Press, 1990

121. Henderson, G., *Survivals in Belief Among the Celts*, Glasgow, J. Maclehose, 1911

122. Henry, P. L, *The Early English and Celtic Lyric*, George Allen & Unwin, 1966

123. Herren, M. J., *The Hisperica Famina*, University of Toronto, 1974

124. Hersh, J., 'Ancient Celtic Incubation', *Sundance Community Dream Journal* vol 3, pp. 80–90, Winter, 1979

125. Highwater, J., *The Primal Mind*, New York, New American Library, 1981

126. Hope, A. D., *A Midsummer Eve's Dream*, Edinburgh, Oliver & Boyd, 1971

127. Hull, E., *Folklore of the British Isles*, Methuen, 1928

128. Hull, E., 'The Hawk of Achill or the Legend of the Oldest Animals', *Folk-Lore* vol 43, pp. 336–409, 1932

129. Hull, E., 'Legends and Traditions of the Cailleach Bheara', *Folk-Lore* vol 38, pp. 225–254, 1927

130. Hull, E., *The Poem-Book of the Gael*, Chatto & Windus, 1912.

131. Hull, E., 'The Silver Bough in Irish Legend', *Folk-Lore* vol 19, pp. 431–445, (1908)

132. Hull, V., 'De Gabail in T-Sida (Concerning the Seizure of the Fairy Mound', *Zeitschrift für Celtische Philologie* vol 19, pp. 53–58, 1931–3

133. Hull, V., 'Two Tales About Find', *Speculum* 16, pp. 329–30, 1941

134. Humphreys, E., *The Taliesin Tradition*, Black Raven Press, 1983

135. Hyde, D., *Legends of Saints and Sinners*, T. Fisher Unwin, 1916

136. Hyde, D., *A Literary History of Ireland*, Ernest Benn, 1967

137. Jackson, A., *The Symbol Stories of Scotland*, Stromness, The Orkney Press, 1984

138. Jackson, K. H., *The International Popular Tale in Early Welsh Tradition*, Cardiff, University of Wales Press, 1961

139. Jarman, A. O. H., 'Dialogue of Myrddin and Taliesin',

A Carmarthenshire Anthology, ed. L. Hughes, Cardiff, Christopher Davies, 1984

140. Jarman, A. O. H., *'Hwimleian, Chwibleian'*, *Bulletin of the Board of Celtic Studies* 26, pp. 71–76, 1955

141. Jones. A. R., and Thomas, G., eds., *Presenting Saunders Lewis*, Cardiff, University of Wales Press, 1973

142. Jones, Bedwyr Lewis, 'The Welsh Bardic Tradition', *Proceedings of the Seventh International Congress of Celtic Studies*, ed. Evans, D. E., Griffith, J. J., and Jope, E. M., Oxford, Oxbow Books, 1986

143. Jones, E., *The Bardic Museum*, A. Strahan, 1802

144. Jones, G. and Jones, T., trans., *The Mabinogion*, J. M. Dent, 1974

145. Jones, O., Williams, E. and Pughe, W. O., eds., *The Myvyrian Archaiology of Wales*, Thomas Gere, Denbigh, 1870

146. Jones, T., 'The Black Book of Carmarthen Stanzas of the Graves', *Proceedings of the British Academy* vol 53, pp. 97–137, 1967

147. Jones, T. G., 'Bardism and Romance', *Transactions of the Honourable Society of Cymmrodorion*, pp. 204–310, 1913/14

148. Jones, T. G., *Welsh Folk-Lore and Folk-Custom*, Methuen, 1930

149. Joyce, P. W., *A Social History of Ancient Ireland* (2 vols), Longmans, Green & Co, 1903

150. Joynt, M., *Feis Tighe Conain*, Dublin, Hodges & Figgis, 1936

151. Jubainville, H. D., *The Irish Mythological Cycle*, Dublin, O'Donoghue & Co, 1903

152. Kalweit, H., *Dreamtime and Inner Space*, Boston and London, Shambhala, 1988

153. Kelly, W. K., *Curiosities of Indo-European Tradition and Folk-Lore*, Chapman & Hall, 1863

154. Kendrick, T. D., *The Druids*, Frank Cass, 1966

155. Kinsella, T. trans., *The Tain*, Oxford University Press, 1970

156. Klindt-Jensen, A. O. *Gundestrupkedelen*, Copenhagen, Nationalmuseet, 1979

157. Knott, E., *The Bardic Poems of Tadhg Dall O hUiginn*, Dublin, Gill, 1926

158. Knott, E. and Murphy, G., *Early Irish Literature*, Routledge & Kegan Paul, 1966

159. Knott, E., *Irish Syllabic Poetry: 1200–1600*, Dublin, Gill, 1957.

160. Koehler, R., 'Taliesin's Little World', *Revue Celtique* 4, pp. 447–449, 1879–80

161. Ledwich, E., *Antiquities of Ireland*, Dublin, John Jones, 1804

162. Le Roux, F. and Guyonvarc'h, C.-J., *Les Druides*, Ouest-France, 1986

163. Lewis, S., 'The Tradition of Taliesin', *Presenting Saunders Lewis*, ed. Jones, A. R. and Thomas, G., Cardiff, University of Wales Press, 1973

164. Lloyd, J. E., *A History of Wales* (2 vols), Longmans, Green & Co, 1911

165. Loffler, C. M., *The Voyage to the Otherworld Island in Early*

Irish Literature, Salzburg, Institut Für Anglistik und Amerikanistik, 1983

166. Lofmark, C., *Bards and Heroes*, Llanerch, Llanerch Enterprises, 1989

167. Lonsdale, S., *Animals and the Origins of Dance*, Thames & Hudson, 1981

168. Loomis, R. S., 'The Spoils of Annwn: An Early Welsh Poem', *Wales and the Arthurian Legend*, Cardiff, University of Wales Press, 1956

169. Lucian, 'Heracles', *Works* vol 1, with an English translation by Harmon, A. M., Heinemann, 1913

170. Macalister, R. A. S., *Lebor Gabala Erenn* (5 vols), Dublin, Irish Texts Society, 1956

171. Macalister, R. A. S., *The Secret Languages of Ireland*, St Helier, Amorica Book Co Amsterdam, Philo Press, 1976

172. McKay, J. G., 'Comh-Abartachd Eadar Cas-Shiubhal-an-t-Sleibhe Agus A' Chailleach Bheurr', *Scottish Gaelic Studies* 3, pp. 10–51, 1934

173. Mackenzie, D. A., *Scottish Folk-Lore and Folk Life*, Blackie & Son, 1935

174. Macneill, E., *Duanaire Finn*, Irish Texts Society, 1908

175. McNeill, F. M., *The Silver Bough*, vol 1, Edinburgh, Canongate, 1989

176. MacQueen, M., 'The Historical Taliesin', *Inner Keltia* No. 6, pp. 90–95, n.d.

177. MacWhite, E. 'Early Irish Board Games', *Eigse* V, pp. 25–35, 1945

178. Mallory, J. P., *In Search of the Indo-Europeans*, Thames & Hudson, 1989

179. Mann, N. R., *The Celtic Power Symbols*, Glastonbury, Triskele, 1987

180. Martin, M., *A Description of the Western Islands of Scotland 1695*, ed. Macleod, D., Stirling, 1934

181. Matthews, C., *Arthur and the Sovereignty of Britain*, Arkana, 1989

182. Matthews, C., *Elements of the Celtic Tradition*, Shaftesbury, Element Books, 1989

183. Matthews, C., *Mabon and the Mysteries of Britain*, Arkana, 1986

184. Matthews, J., *A Celtic Reader*, Wellingborough, Aquarian Press, 1990

185. Matthews, J,. *The Celtic Shaman: A Handbook*, Shaftesbury, Dorset, Element Books, 1991

186. Matthews, J., *Fionn MacCumhail*, Poole, Dorset, Firebird Books, 1988

187. Matthews, J., *Gawain, Knight of the Goddess*, Aquarian Press, 1990

188. Matthews, J., 'Incubatory Sleep and Precognitive Dreaming

in the Celtic World', *The Fourth Book of Merlin*, ed. Stewart, R. J., Shaftesbury, Dorset, Element Books, 1991

189. Matthews, J., *The Song of Taliesin*, Unwin Hyman, 1991

190. Matthews, J. and Matthews, C., *The Aquarian Guide to British and Irish Mythology*, Wellingborough, Aquarian Press, 1988

191. Matthews, J. and Matthews, C., *The Celtic Book of the Dead*, forthcoming, 1991

192. Matthews, J. and Matthews, C., *Ladies of the Lake*, Aquarian Press, 1991

193. Matthews, J. and Matthews, C., *The Western Way* (2 vols), Arkana, 1987–8

194. Meek, D. E., 'The Banners of the Fian in Gaelic Ballad Tradition', *Cambridge Medieval Celtic Studies* No. 11, pp. 30–69, Summer, 1986

195. Megaw, R. and Megaw, V., *Celtic Art*, Thames & Hudson, 1989

196. Melia, D. F., 'The Irish Saint as Shaman', *Pacific Coast Philology* vol 18, pp. 37–42, 1983

197. Mercer, V. *The Irish Comic Tradition*, Oxford, The Clarendon Press, 1962

198. Meroney, H., 'Early Irish Letter Names', *Speculum* XXIV, pp. 19–43, 1955–6

199. Michell, J., *Secrets of the Stones*, Rochester, Inner Traditions International, 1990

200. Monad, J., *A Druidic Calendar: The Coligny Calendar as Cleared Up*, unpublished translation, n.d.

201. Merry, E., *The Flaming Door*, Edinburgh, Floris Books, 1983

202. Meyer, K., 'The Boyish Exploits of Finn', *Eriu* I, pp. 180–190, 1904

203. Meyer, K., 'The Colloquy of Colum Cille and the Youth at Carn Eolairg, *Zeitschrift für Celtische Philologie* vol 2, pp. 313–317

204. Meyer, K., *Fianaigecht*, Dublin, Hodges & Figgis, 1910

205. Meyer, K., 'Finn and the Man in the Tree', *Revue Celtique* XXV, pp. 344–349, 1904

206. Meyer, K., [ed. and trans.] *Hibernica Minora*, Oxford, The Clarendon Press, 1894

207. Meyer, K., *The Triads of Ireland*, Dublin, Royal Irish Academy Lecture Series XIII, 1906

208. Meyer, K., [ed. and trans.] *The Vision of MacConglinne*, D. Nutt, 1892

209. Meyer, K., *The Voyage of Bran son of Febal* (2 vols), D. Nutt, 1895

210. Miles, D., *The Royal National Eisteddfod of Wales*, Swansea, Christopher Davies, 1977

211. Morgan, P., *Iolo Morganwg*, Cardiff, University of Wales Press, 1975

212. Morgannwg, Iolo, *The Triads of Britain*, Wildwood House, 1977

213. Morris, J., *The Age of Arthur*, Weidenfeld & Nicholson, 1973
214. Morris, J., *The Matter of Wales*, Oxford University Press, 1984
215. Morris, L., *Celtic Remains*, J. Parker, 1878
216. Morris, W. B., *The Prehistoric Rock-Art of Argyll*, Poole, The Dolphin Press, 1977
217. Murphy, G. *Early Irish Lyrics*, Oxford University Press, 1956
218. Murphy, G., 'Finn's Poem on May-Day', *Eriu* 17, 1955
219. Murray, L. and Murray, C., *The Celtic Tree Oracle*, Rider, 1988
220. Naddair, K., *Keltic Folk & Faerie Tales*, Century, 1987
221. Naddair, K., *Ogham, Koelbren & Runic* (2 vols), Edinburgh, Keltia Publications, 1986/87
222. Nagy, J. F., 'The Wisdom of the Geilt', *Eigse* vol 19, pp. 44–60, 1982
223. Nagy, J. F., *The Wisdom of the Outlaw: The Boyhood Deeds of Fionn in Gaelic Narrative Tradition*, Berkley, University of California Press, 1983
224. Nash, D., 'Reconstruction Posidonius', *Britannia* vol VII, pp. 111–126, 1976
225. Nennius, *British History and the Welsh Annals*, ed. and trans. J. Morris, Phillimore, 1980
226. Nichols, R., *The Book of Druidry*, Wellingborough, Aquarian Press, 1990
227. Nichols, R. and Kirkup, J., *The Cosmic Shape*, The Forge Press, 1946
228. Nicholson, S., *Shamanism*, Theosophical Publishing House, 1987
229. O'Boyle, S., *Ogam, the Poet's Secret*, Dublin, Gilbert Dalton, 1980
230. O'Conor, C., *Dissertations on the History of Ireland*, Dublin, G. Faulkner, 1766
231. O Croinin, D., 'The Oldest Irish Names for the Days of the Week', *Eriu* 32, pp. 95–114, 1981
232. O'Curry, E., *Manners and Customs of the Ancient Irish* (3 vols), Williams & Norgate, 1873
233. O'Donovan, J., *Cormac's Glossary*, edited, with notes and indexes, by Whitley Stokes, Calcutta; Irish Archaeological & Celtic Society, 1868
234. O'Driscoll, R., ed., *The Celtic Consciousness*, Edinburgh, Cannongate Publishing; Portlaoise, The Dolmen Press, 1982
235. O'Flaherty, R., *Ogygia: or a Chronological Account of Irish Events*, Dublin, W. McKenzie, 1793
236. O'Grady, S., ed. and trans., *Silva Gadelica* (2 vols), Williams & Norgate, 1892
237. O hOgain, D., *The Hero In Irish Folk History*, Dublin, Gill & Macmillan, 1985
238. O hOgain, D., *Fionn mac Cumhail: Images of the Gaelic Hero*, Dublin, Gill & Macmillan, 1988

239. O'Keeffe, J. G. ed. and trans, *Buile Suibne*, D. Nutt, 1913

240. Olmstead, G. S., 'Gaulish and Celtiberian Poetic Inscriptions', *Mankind Quarterly* XXVIII, No. 4, pp. 339–387, 1988

241. Olmstead, G. S., *The Gundestrup Cauldron*, Brussels, Latomus, 1979

242. Olmstead, G. S., 'The Use of Ordinal Numbers on the Gaulish Coligny Calendar', *Journal of Indo-European Studies* vol 16, pp. 267–339, 1988

243. Oosten, J. G., *The War of the Gods: The Social Code in Indo-European Mythology*, Routledge & Kegan Paul, 1985

244. O'Rahilly, T. F., *Early Irish History and Mythology*, Dublin Institute for Advanced Studies, 1976

245. Parry, J. J. ed. and trans., *The Vita Merlini*, University of Illinois, 1925

246. Parry, T., *A History of Welsh Literature*, Oxford, The Clarendon Press, 1955

247. Parry-Jones, D., *Welsh Legends and Fairy Lore*, Batsford, 1953

248. Patch, H. R., *The Other World*, Cambridge, Mass., Harvard University Press, 1950

249. Peate, I. C., 'The Gorsedd of the Bards of Britain', *Antiquity*, pp. 13–15, 1950/1

250. Pennar, M., *The Black Book of Carmarthen*, Llanerch, Llanerch Enterprises, 1989

251. Piggott, S., *Ancient Britons and the Antiquarian Imagination*, Thames & Hudson, 1989

252. Plummer, C., 'On the Meaning of Ogam Stones', *Revue Celtique* XL, pp. 387–90, 1923

253. Powel, T., 'Finn and Gwynn', *The Academy* XXVII, p. 65, 1885

254. Powell, T. G. E., *The Celts*, Thames & Hudson, 1958

255. Powell, T. G. E., 'From Urartu to Gundestrup: the Agency of Thracian Metal-work', *The European Community in Later Prehistory: Studies in Honour of C. F. C. Hawkes*, ed. J. Boardman et al., Routledge & Kegan Paul, 1971

256. Price, G., *Ireland and the Celtic Connection*, Colin Smythe, 1987

257. Reed, H., 'Dream Incubation', *Sundance Community Dream Journal* vol 2, pp. 9–26, 1978

258. Rejhon, A. C., 'Hu Gadarn: Folklore and Fabrication', *Celtic Folklore and Christianity*, ed. P. K. Ford, Macnally & Loftin, Santa Barbara, 1983

259. Rhys, J., *Celtic Folk-Lore, Welsh & Manx* (2 vols), Wildwood House, 1980

260. Rhys, J., *Lectures on the Origin and Growth of Religion as Illustrated by Celtic Heathendom*, Williams & Norgate, 1888

261. Richards, M., trans., *The Laws of Hywel Dda*, Liverpool University Press, 1954

262. Richardson, L. J. D., 'The Word Ogham', *Hermathena* LXII, pp. 9–15, 1943
263. Ritchie, A., 'Painted Pebbles in Early Scotland', *Proceedings of the Society of Antiquaries of Scotland* vol 104, pp. 297–301, 1972
264. Ritchie, A., *Picts*, Edinburgh, H.M.S.O. 1989
265. Roberts, B. F., ed., *Early Welsh Poetry: Studies in the Book of Aneurin*, Aberystwyth, National Library of Wales, 1988
266. Roberts, P., *The Cambrian Popular Antiquities*, E. Williams, 1815
267. Robinson, F. N., 'Satirists and Enchanters in Early Irish Literature', *Studies in the History of Religion Presented to C. H. Toy*, ed. Lyon, D. G., and Moore, F. G., Macmillan, 1912
268. Ross, A., 'Chartres: the Locus of the Carnutes', *Studia Celtica* 14/15, pp. 260–269, 1979/80
269. Ross, A., 'The Divine Hag of the Pagan Celts', *The Witch Figure*, ed. Newall, V., Routledge & Kegan Paul, 1973
270. Ross, A., *Pagan Celtic Britain*, Cardinal, 1974
271. Ross, A. and Robins, D., *The Life and Death of a Druid Prince*, Rider, 1989
272. Rowland, J., *Early Welsh Saga Poetry*, Cambridge, D. S. Brewer, 1990
273. Rowlands, R. F., 'Bardic Lore and Education', *The Bulletin of the Board of Celtic Studies* vol 32, pp. 143–155, 1985
274. Rust, J., *Druidism Exhumed*, Edinburgh, Edmonston & Douglas, 1871
275. Sanders, N. K., *Prehistoric Art in Europe*, Harmondsworth, Penguin Books, 1968
276. Santillana, G. and von Dechend, H., *Hamlet's Mill*, Macmillan, 1969
277. Sayers, W., 'Cerrce, Anarchair: Epithets of the Dagda, Cernunnos and Conal Cernach', *Journal of Indo-European Studies* vol 16, pp. 341–364, 1988
278. Schofield, W. H., *Mythic Bards*, Cambridge, Harvard University Press, 1920
279. Scott, R. D., *The Thumb of Knowledge in Legends of Fionn, Sigurd and Taliesin*, Publications of the Institute of French Studies, Columbia University, New York, 1930
280. Simms-Williams, P., 'The Evidence for Vernacular Irish Literary Influence on Early Medieval Welsh Literature', *Ireland in Early Medieval Europe*, ed. Whitlock, D. et al., Cambridge University Press, 1976
281. Sjoestedt, M. L., *Gods and Heroes of the Celts*, Berkley, Turtle Island Foundation, 1982
282. Sjoestedt, M. L., 'Seige De Druim Damhgaire', *Revue Celtique* vol 44, pp. 157–186, 1927
283. Smyth, M., 'Isidore of Seville and Early Irish Cosmography', *Cambridge Medieval Celtic Studies* No. 14, pp. 69–102, Winter, 1987
284. Snyder, G., *Good, Wild, Sacred*, Five Seasons Press, 1984

285. Spaan, D. B., *The Otherworld in Early Irish Literature*, University of Michigan, 1969

286. Stephens, M. ed., *The Oxford Companion to the Literature of Wales*, Oxford University Press, 1986

287. Stevens, J. and Stevens L. S., *Secrets of Shamanism*, New York, Avon Books, 1988

288. Stewart, R. J., *The Elements of Creation Myth*, Shaftesbury, Element Books, 1989

289. Stewart, R. J., *The Mystic Life of Merlin*, Arkana, 1986

290. Stewart, R. J., *The Prophetic Vision of Merlin*, Arkana, 1986

291. Stewart, R. J., *The Underworld Initiation*, Wellingborough, Aquarian Press, 1985

292. Stewart, R. J., *The Waters of the Gap*, Shaftesbury, Element Books, 1989

293. Stokes, W., 'The Borama', *Revue Celtique* 13, pp. 33–124, 1892

294. Stokes, W., *The Calendar of Oengus*, Dublin, Hodges, Fisher and Figgis, 1880

295. Stokes, W., 'The Colloquy of the Two Sages', *Revue Celtique* vol 26, pp. 4–64pp, 1905

296. Stokes, W., 'Find and the Phantoms', *Revue Celtique* VII, pp. 289–307, 1886

297. Stokes, W., 'The Prose Tales in the Rennes Dindsenchas', *Revue Celtique*, pp. 272–484

298. Stokes, W., 'The Siege of Howth', *Revue Celtique* VIII, pp. 47–64, 1887

299. Stokes, W. and Windisch, E., 'The Irish Ordeals' and 'The Fitness of Names', *Irische Texte* (3rd Series, vol 1) Leipzig, Verlag von S. Hirzel, 1891

300. Strabo, *Geographica*

301. Suckling, N., *Fidchell (Celtic Chess)*, issued privately, 1989

302. Sutherland, E., *Ravens and Black Rain: The History of Highland Second Sight*, Constable, 1985

303. Tacitus, *Germania*, trans. H. Mattingly, Harmondsworth, Penguin Books, 1948

304. Tatlock, J. S. P., *The Legendary History of Britain*, New York, Gordian Press, 1979

305. Taylor, R. T., *The Political Prophecy in England*, Columbia University Press, 1911

306. Thomas C., 'The Animal Art of the Scottish Iron Age', *Archaeological Journal* 143, pp. 14–64, 1961

307. Tierney, J. J., *The Celtic Ethnography of Posidonius*, Dublin, Proceedings of the Royal Irish Academy, 1960

308. Tolstoy, N., *The Quest for Merlin*, Hamish Hamilton, 1985

309. Travis, J., *Early Celtic Versecraft*, Shannon, Irish University Press, 1973

310. Trevelyan, M., *Folk-Lore and Folk-Stories of Wales*, Eliot Stock, 1909

311. Van Hamel, A. G., *Aspects of Celtic Mythology*, British Academy, 1935

312. Van Hamel, A. G., 'The Game of the Gods', *Arkiv for Nordisk Filologie* VI, pp. 218–242, 1934

313. Wace, *Chronicles* (in) *Arthurian Chronicles*, trans. E. Mason, London, Dent, 1962

314. Wagner, H., 'The Origins of Pagan Celtic Religion', *Zeitschrift für Celtische Philologie* XXXVIII, pp. 1–28, 1981

315. Wagner, H., 'Studies in the Origins of Early Celtic Tradition', *Eriu* XXVI, pp. 1–26, 1975

316. Watkins, C., 'Indo-European Metrics and Archaic Irish Verse', *Celtica* VI, pp. 194–249, 1963

317. Watson, W. J., *The History of the Celtic Place Names of Scotland*, Dublin Irish Academic Press, 1986

318. Webster, K. G. T., 'Arthur and Charlemagne: Notes on the Ballad of King Arthur and King Cornwall and on the Pilgrimage of Charlemagne', *Englische Studien* 36, 1905

319. Wentz, W. Y. Evans, *The Fairy Faith in Celtic Countries*, New York, Lemma Publishing Co, 1973

320. Whatmough, J., *The Dialects of Ancient Gaul*, Cambridge, Mass., Harvard University Press, 1970

321. Wheeler, R. E. M., *Report on the Excavation of the Prehistoric Roman and Post-Roman Site in Lydney Park, Gloucestershire*, Oxford, The Society of Antiquaries, 1932

322. Williams, G., *An Introduction to Welsh Poetry*, Faber & Faber, 1953

323. Williams, G. J., 'Tri Chof Ynys Brydain', *Llen Cymru* vol 3, pp. 234–239, 1955

324. Williams, I., *Armes Prydein: The Prophecy of Britain* (English version by Rachel Bromwich), the Dublin Institute for Advanced Studies, 1982

325. Williams, I., *The Beginnings of Welsh Poetry*, ed. R. Bromwich, Cardiff, University of Wales Press, 1980

326. Williams, I., *Lectures on Early Welsh Poetry*, Dublin, Institute for Advanced Studies, 1970

327. Williams, M., 'An Early Ritual Poem in Welsh', *Speculum* 13, pp. 38–51, 1938

328. Williamson, R., *The Craneskin Bag: Celtic Stories and Poems*, Edinburgh, Canongate, 1979

329. Wood, J., 'The Elphin Section of Hanes Taliesin', *Etudes Celtiques* vol 18, pp. 229–244, 1981

330. Wood, J., 'The Folk-Lore Background of the Gwion Bach Section of Hanes Taliesin', *Bulletin of the Board of Celtic Studies* 30, pp. 621–634, 1983/4

331. Wood, J., 'Maelgwn Gwynedd: A Forgotten Welsh Hero', *Trivium* vol 19, pp. 103–117, 1984

332. Wood, J., 'Versions of Hanes Taliesin by Owen John and Lewis Morris', *Bulletin of the Board of Celtic Studies* vol 29, pp. 285–294, 1981/2

333. Wood, J., 'Virgil and Taliesin: The Concept of the Magician in Medieval Folk-Lore', *Folklore* vol 94, pp. 91–104, 1983

3 Supplemental

334. Bromwich, R., *Triodd Ynys Prydein* (The Welsh Triads), Cardiff, University of Wales Press, (2nd Edition, 1978)
335. Morgannwg, I., *Barddas*, ed. J. Williams ab Ithel, Llandovery, D. J. Roderic, 1862
336. Morgannwg, I., *Iolo MSS*, ed. T. Williams, Llandovery, William Rees, 1848
337. Rees, A. and Rees B., *Celtic Heritage*, Thames & Hudson, 1961
338. Herbert, A., *Britannia After the Romans*, H. G. Bohn, 1836
339. Plutarch, 'The E. in Delphi', *Moralia* vol 4, trans. F. C. Babbitt, Heinemann, 1957
340. Griffiths, M., *Early Vaticination in Welsh with English Parallels*, Cardiff, University of Wales Press, 1937
341. Geoffrey of Monmouth, *History of the Kings of Britain*, trans. L. Thorpe, Harmondsworth, Penguin Books
342. Caldecott, M., *Taliesin and Afagddu*, Brans Head, Frome, 1983

Index

Mogh Ruith 44-6, 52, 62
Monard, Jacques 241
Mongan 112, 153
Morann Mac Main
    collars of 72
    ogam of 215-16
Morda 14, 15, 25, 79
Morfran (see also *Afagddu*) 14, 24ff
Morgen 253
Morrigan 26, 160, 223
Morris, Lewis 20, 66
Morris-Jones, Sir John 92, 94
Mother of the Animals 36
Murias 87
Murray, Colin 221
Mwys (*see also* weir) 8, 89, 307
Myfyrian Archaiology 226, 227, 261, 271
Mynawg 293, 305, 306
Myrddin *see* Merlin
Myreur des Histors 273

Naddair, Kaledon 220
Nash, D. W. 94, 277, 288
Native American tradition 59, 71, 155-6
Nechtan
    well of 117, 187, 191
    wife of 79, 130
Nede 79, 110, **128-39**, 140-2
neladoracht (cloud divination) 192-3
Nemea 142
Nemedians 53, 161
nemeton (sacred grove) 234
Nennius 11
Nicander 50
nine maidens 24, 251, 253
Ninine 230
Nodens 56-7, 58
Nuadu Airgetlam (Silver-Hand) 56, 87, 250
    wife of 79, 130
number lore 246, 248

O'Carolan, Turlough 188
O'Conor, Charles 220

O'Curry, Eugene 121, 189
O'Flaherty, Roderic 220
O'Hogain, Daithi 167
Ochenn 51
Odin 159
Odysseus 247
Oengus Mac ind Og 33, 79, 130, 132, 136, 137, 173
    ogam of 216
ogam/ogham 55, 85, 109, 113, 121-2, 168, 189, 210, 211-36, 242
    alphabet *214-15*, 300
    alternative 218
    as grave markers 211
    as sign language 218
    extra letters of 218
    of Mac Ind Oic 216
    of Morann Mac Main 215-16
    order of 219-20
    origins of 212-14
    Pictish 242-3
Ogam Tract (Duil Feda) 212, 213, 223
Ogma mac Elatha 212-13, 250
Ogmios 213
Ogyrwen (Goddess of Inspiration) 78, 102, 104, 254, 293, 310
Oisin 81, 82, 245
Old Kveldulfr 181
oldest animals 156-72, *170*
Olmstead, Garrett 241
Olwen 239, 267
or firindi (true speech ritual) 183
Oran 61-2
ordeals 70-3
Orkneys 240
Orphic instruction 118
Oscur mac Crimthann 30-1
Otherworld 30, 34, 35ff, 46, **48**, 50, 70, 83, 109, 128, 136, 142-4, 188, 244, 245, 250ff, 268
    as Summer Country 237, 271
    egress thither by water 50, 87